Interference Fringe

—

Tallur L.N.

Interference Fringe

—

Tallur L.N.

Chaitanya Sambrani

Gary Garrido Schneider

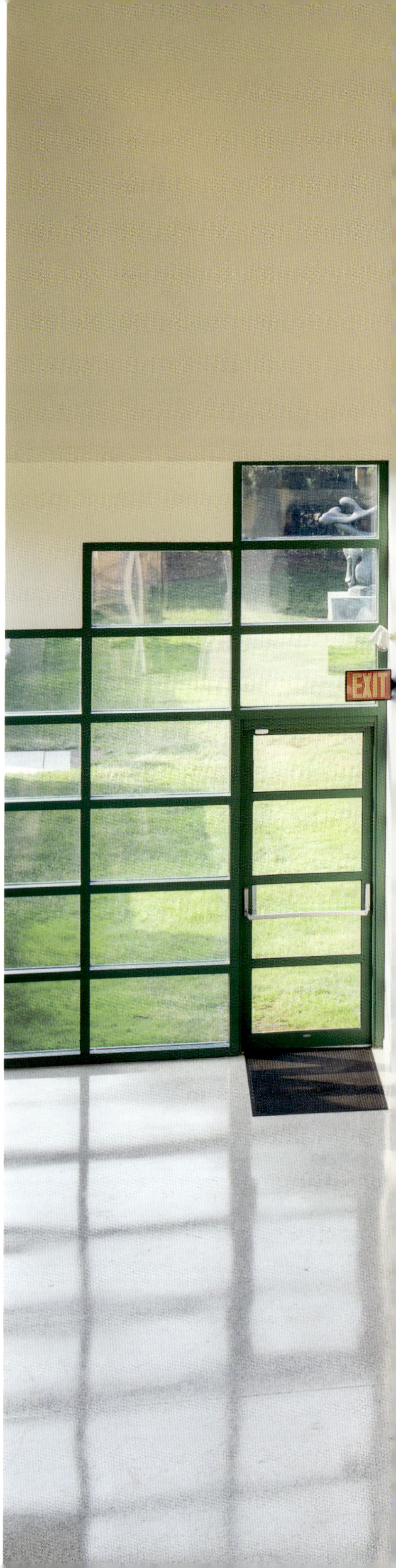

Grounds For Sculpture

Hamilton, New Jersey

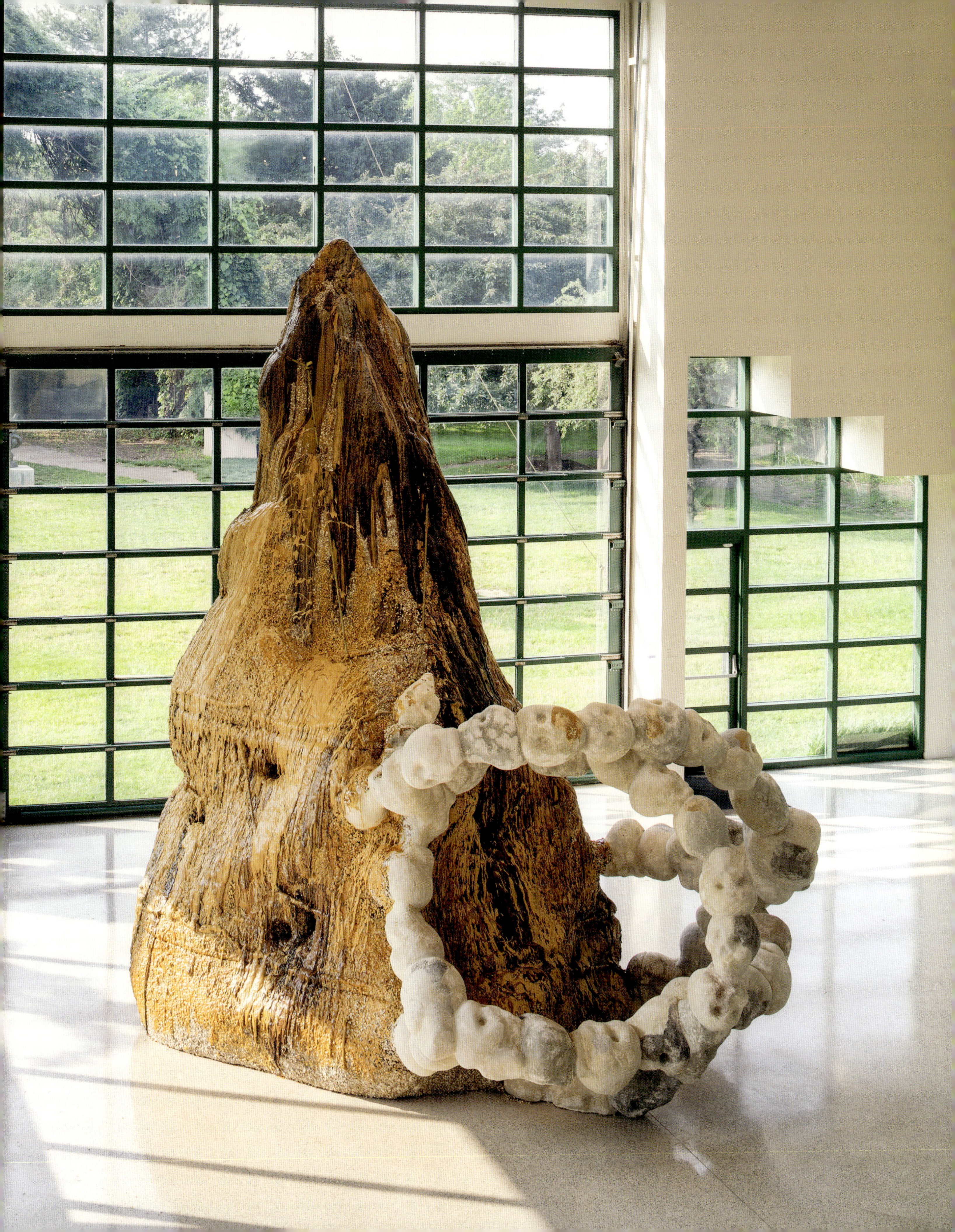

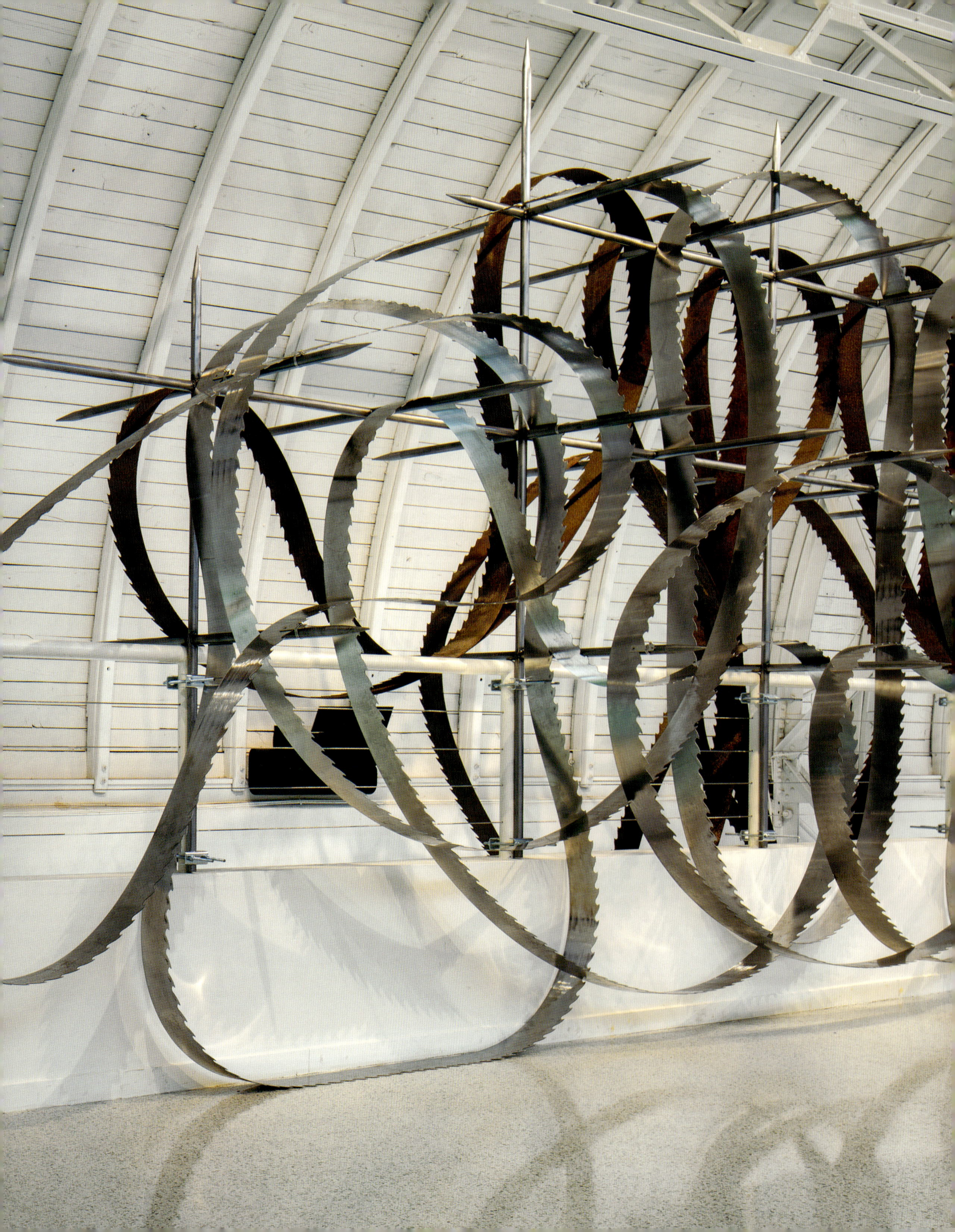

Contents

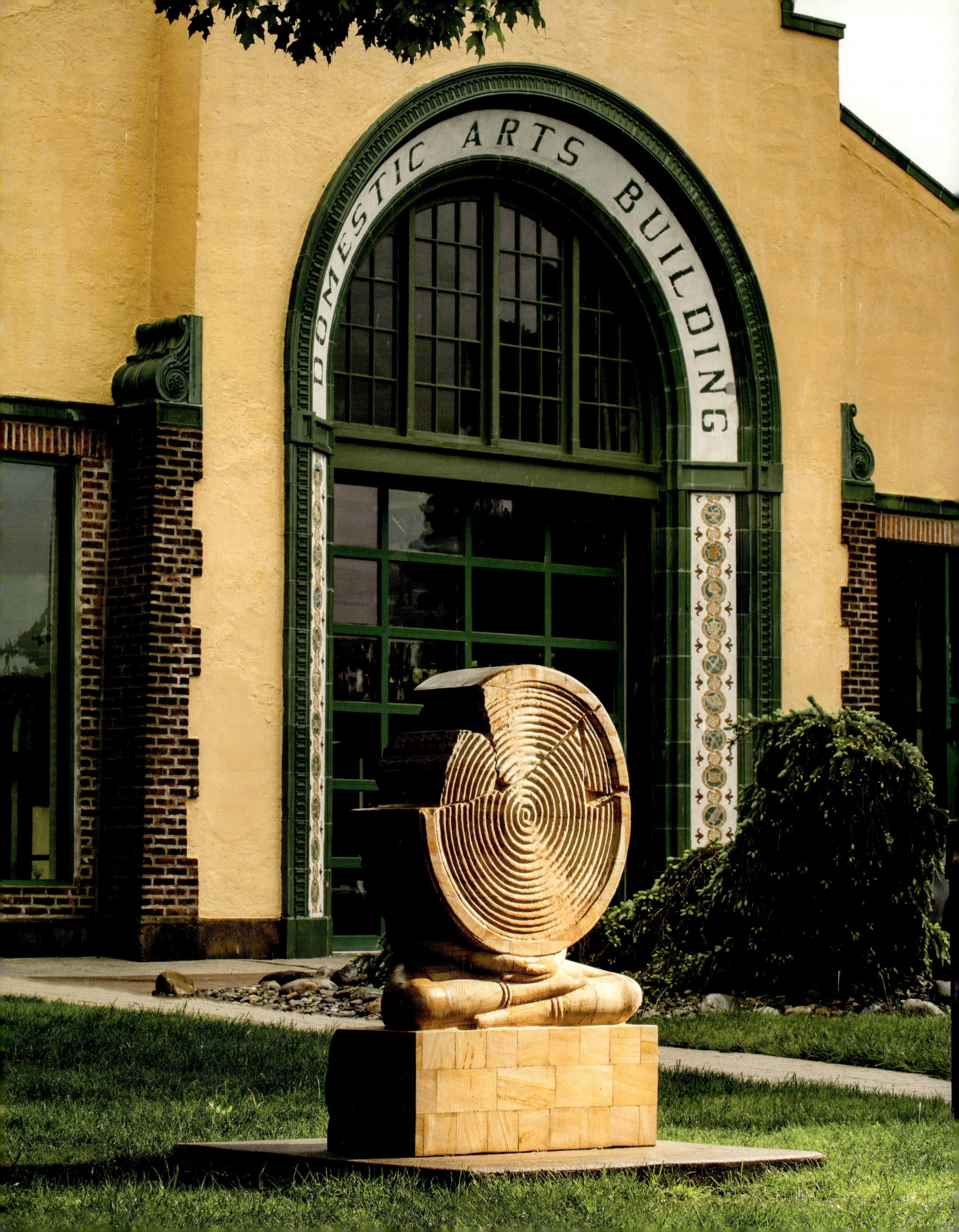
DOMESTIC ARTS BUILDING

Foreword and Acknowledgments

This volume is published on the occasion of the exhibition *Interference Fringe | TALLUR L.N.*, organized by Grounds For Sculpture. This project affirms Grounds For Sculpture's commitment to broadening our exhibition program and collection in ways that reflect the diversity of the region and the dynamic world around us. It opens at a time when society is at odds with itself and the lines between fact and fiction have blurred. Filled with twenty-seven works created in a range of media, interactive sculptures, and site-specific installations that extract witty wordplay from our contradictions and follies, this survey show beckons us to mine the paradoxes of life while looking critically at forces of history, capitalism, and globalization.

Tallur L.N.'s works reference ancient and popular icons, myths, and symbols, yet he subverts their easy categorization by exposing the universal humor and parody in our relationships to objects across cultures. An artist with a strong background in museology and deep knowledge of materials and conservation techniques, Tallur is known for making works that allude to their eventual decay or transformation despite our best attempts to preserve them. He reminds us that what we value is always in physical and psychological flux.

This exhibition grew out of the acquisition of the sculpture *Obituary Note* (2013; cat. 9), a work brought to my attention by my wife, the artist Gwen Charles. It was among the first pieces acquired as I began my tenure as the executive director of Grounds For Sculpture. I was looking for artists whose work expanded the scope of our collection in a variety of dimensions. When I arrived, *Prana 7* (1992) by Lalitha Shankar was the sole sculpture in the collection by an artist from India. The works an institution acquires and the artists it supports are a direct reflection of its values. Given the expanding South Asian community in New Jersey and among our audience, it became a priority to thoughtfully address that deficiency. Our board president, Eric Ryan, who has a profound affinity for India and Hinduism, was an early champion of this exhibition. He joined me for a research trip throughout India and his insight has deeply informed this project.

Over the last two decades, Tallur has established himself as one of India's most prolific and innovative sculptors. His practice has benefited from a global network of collectors and gallery representation beginning early in his career. We are appreciative of Arario Gallery (Seoul), Gallery Chemould (Mumbai), Nature Morte (New Delhi), and Jack Shainman Gallery (New York) for their support of Tallur. We particularly want to acknowledge Peter Nagy, Aparajita Jain, and Jessica Arisohn

Tolerance, 2019 (cat. 15)

at Nature Morte for their partnership, valuable perspective on Tallur's work, assistance in securing loans, advice on international shipping, and help to raise critical awareness around the exhibition.

A project of this magnitude is not possible without the commitment of many funders whose support demonstrates the significance of this endeavor and affirms the relevance of Tallur's work to our contemporary world. I want to express my appreciation to our Board of Trustees for their unfaltering belief in this important project. We are pleased to acknowledge the following for their major support of the exhibition and the catalogue: the National Endowment for the Arts, Art Works; Bank of America; New Jersey Department of State, Division of Travel & Tourism; Chemould Prescott Road; Marriott Princeton; Nature Morte; Frank and Sharon Lorenzo; Umesh and Sunanda Gaur. We are grateful to the following Exhibition Supporters: Gordon and Lulie Gund, Barbara Lawrence and Allen Laskin, and Eric B. Ryan.

The exhibition includes the premiere of an important new work and the exhibition's partial namesake, *Fringe* (2019; cat. 18), a towering eighteen-foot-tall, site-specific installation coated in bone meal, bone char, and crushed bone, which was inspired by historic Indian temple fragments in the collection of the Philadelphia Museum of Art. Grounds For Sculpture and the artist wish to acknowledge Darielle Mason, the Stella Kramrisch Curator of Indian and Himalayan Art at the Philadelphia Museum of Art, for embracing the project and providing access to their collection.

The commissioned work was produced with the support of Jon Lash, John Rannou, and Fred Morante of Digital Atelier and Jim Mills of Sculpture Cast, and we thank each of them for their deep understanding of artists and for their collaboration. Also debuting in the exhibition is a video work, *Interference* (2019; cat. 17), which was made in partnership with the Junagadh Museum in Gujarat, India, with special thanks to Varia Kiran, videography; Vandita Jain, sound engineer; and Bhanu Pratap Singh.

We offer profound gratitude to the following for generously loaning work to the exhibition: Ashish Jain, 21c Museum Hotels, Laura Lee Brown and Steve Wilson, Robert B. Feldman, Kiran Nadar Museum of Art, Ozlo Collection, Rajshree Pathy, and the Philadelphia Museum of Art.

This catalogue, of which I couldn't be prouder, was expertly brought about through the persistent support and guidance of Donna Wingate and her colleagues at Lucia|Marquand. I would like to thank Lucia|Marquand's Design Director Tom Eykemans for his thoughtful and striking book design, and Leah Finger and Meghann Ney at Lucia|Marquand, who provided production coordination. Special thanks to Kristin Swan for copyediting this book and to Nicholas Knight for photography. I am particularly grateful to Chaitanya Sambrani for his insightful essay.

As an executive director organizing a large international survey while balancing many other responsibilities, I have had the benefit of an incredible leadership team who not only supported my investment in this project but leveraged it to move the institution forward. I wish to personally thank my colleagues: Mark Baird, Manager of Guest Services; Heather Brady, Director of Education and Engagement; Rhonda DiMascio, Director of Development; Coby Green-Rifkin, Director of Marketing; Rob Gross, Chief Financial

Officer; Tom Moran, Chief Curator; Alex Silagyi, Director of Guest Services; and Matt Smith, Director of Facilities.

It is with great appreciation that I acknowledge Faith McClellan, Director of Collections and Exhibitions, for expertly managing all details of this complex project and serving as my principal partner throughout. This project was aided by Ami Mehta, who served as Associate Curator while securing loans, conducting research, and developing interpretive material. Special thanks to Lindsey Young-Lockett, Manager of Exhibition Production, for her endless research and ingenuity in supporting the creation of a number of commissioned works, many using unconventional materials (industrial scaffolding, crushed bone, bone meal, used car tires, etc.), with the help of Dani Edgar, Assistant Registrar, and Tracy Lee, Assistant Preparator. Harry Gordon and Eric Schultz of Harry Gordon Studios lent significant expertise with great patience throughout the installation process.

Finally, I would like to thank Tallur for dedicating such significant time to this exhibition and for sharing his subversive, interactive, and complex body of work with our audience. It has been my honor and pleasure to walk side by side with him on this journey, and through his perspective, to widen my way of seeing.

Gary Garrido Schneider
Executive Director

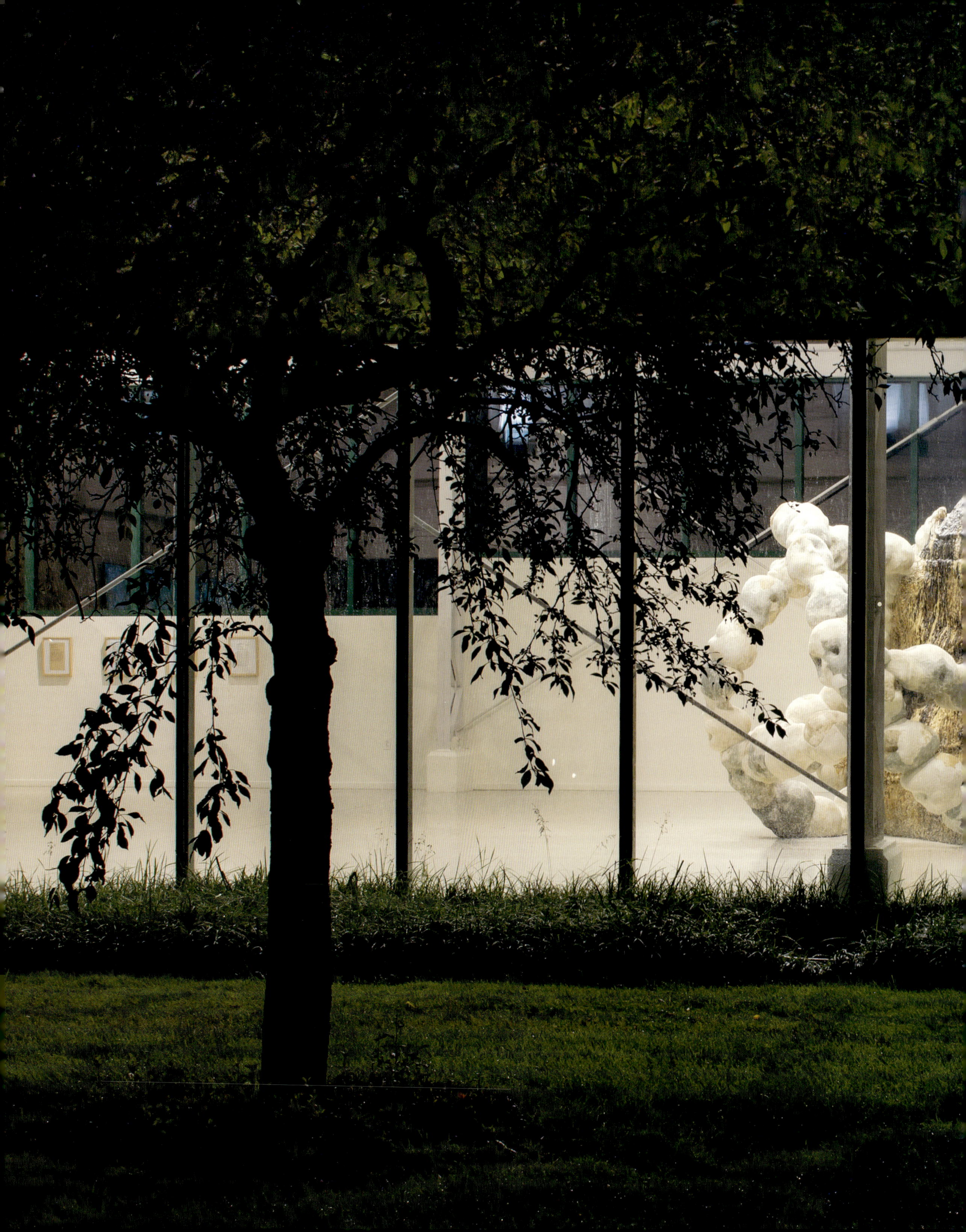

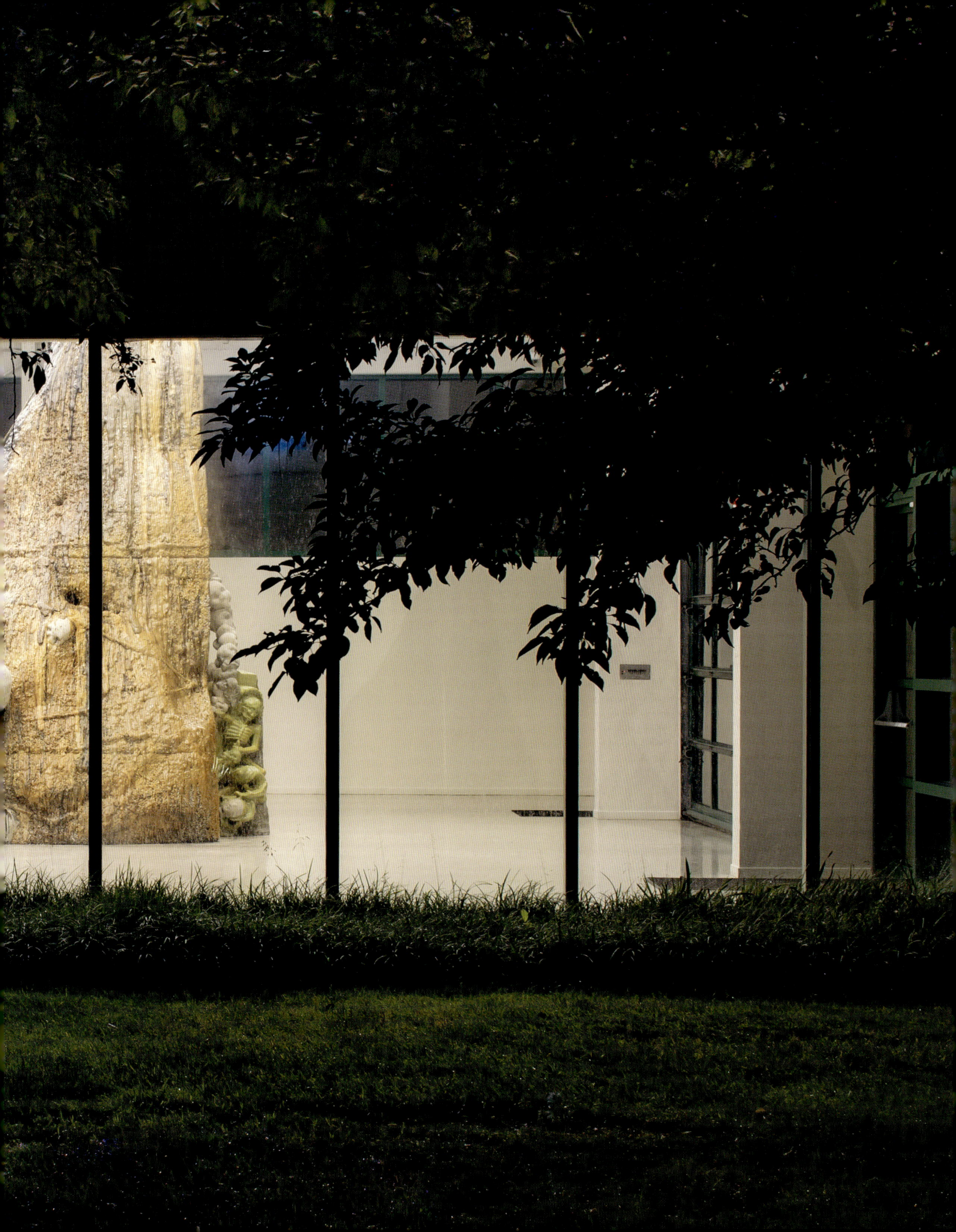

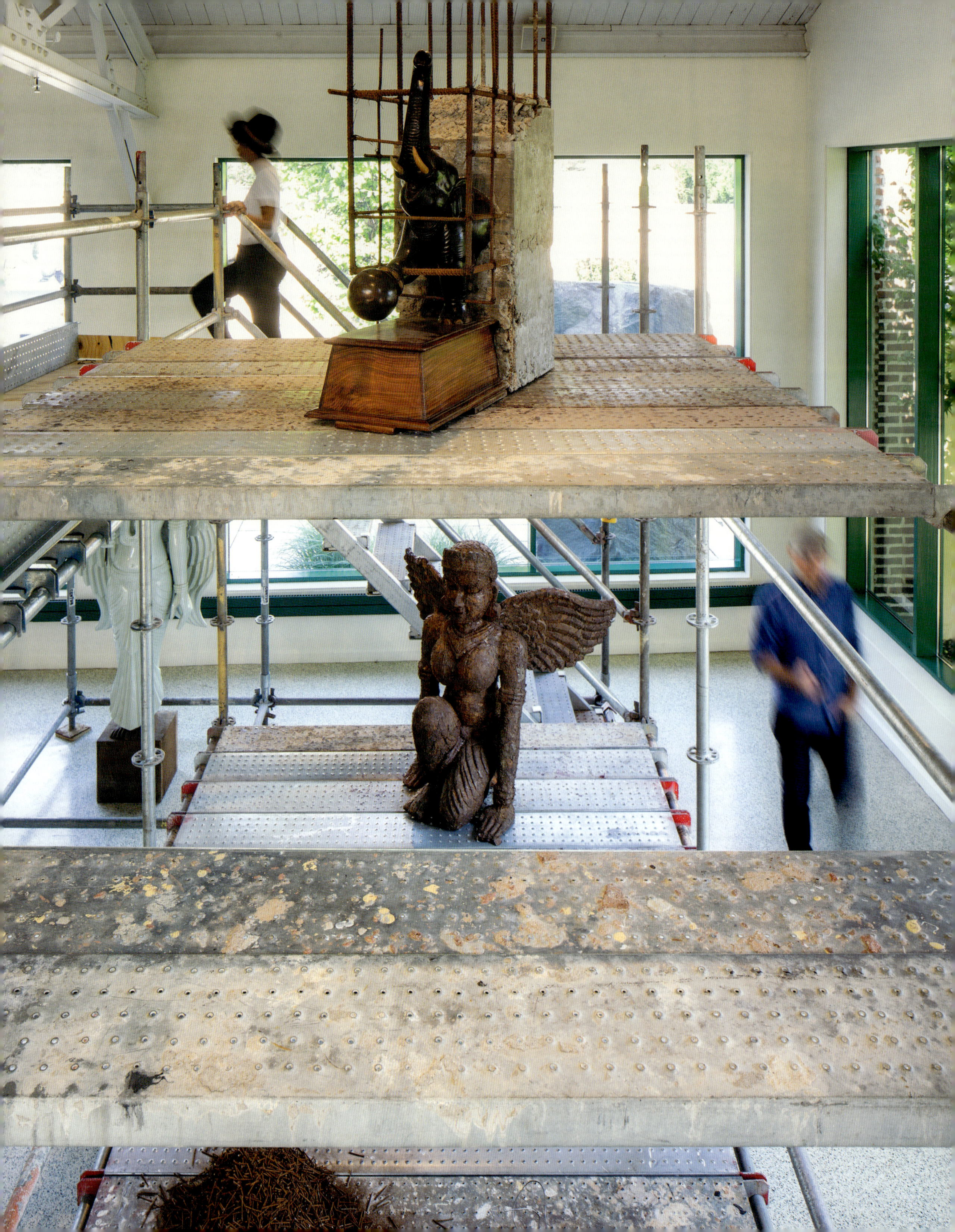

Interference Fringe

—

Symbols, Signals and Noise

Gary Garrido Schneider

The importance of memory in the contemporary context is demonstrated through the construction of collective memory and its presentation through an official history. We look at history and collective memory as one of the most important elements in the construction and homogenization of modern democratic communities. Collective memory is established through the assumption that each society develops the memory of its own past and transmits it to future generations. Meanwhile, political and social context contribute to a collective amnesia of the past. Collective amnesia is the effacement of minority histories from dominant narratives and the negotiation of collective identities.

—Tallur L.N.

In 1999 Tallur L.N. had his first solo exhibition, *Past-Modern, Interactive Art Objects*, which opened at the venerable Gallery Chemould in Mumbai and secured him an Emerging Artist Award from Bose Pacia Modern. The award included an opportunity to bring this exhibition to New York City. The Bose Pacia Modern gallery, which opened in New York in 1994, had a dedicated focus on South Asian contemporary art and was instrumental in introducing the artwork from this geographic region to the international arts community. Tallur's debut in these two important platforms marked a promising start for the artist, and the work he exhibited established thematic undercurrents that have continued throughout his creative practice.

This important early exhibition included an installation of eight finely crafted wooden containers, which the viewer was invited to explore both manually and visually.[1] Most of the objects had hinged lids and drawers that opened to reveal a compartmentalized selection of images and objects, like miniature cabinets of curiosity. The participant was guided through an intellectual and emotional journey of semantic and visual contradictions that were simultaneously amusing and thought provoking. The work titled *Dinosaur Egg* (1999; figs. 1–3) opened to reveal a technical drawing of a dinosaur embryo evoking the field of scientific observation. Its purported objectivity was immediately challenged in the subsequent drawers, which revealed a commercial tray of counterfeit eggs and a fried egg ready for consumption. The final compartment contained a stone ironically inscribed with the words "temporarily removed for restoration." This participatory exploration of contradictory evidence destabilized the notion of truth while exposing our susceptibility and willingness to be led to fabricated conclusions.[2]

The materials, symbols, and actions Tallur employs in his conceptual body of work all operate as signals of transmission and reception. These waves of communication deliver a series of tensions—the sacred and the secular, handmade and mass produced, authentic and counterfeit, and creative and destructive, which

Scaffold, 2019 (cat. 20)

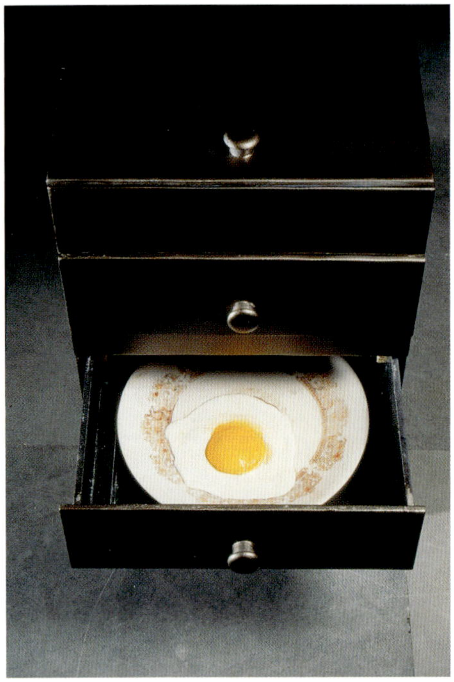

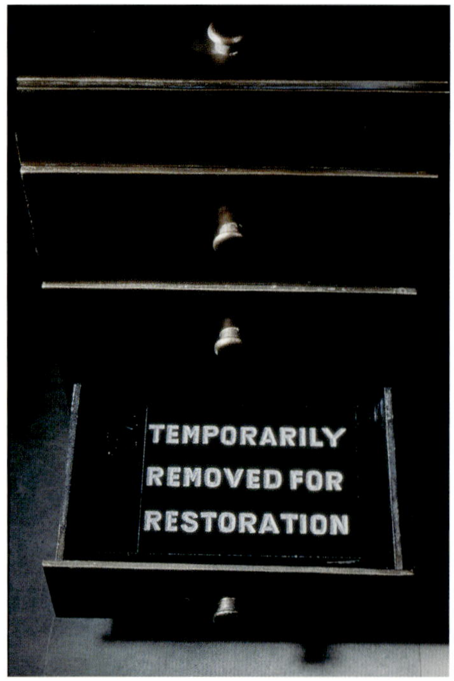

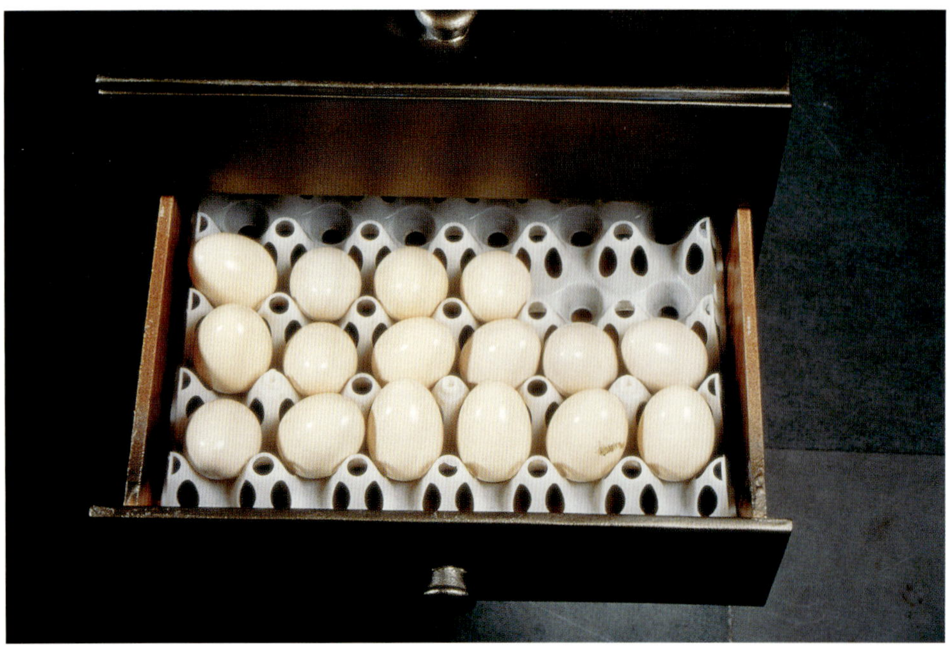

Figs. 1–3
Dinosaur Egg, 1999
mixed media, wood, stone
39 × 12½ × 15 inches
Courtesy of the artist

are continually at play in his work. It is in the ebb and flow of these contradictions and at the threshold of their intersection that the meaning and consequence within Tallur's work resides. He purposefully introduces interference into his equation, conceptual noise that disrupts easy consumption. He employs wit, irony, and ambiguity in ways that add nuance to the reading of his work. The mixed signals imbedded in his material, the feedback loops inherent in his appropriated iconography, and the clever wordplay in his titles all provide clues to help unpack the layers of meaning while equally serving as a fair warning for the deceptive twists that lie ahead. The alternating wavelengths and channels of information complicate, contradict, and confound any easy assignment of meaning.

It is perhaps important to note that Tallur studied museology, receiving a master's degree at the University of Baroda, a formative experience that introduced an enduring fascination with the practice of museums and fuels the artist's skepticism about the politics of display and representation. This educational foundation and the echoes of his earliest exhibition are particularly resonant in the installation *Scaffold* (2019; cats. 20–28), conceived for *Interference Fringe | TALLUR L.N.* as a physical and conceptual framework to present a retrospective body of the artist's work. The scaffold grew out of an impulse to ensure that the artwork commanded the space in a way that moved beyond the conventional pedestal, asserted itself against the dominant architecture of the site, and ultimately enabled the artist to see his work anew. This site-specific installation consists of eight preexisting artworks that have been assembled on a multilevel structure composed of construction scaffolding, forming a recursive exhibition within an exhibition. The installation serves as an index and cognitive map for the complex system of ideas embedded throughout the exhibition.

The inherent meaning denoted by a material is central to Tallur's artwork and is often a point of ignition.[3] In this case, the industrial scaffold represents a decidedly utilitarian material that provides stability and protection while being deployed in acts of construction and deconstruction. The steel structure is marked and worn from previous use, providing a patina of time, labor, and authenticity. Whereas a pedestal functions as a static and stable repository, the scaffolding is transitory, iterative, and dynamic, alluding to an ongoing development and evolution. It is erected to hold people and materials in the service of assembling and fabricating.

Many of Tallur's works demand, via their systems and structure, that they be understood through multiple perspectives and disciplinary lenses. The physicality of the scaffold beckons the viewer to circulate around, walk through, and ascend to a series of viewing platforms that viscerally afford varying vantage points. The sculptures are presented as a sequence of objects that are framed and held in correspondence by a network of conceptual and aesthetic associations. While reinforcing connections between the artworks, the structure also challenges the viewer with obscured views and partial access. Much like the work it holds, the scaffolding deliberately makes it difficult to decipher the cultural and religious symbols that many of the sculptures appropriate. Tallur purposefully obscures, transforms, and subverts the traditional reading of these historic references as he creates conceptual metaphors through the manipulation and integration/dis-integration of materials. This fragmentary experience of the work sets up a situation in which meaning is always "differential" and "postponed," never complete and total.[4]

A central artwork within the scaffold structure is *Hatha Yoga* (2012; cat. 27) an

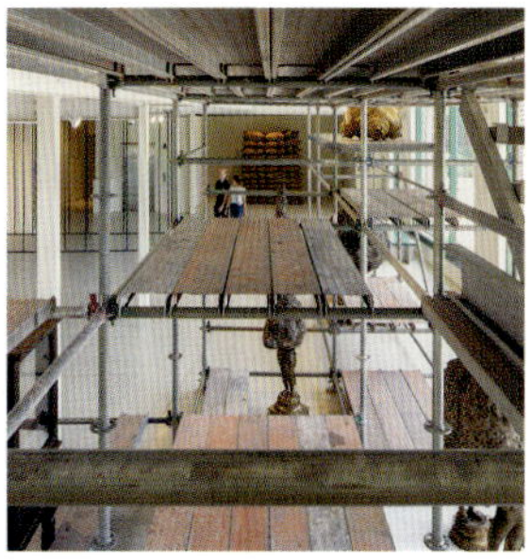

Scaffold, 2019 (cat. 20)

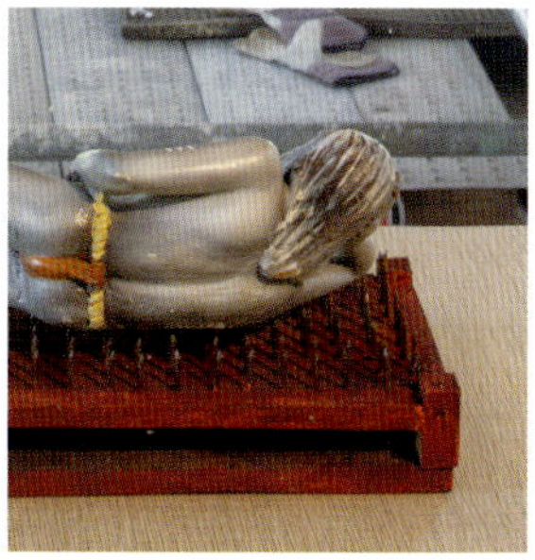

Hatha Yoga, 2012 (cat. 27)

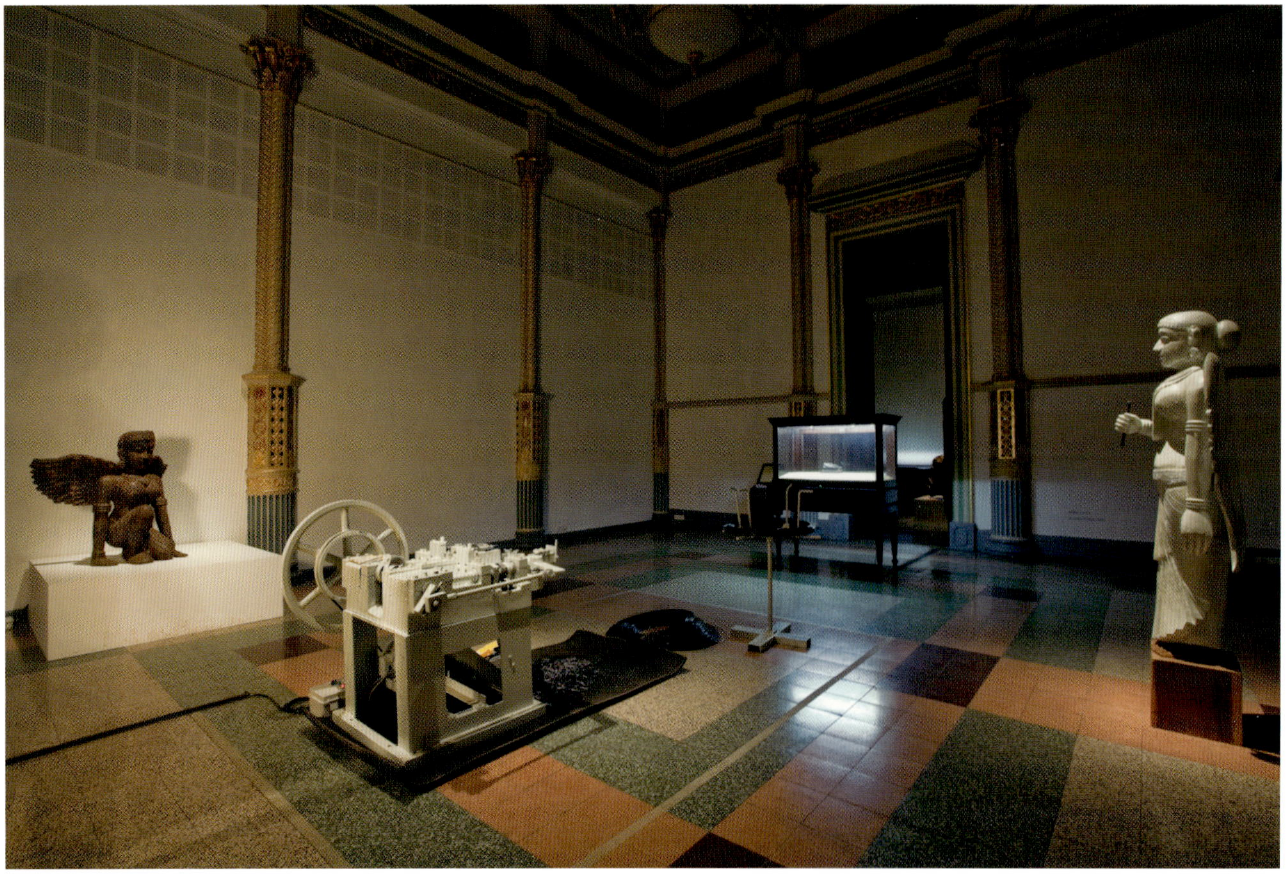

Fig. 4
Quintessential at Dr. Bhau Daji Lad Mumbai City Museum, Mumbai, India, installation photo, 2011

installation composed of four objects that was originally created for the exhibition *Quintessential* at the Dr. Bhau Daji Lad Museum in Mumbai in 2011 (fig. 4). This seminal exhibition consisted of multiple site-specific interventions and interactive sculptures that responded critically to the museum's permanent collection, much of which reflects the legacy of the colonial era in which it was founded. These cultural artifacts expose the unreliable narration of the British colonizer recording the colonial subject. For *Hatha Yoga*, Tallur made a replica of a clay figurine, part of the ethnographic collection, that depicts a yogi reclining on a bed of nails. He placed this trope, symbolic of orientalist stereotypes of India, on display within one of the museum's colonial-era wooden vitrines. By subverting the institutional language of presentation and reversing the gaze, he calls into question the exoticizing of Indian culture and the perversion of yoga as it becomes a transnational commodity.

This vitrine with the yogi on a bed of nails is paired with two sculptures of winged celestial beings that incorporate nails, along with an industrial nail-making machine. The nail, a material signifier with varying contextual implications, provides the narrative through line for the disparate sculptural components of this work. One figure is inspired by a Christian angel holding two large nails, symbolic of the crucifixion, which the artist encountered at the Metropolitan Museum of Art in New York. In an attentive reversal of the subject and observer, the artist brought the image back to India and employed local craftsmen to produce an enlarged version of this sculpture, the results best described as a translation in which proportions and attire are subtly affected by the vernacular rules for sculpture production. The second figure, coated in an armor of nails, is in the image of Garuda, an avian creature from Hindu mythology with a mix of eagle and human features. Just as the nail can have varying symbolic meanings attached to it depending on the context, so, too, do these winged figures. Perhaps in this case the similarities of the winged forms point to the difficulty in establishing the provenance of cultural ideas and the debts one culture may owe to another in the continual circulation of ideas. Tallur's work reminds us that the meaning we assign to objects is not static; it is in a constant state of transaction, translation, and misinterpretation.

The functional nail-making apparatus—complete with a coil of metal wire that traverses the machine, emerging as newly minted nails deposited at the base of the device—functions as a counterpoint within *Hatha Yoga*. The pile of new nails sits next to a mound of rusty older nails, establishing a tension between past and present, the functional and obsolete. The production of the nail becomes a meditation on the singularity of this object. In this situation, the nail becomes the most tangible, uncomplicated, and earnest truth, proffering its utility to secure, to construct, and to fix in place. Tallur's assembly destabilizes not only the different perspectives on the authentic but the entire notion of the authentic at all. These concerns of authorship, veracity, and representation reverberate throughout his enterprise.

On the second level of *Scaffold* is *"?"* (2011; cat. 24), in which the artist assembles a series of six sculptural pedestals welded together to form a jack or six-pointed, star-like arrangement. The new form destabilizes the very balance intended by the component bases. Each of the pedestals, acquired from a manufacturer of mass-produced religious sculptures, is topped by a pair of feet, with the rest of the figure absent above the ankles. The effect gives the impression that the figure was violently removed where, in fact, these pedestals are fabricated to be interchangeable; any deity could be assigned and welded onto the generic feet. This standardized economic efficiency, a cutting of corners, is introduced at the very foundation of the representation and the commodification of the divine. In related works, including *Unicode* (2011; cat. 25), *Pedestal on Pedestal* (2012; cat. 26), and *Victory Pillar* (2012; cat. 28), we see similar replicas of religious symbols buried and burdened under concrete, coins, and construction materials. These materials symbolic of modern development are set in dynamic tension with the traditional. They allude to the global economic system of overproduction and overconsumption that is at risk of collapsing under its own weight, and expose a homogenizing tendency in

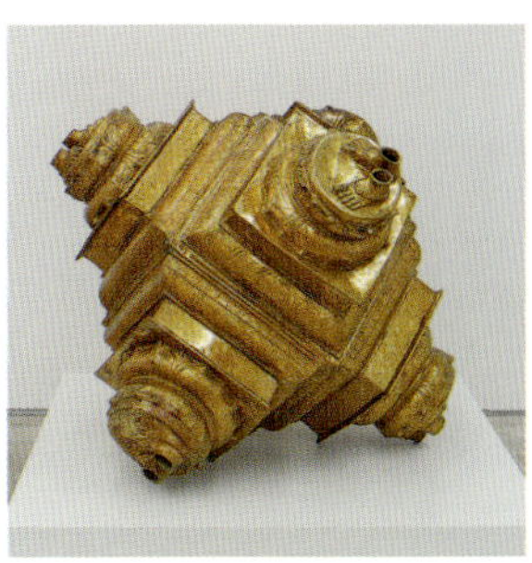
"?", 2011 (cat. 24)

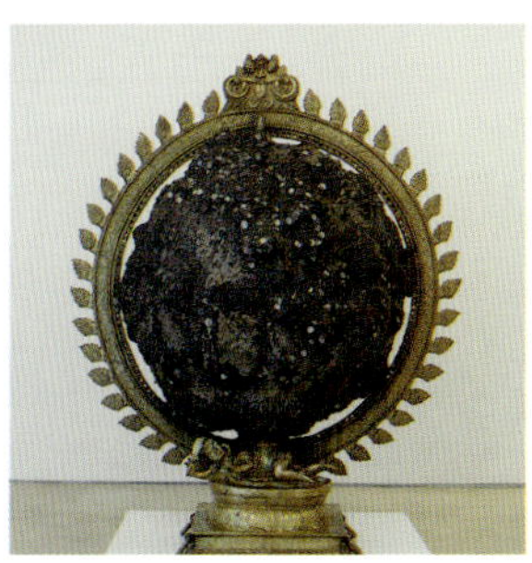
Unicode, 2011 (cat. 25)

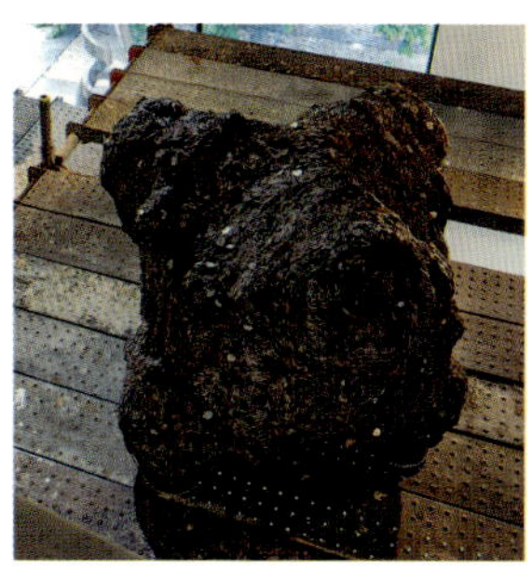
Pedestal on Pedestal, 2012 (cat. 26)

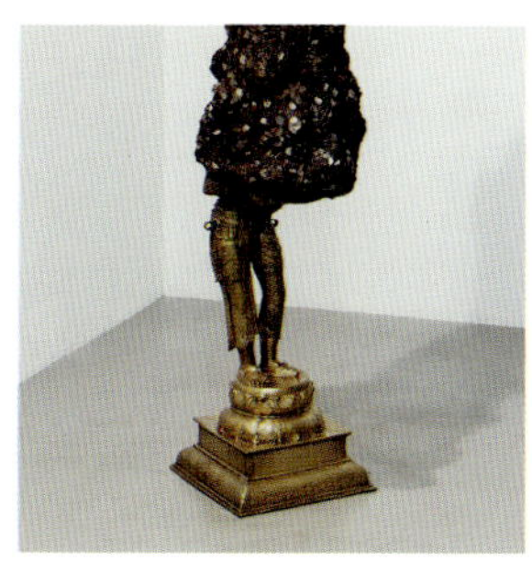
Victory Pillar, 2012 (cat. 28)

the aspiration of progress that may prove to be all consuming.

Anxiety around money and the greed it fuels carries throughout the exhibition. The work *Chromatophobia* (2012; cat. 7) presents a therapeutic solution to the irrational fear of money. Visitors are invited to hammer coins into a giant log that seemingly has crashed over a stone sculpture of Budai, a tenth-century Chinese monk known for his abundance, contentment, and generosity. Over the centuries, this symbol of good fortune has evolved into a patron deity of shopkeepers and is familiar as a mass-produced tourist trinket. The base of the stone figure is engraved with the text "Made in China" and "Made in America." These contested claims of production designate the cultural artifact as a globalized commodity, reminding us of the attrition, redistribution, and accrual of meaning that results in this exchange. The hammering of the coin is evocative of both the tradition, in parts of India, of nailing currency into the threshold of the home as an invocation of prosperity, and the ritualized activity of throwing a coin into a fountain—a shared notion of giving something up to gain wish fulfillment. This playfully interactive work gently mocks society's tendency for empty idol worship and obsession with ritual. Over the course of time, the log has increasingly become embossed with coins, evidence of the audience's faith in this artwork's therapeutic claims—or at least their willingness to hedge their bets.

In the work *Apocalypse* (2010; cat. 5) visitors can cross the threshold into a caged vault where a commercial-grade machine similar to those used for polishing precious stones is co-opted for an installation in which visitors are invited to deposit their currency. With characteristic humor, the artist guarantees the resulting polished coins will emerge certifiably civilized. These deposits are burnished until their denomination and signifiers of national identify are slowly worn away as the monetary value of the coins returns to that of their base metals. In this act of refinement, one gets back less than one puts in, a contradiction that points to the subjectivity inherent in establishing what is "civilized," as well as the power imbalance and loss involved in the extraction of value from one culture by another. This negation underscores the irony that sometimes our human desire for progress can have the inverse result and alerts us to the inherent violence in the drive for equivalence. The title suggests the religious conception of the end of the world, a revelation, in which the power of evil is destroyed at the threshold of the divine. In our contemporary sense, the term has all-too-human implications—the destruction of the world through large-scale catastrophic events resulting from environmental crisis, dehumanizing technological progression, and an economic system with inequitable distribution of resources that may prove to be dangerously unsustainable.

The strategy of physically deconstructing objects as a conceptual act carries through much of Tallur's work. He deploys natural forms of erosion and decomposition as well as manufactured acts of destruction that provide a wide

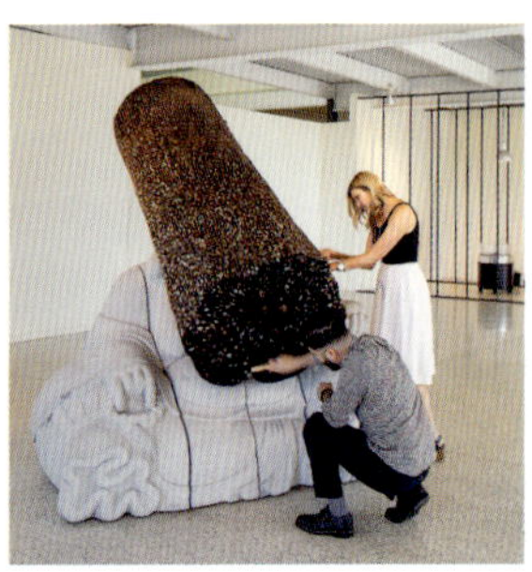

Chromatophobia, 2012 (cat. 7)

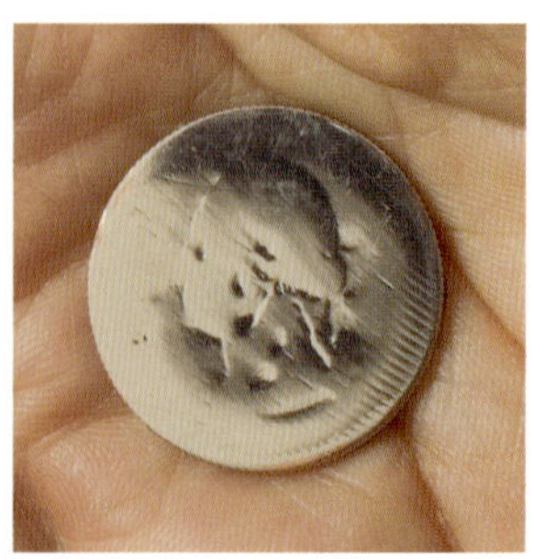

Apocalypse, 2010 (cat. 5)

range of metaphoric and poetic associations. In *Milled History* (2014; cat. 12), the artist employs termites to digest parts of a wooden icon in a controlled process of decay. The procedure draws inspiration from a practice utilized by natural history museums that deploy flesh-eating dermestid beetles to clean animal bones in preparation for display, a process more delicate and cost-effective than assigning humans to the task. The termites' act of consumption, digestion, and destruction of a religious or cultural icon stands in as proxy for human behavior. The work contends with our impulse to preserve, as the partially decomposed wooden sculpture is then digitally scanned to produce renderings used to carve the degraded form in yellow teakwood sandstone. This material was chosen for the similarity between its sedimentary layers and the wood grain of the original. The resulting sculpture mimics (and mocks) an archeological fragment surgically excavated from its original context and destined for museum display, subject to the questions of ownership and representation inherent in this exploit. The recent repatriation of illicitly acquired Roman artifacts by museums abroad and France's restitution of cultural artifacts looted from Africa during the colonial period speak to this contested control over the historical record.

The warm tonality of the sandstone visually calls to mind the archeological site of Petra and its own erosion, affected by environmental factors, neglect, and the impact of heavy tourism. Tallur's intentional act of destruction is likewise a somber reminder of the cultural defacement and eradication that often results from human conflict and military domination, as evidenced by the recent demolition of the Buddhas of Bamiyan by the Taliban. *Milled History* contains two holes, punctuations in the surface that serve as portals visually urging the viewer to consider what is on the other side. While the coarsely textured front side of the sculpture visualizes the natural process of decay, the rear is sheer and polished, the quarried stone clearly manipulated. Even so, the highly refined surface calls our attention to the natural processes that formed the stone, with its sedimentary layers on full display. The front of the work speaks to the archeological record of human society and the fragility of historical veracity. The materiality of the stone offers a humbling reminder of a grander geological timeline of which we are but a layer.

The act of cultural effacement continues with *Enlightenment Machine (Beta Version 3.0)* (2019; cat. 16). In this work the viewer is invited to reshape replicas of cultural, civic, and religious iconography by carving them on a manually operated grinder at the center of the sculpture's two giant wooden wheels. Tallur subjects these cheap reproductions to the mechanical destruction inherent in their mass production. He provokes audiences to consider how objects and symbols can be leveraged to peddle edited or manufactured versions of history.[5] The three editions of this sculpture exhibited in India, China, and the United States have utilized domestic souvenirs from the site country, requiring the local audience to have some skin in the game. The versions

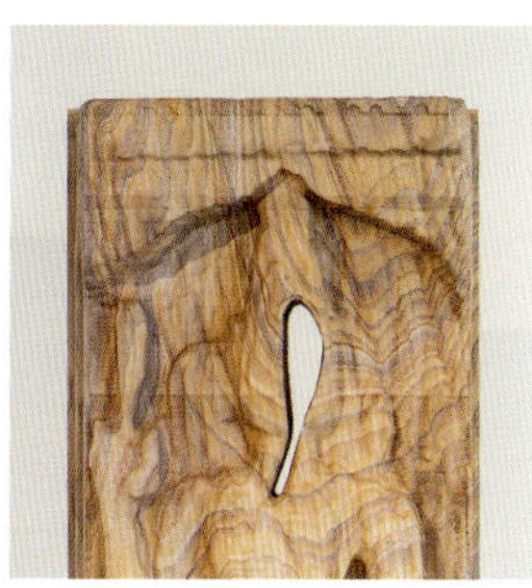

Milled History, 2014 (cat. 12)

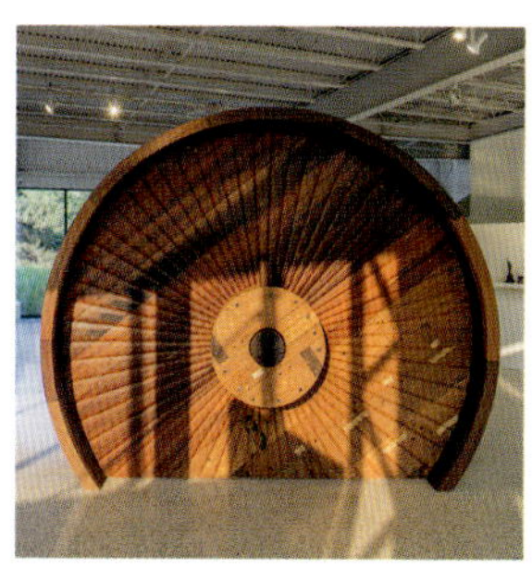

Enlightenment Machine (Beta Version 3.0), 2019 (cat. 16)

in India and China from 2011 utilized religious deities commodified for tourist consumption, whereas the new version in the United States invites visitors to reshape souvenirs of the Statue of Liberty and the Liberty Bell. The title's implications stretch from the dharma wheel representing the path to spiritual enlightenment (Nirvana) to the Western ideal of liberty as defined in the Age of Enlightenment.

In the current version, the interrogation of the Statue of Liberty comes amidst the political tensions in the United States, and globally, around mass migration and the resultant rise of nationalism and isolationism. Initially a gift to the United States from France, the monumental version of the Roman goddess Libertas was intended to commemorate the abolition of slavery in the United States. Not visible from the ground—and notably omitted from the tourist trinkets—are a broken chain and shackle at the statue's feet. It is important to note that the promise of universal liberty was far from a reality for people of color and women during the late nineteenth century when the statue was first conceived. Over time, the monument has become more commonly associated with immigration than emancipation. Yet even in the early twentieth century, when this symbolism arose from the statue's proximity to the Ellis Island port of entry, discriminatory immigration quotas meant this welcome was extended to some but not all. The meaning of cultural symbols is never fixed, as we are continually shaping, reshaping, and recasting them to our present moment and needs. By luring visitors to participate in contradictory acts of re-creation and erasure, Tallur parodies the ways that we are all complicit in the dissolution of the very values our monuments allegedly uphold.

The work *Eraser Pro* (2012; cat. 8) takes its title from a software technology used to permanently remove data from a hard drive. The artist has applied the expunging of memory to a store-bought, mass-produced bronze sculpture of Mahatma Gandhi. In Tallur's adaptation, this sculpture has been burnished fervently, applying a mechanical grinding process to an extreme until much of the figure is violently worn away. The figure stands in a state of disintegration, with its resemblance to the original on the threshold of recognition, suggesting the way that obsessive reverence contributes to the erosion of our collective memory. Gandhi, emblematic of India's independence, was—like many of our heroes—a far more complicated figure than his idealized place in history has often allowed. This work seems to acknowledge and to unseat that generally unquestioned position. However, the direction of critique in both *Eraser Pro* and *Enlightenment Machine* is not so easy to isolate. The interrogation of these symbols so closely tied to national identity clearly reverberates for the viewer within a globally contested political landscape, yet one gets the sense that for the artist, perhaps our collective emotions and behaviors—irrespective of the distinctions of nation state or affiliation—are as much the substance and target of these works.

The corrosive veneration of *Eraser Pro* and the self-contradictory action in *Apocalypse* find a level of sublime conceptual refinement in *Threshold* (2015/2019; cat. 13). This work takes as its starting point the simple paradox that as one sharpens the blade of a knife it grows more effective in its function but is also slowly eroded, until the tipping point when it is no longer usable. Tallur extends this action through the appropriation of an

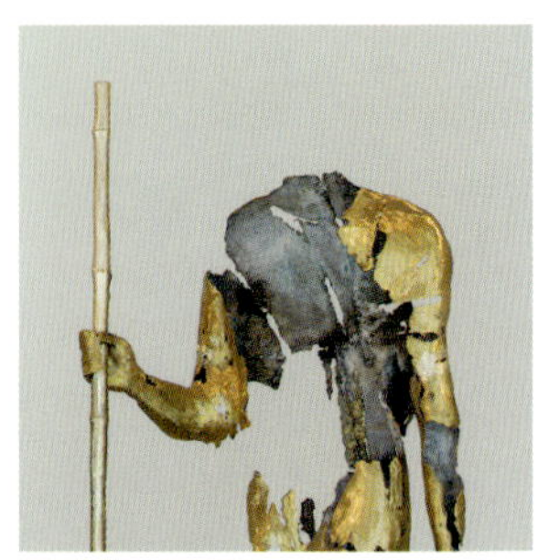

Eraser Pro, 2012 (cat. 8)

obsolete industrial machine designed to mechanically sharpen the individual teeth on a large band saw blade. The grinder wheel on the machine has been adjusted, tampered with, so that rather than sharpen, it rhythmically hammers down and erodes the teeth. Like the Egyptian symbol Ouroboros depicting a serpent eating its own tail, the machine circulates the saw blade, and with attendant sparks and sharp noise it slowly consumes and blunts the function. Over time, artists have invariably employed machines as a metaphor for idealized human progress or, conversely, as a dystopian warning against transgressions. In *Threshold*, the autonomous action of the machine serves as a physically poetic gesture—a circular reference, a statement of fact in the act of referencing and negating itself.

The moment of impact where creation meets destruction occurs throughout Tallur's body of work, including in the large-scale sculpture *Fringe* (2019; cat. 18). This work was commissioned for this exhibition and was inspired by a tenth-century temple fragment from the South Asian collection of the Philadelphia Museum of Art known as *Terrifying Attendant Spirits* (cat. 2). Tallur was permitted to digitally scan the original sculpture, and he used the resulting digital files as the basis to create this new monumental work. Tallur sees this process as a direct conversation with the original artist, a dialogue carried out not in verbal language but in a visual and material format. *Fringe* builds upon the garland of skulls and attendant skeletal figures that are believed to have originally stood on the peripheral edges of a sculpture of the Hindu goddess Kali, who embodies the duality of creation and destruction. Fearsome and renowned for her garland of skulls, she is the great Creator-Destroyer, the incarnation of time. In *Fringe*, a labyrinthine helix of skulls erupts from this mountain-like form, the absolute void from which everything arises, the absolute fullness into which it returns. The visceral bone meal, crushed bone, and charred bone the sculpture is made from secrete, discharge, and protrude in ways that are mesmerizing, disturbing, and terrifying.

The work *Coherence* (2019; cat. 14) also part of the partnership with the Philadelphia Museum of Art, takes its inspiration from a ninth- or tenth-century sculptural fragment identified as the lower portion of a stele with a deity in Samapada Sthanika flanked by female and male attendants (cat. 1). This stone carving consists of two figures flanking a missing central deity, indicated only by the remains of its feet. The sculpture is severely weathered on all surfaces, making definitive attribution of the provenance and identify difficult. As with the work that inspired *Fringe*, Tallur was specifically drawn to the stele's fragmented forms with their physical and conceptual negative space. In his new creation, he reconceives the void, giving

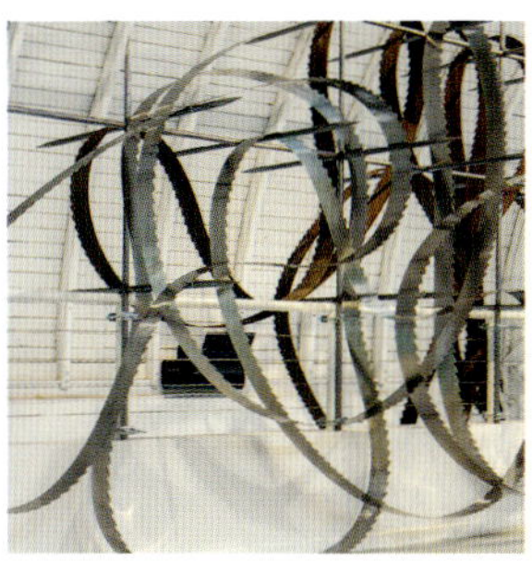

Threshold, 2015/2019 (cat. 13)

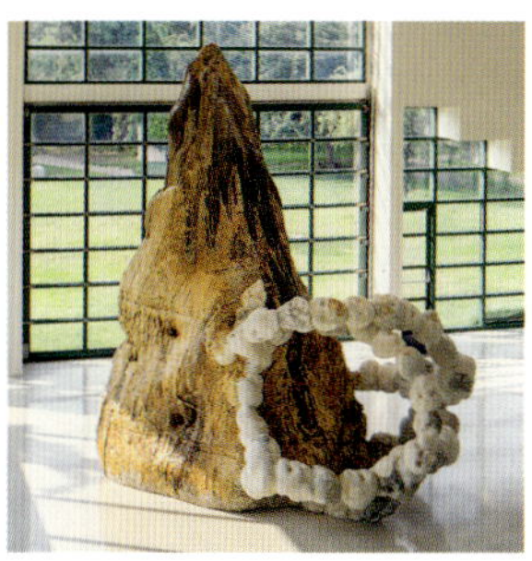

Fringe, 2019 (cat. 18)

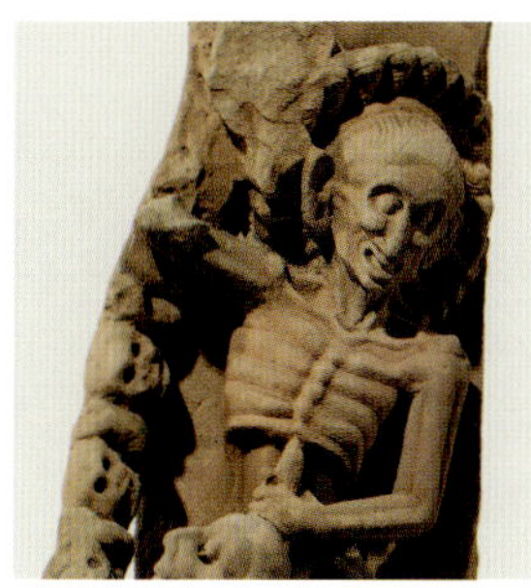

Artist Unknown, India, **Terrifying Attendant Spirits**, ca. 10th century (cat. 2)

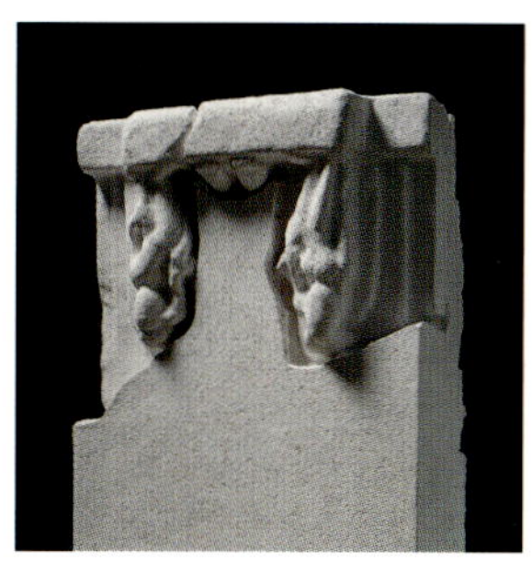

Coherence, 2019 (cat. 14)

it physical form again. The sculptural fragment underwent a series of recursive procedures typical of Tallur's methodology, including multiple interactions of digital scanning, computer-assisted carving, and manual manipulation of the material. The resulting sculpture cast in marble dust gives the illusion of being made of inexpensive and pedestrian Styrofoam. This faux Styrofoam signals, with its crumbling texture, a tentative fragility and is at odds with the value of permanence often associated with marble. The sculpture includes an inverted replication of the original artifact, with the vacant space underneath filled in, this new volume filling the void like packing materials protecting valuable commercial goods. The sculpture makes the viewer feel the absence of the main figure and represents a generous effort to bring forth that which was lost.

This process of excavating the past and making it visible in new forms manifests itself in the work *Interference* (2019; cat. 17), made for this exhibition in partnership with the Junagadh Museum in the state of Gujarat, India. This slow-motion video captures the manual cleaning of a rug originally installed at a palace in Junagadh. The ornate textile, with its geometric floral pattern, was initially produced in the late nineteenth century by inmates believed to be imprisoned for their role as freedom fighters in the ongoing struggle for independence from colonial Great Britain. A surprising amount of dust is exhumed in this beating process, creating billowing smoke-like plumes that envelop the scene, the laborers, and this cultural artifact. The work alludes to the sediment of time and a release of that which is embedded underneath the surface of our dominant narrative. The sound is slightly off register with the action, creating an echoing effect not unlike that of mortars discharging in the distance, while the image of the dust clouds calls to mind a city under aerial bombardment (carpet bombing). This suggests an association between the act of cleaning or cleansing and the violent and destructive conflicts in places such as Iraq, Afghanistan, and Syria. At the culmination of the video, the action ceases, the figures depart, and the dust settles, accompanied by a calm that is devoid of human presence.

This new video work has direct connections to an earlier work titled *Thatwamasi (that thou art)* (2011; figs. 5 and 6), which was created for the exhibition *Quintessential* at the Dr. Bhau Daji Lad Museum in Mumbai. Like *Hatha Yoga*, this work modifies a historic wooden museum vitrine, converting it into a functioning vacuum cleaner that deposits clouds of dust into the glass case. This sculpture is decidedly functional and was used simultaneously to clean, collect, and display the dirt of the museum. The piece accomplishes its institutional critique with simplicity and a good degree of humor. The title, *Thatwamasi (that thou art)*, references the Vedic verse that suggests God is everywhere in all living and nonliving things. By extension, the work is suggestive of the divine—and art—in even the smallest of particles. This points to Tallur's ability to elevate elemental materials to create situations that are simultaneously irreverent, critical, and spiritually reverential.

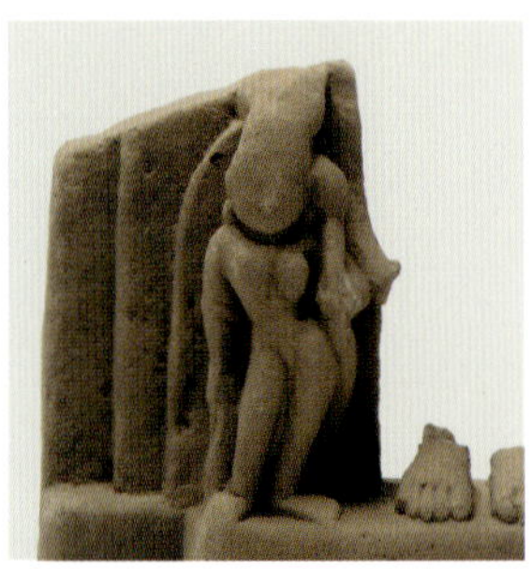

Artist Unknown, India, **Lower portion of a stele with deity in Samapada Sthanika flanked by female and male attendants**, 9th–10th century (cat. 1)

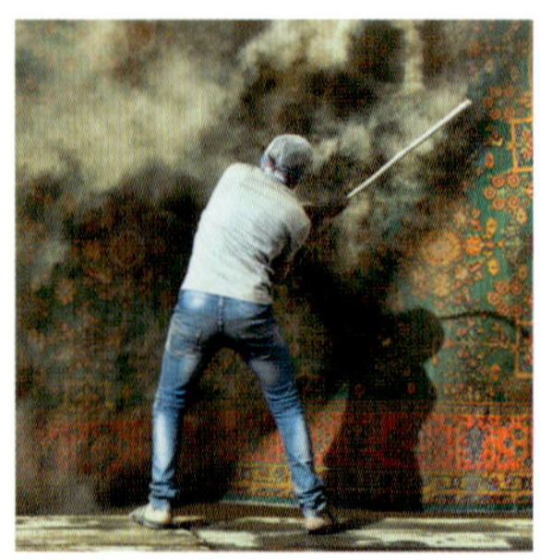

Interference, 2019 (cat. 17)

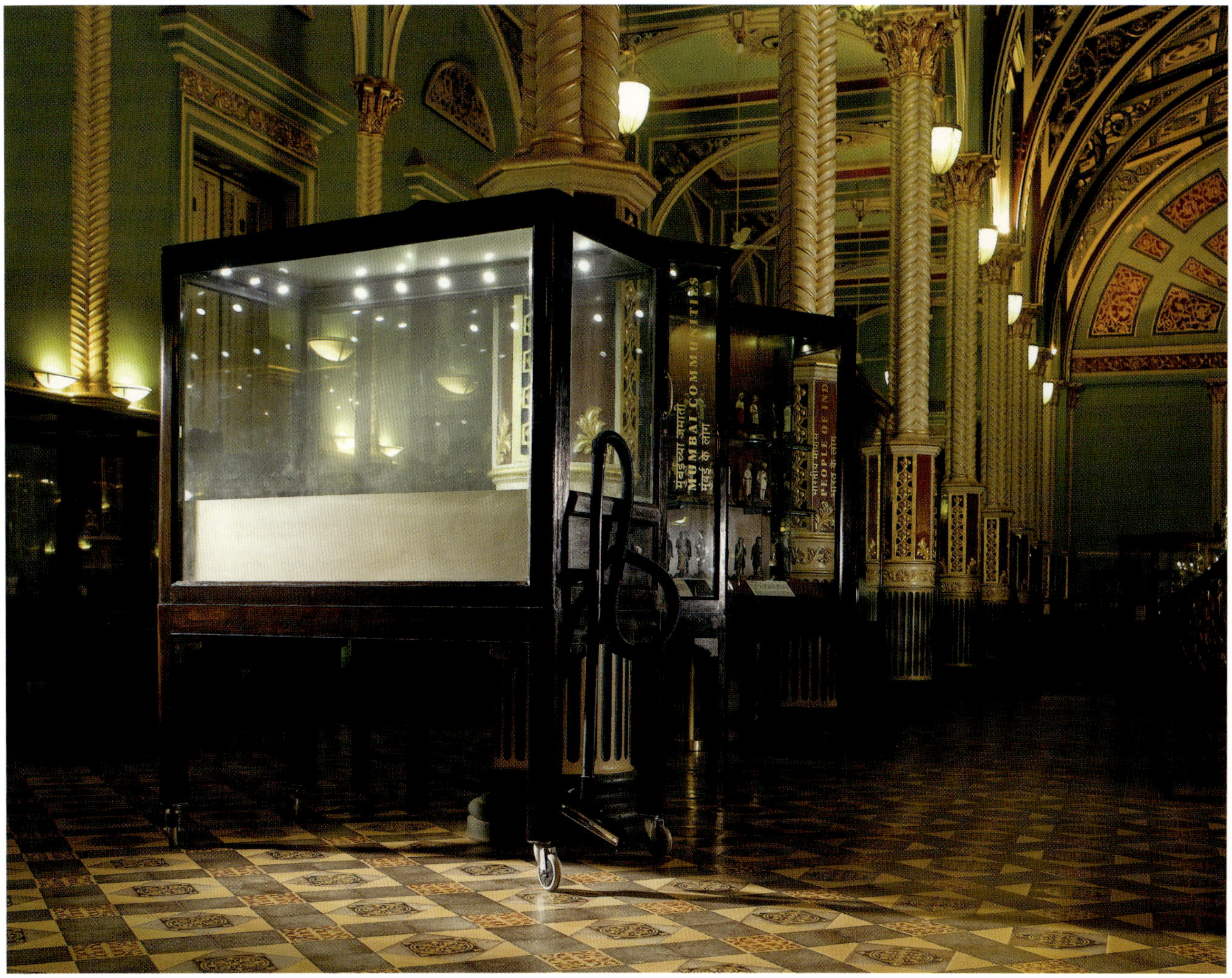

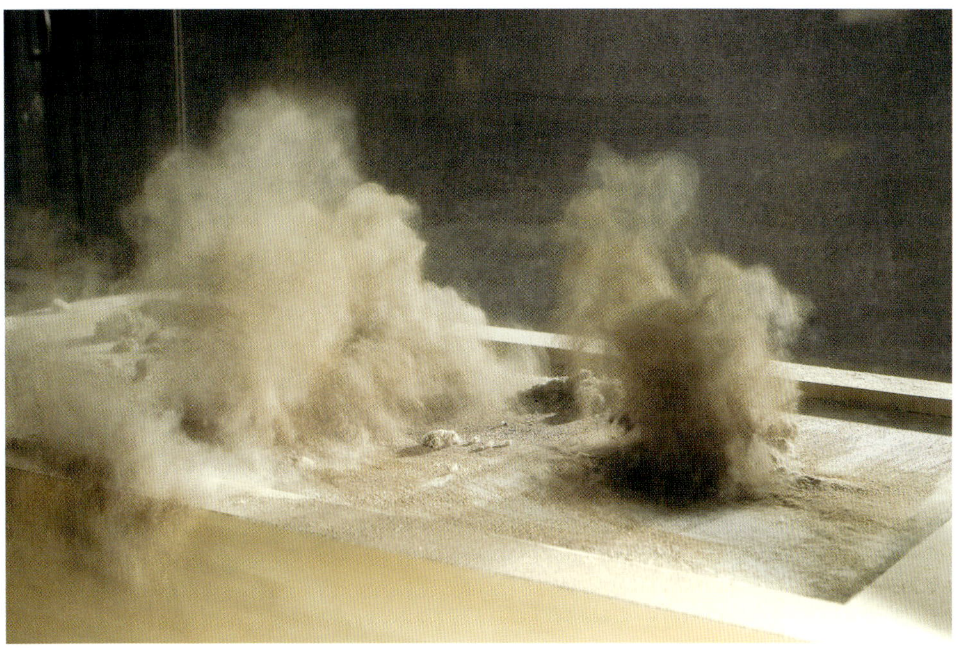

Figs. 5 and 6
Thatwamasi (that thou art),
2011
museum vitrine, vacuum cleaner
71 × 55 × 27 inches
Courtesy of the artist

Tallur's exploration of the symbolic potential of material and action continues with *Path Breaker* (2019; cat. 19). This commanding installation incorporates three automobile tires affixed to a mechanism that drives them to spin relentlessly within a large basin of mud. A glass portal bisects the basin, permitting the viewer to cut through the center of the structure. The centrifugal force of the wheel hurls mud onto both the adjacent walls and the glass partition, causing the soil to slowly build up over time. The partially submerged tires stand in tension with the wheel, one of the earliest of human tools, which implies forward motion and mobility. Despite their incessant spinning, despite the application of force, the tires remain perpetually stuck in the mud. However, the object is not static, and the work advances over time as the sedimentary deposit on the surrounding wall marks and leaves a trace of its action. Through the simple mechanical churning of raw material into symbolic sediment, Tallur conjures a level of consequence out of the seemingly inconsequential.

With pointed humor and incisive visual commentary, Tallur L.N. confronts our belief systems, questioning the value we assign to money, icons, and artifacts, and he reminds us, through the inevitable process of decay and renewal, mortality and metamorphosis, that meaning is never fixed. *Interference Fringe* alludes to the notion that we simultaneously carry forward and censor memories of the past, and that this subjective retelling becomes history. As Tallur explained, in physics, "interference" is a phenomenon in which two waves come together. If their frequency and wavelength are in sync, they can amplify, diminish, or negate one another. The idea of conflicting signals speaks to the competing stories, celebration of select relics, and contradictory meanings we bestow. At a time when society is at odds with itself and the lines between fact and fiction have blurred, Tallur asks us to looking critically at the forces of history, capitalism, and globalization and to mine the paradoxes of life, always mindful of our willing or unwitting participation as architects and arbiters of collective memory and collective amnesia.

Notes

The title of this essay derives from John R. Pierce, *Symbols, Signals and Noises: The Nature and Process of Communication* (New York: Harper and Row, 1965).

Epigraph: Tallur L.N., excerpt from the artist's conceptual statement "Collective Memory v/s Collective Amnesia," developed for the exhibition *Interference Fringe*, emailed to the author March 2, 2019.

1. For more on this exhibition, see Holland Cotter, "Art in Review: L.N. Tallur," *New York Times*, May 7, 1999.

2. Bose Pacia Modern, "Press Release: Past-Modern, Interactive Art Objects," 1999, http://www.bosepacia.com/exhibitions/1999-04-24_ln-tallur/press-release/.

3. Tallur L.N., *Placebo: Tallur L.N.*, exh. cat. (Seoul, Korea: Arario Gallery; Mumbai, India: Chemould Prescot Road, 2009), 45.

4. Ella Shohat, *Taboo Memories, Diasporic Voices* (Durham, NC: Duke University Press, 2006).

5. Ami Mehta, interpretive text for *Interference Fringe | TALLUR L.N.*, Grounds For Sculpture, 2019.

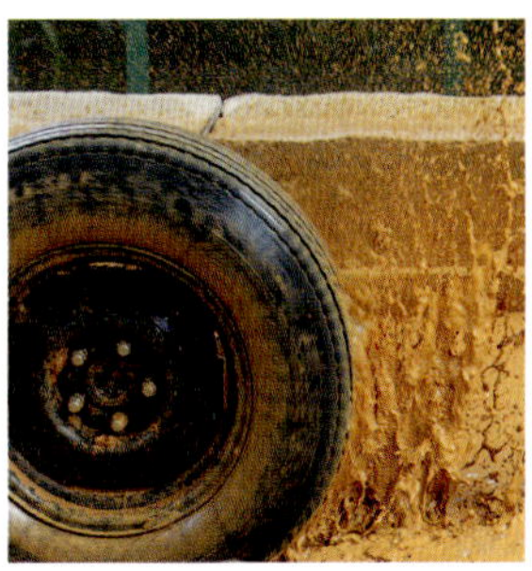

Path Breaker, 2019 (cat. 19)

Plates

—

Scaffold Installation

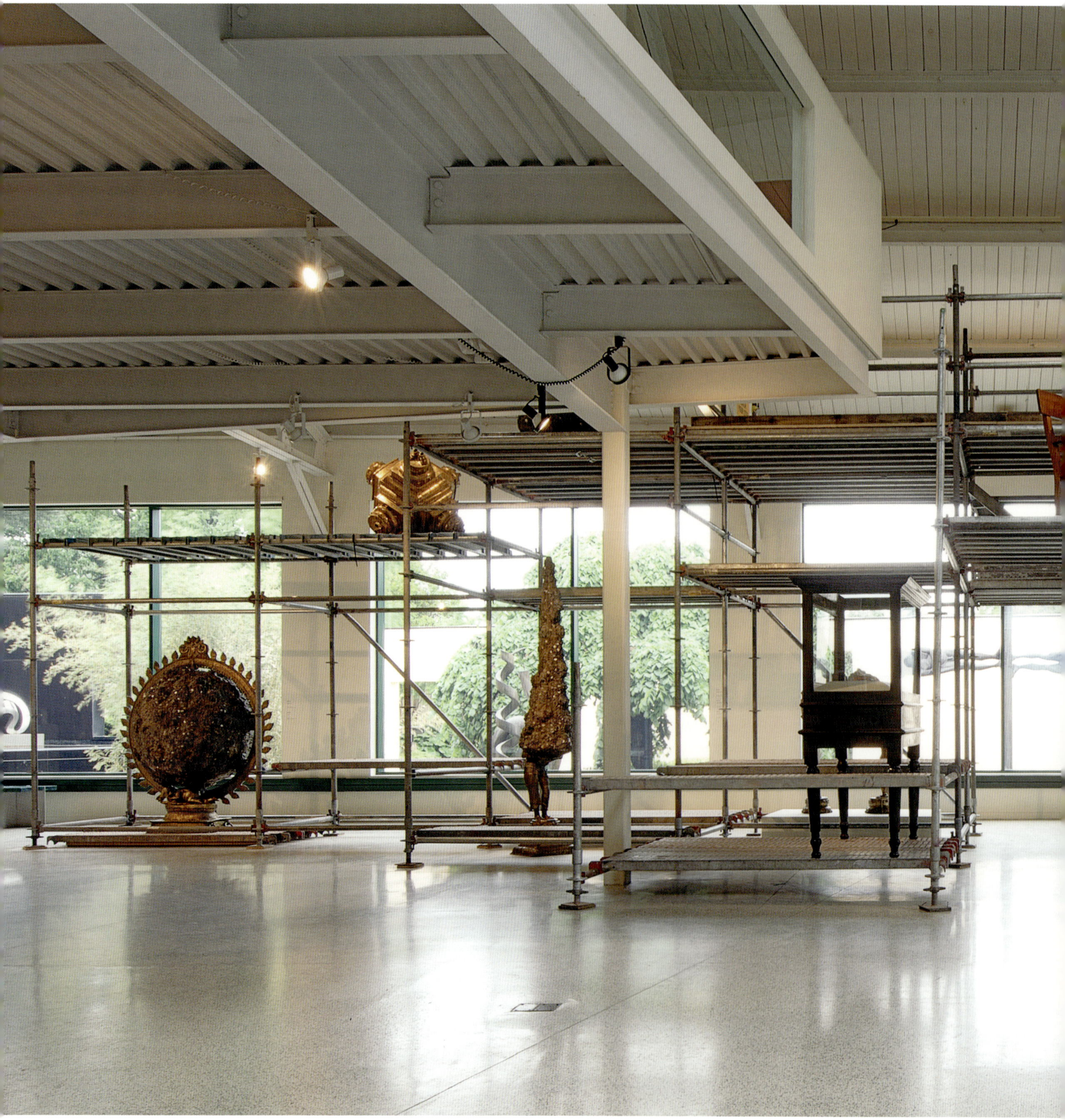

Scaffold, 2019 (cat. 20)

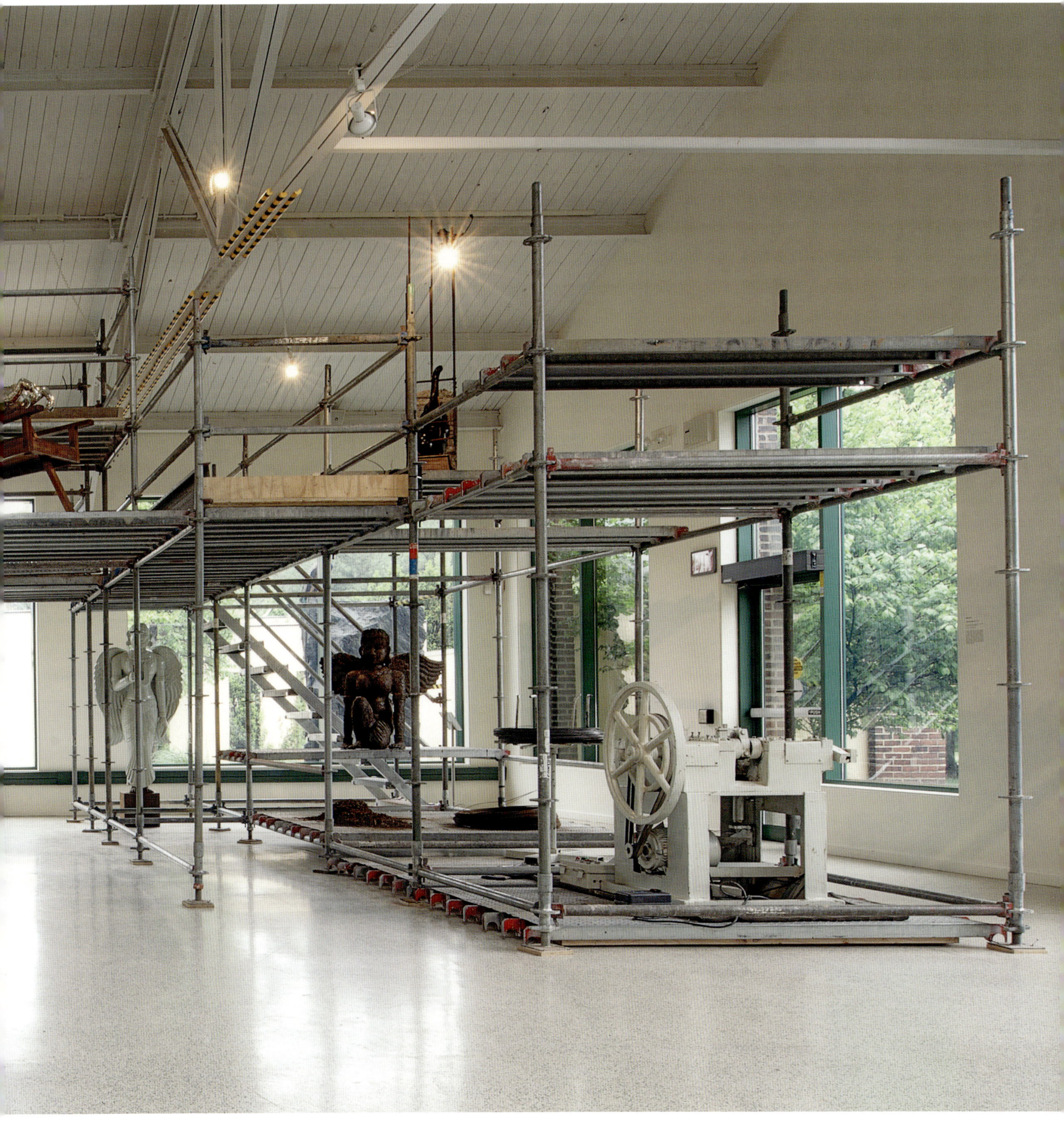

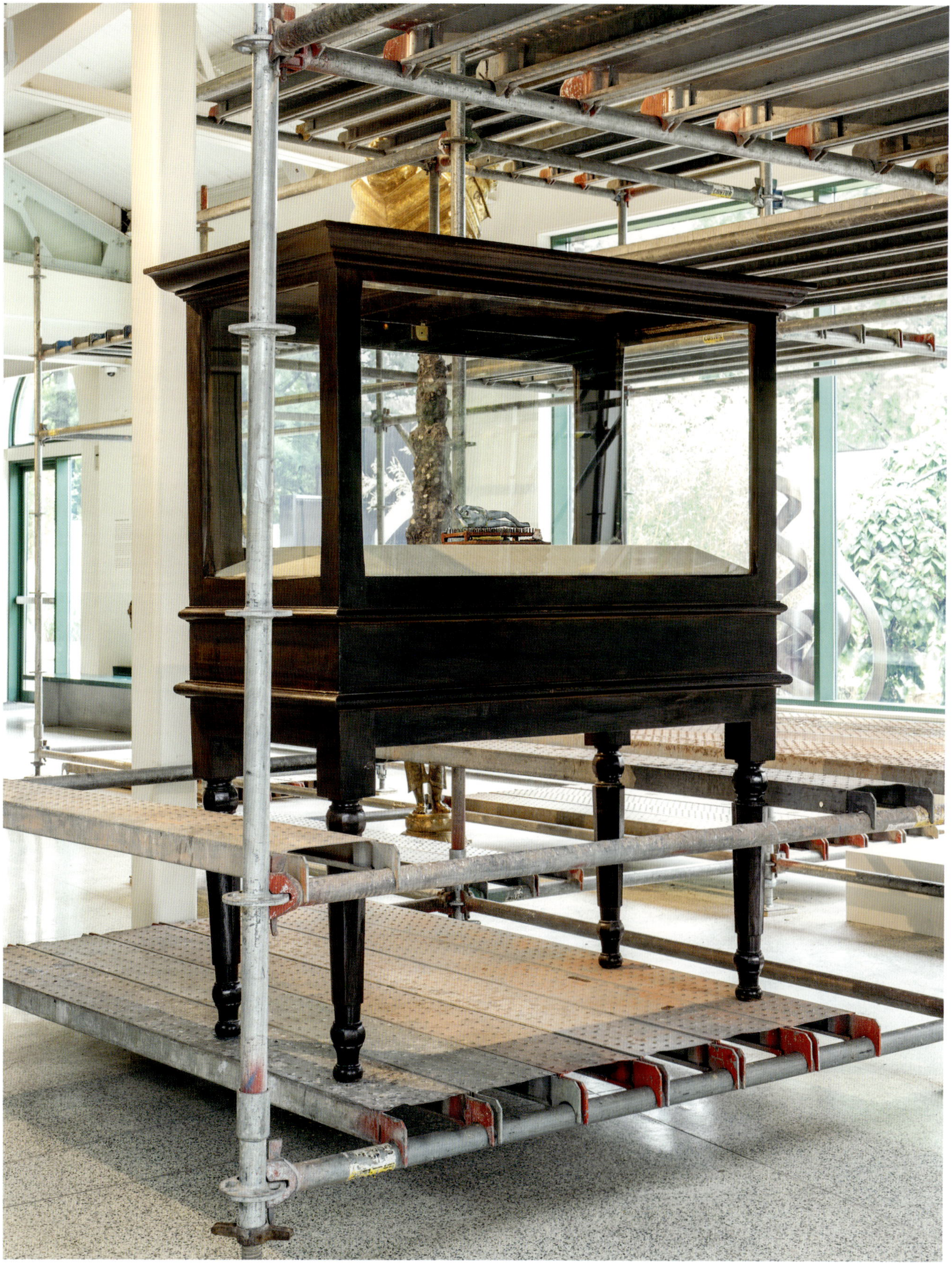

Hatha Yoga, 2012 (cat. 27)

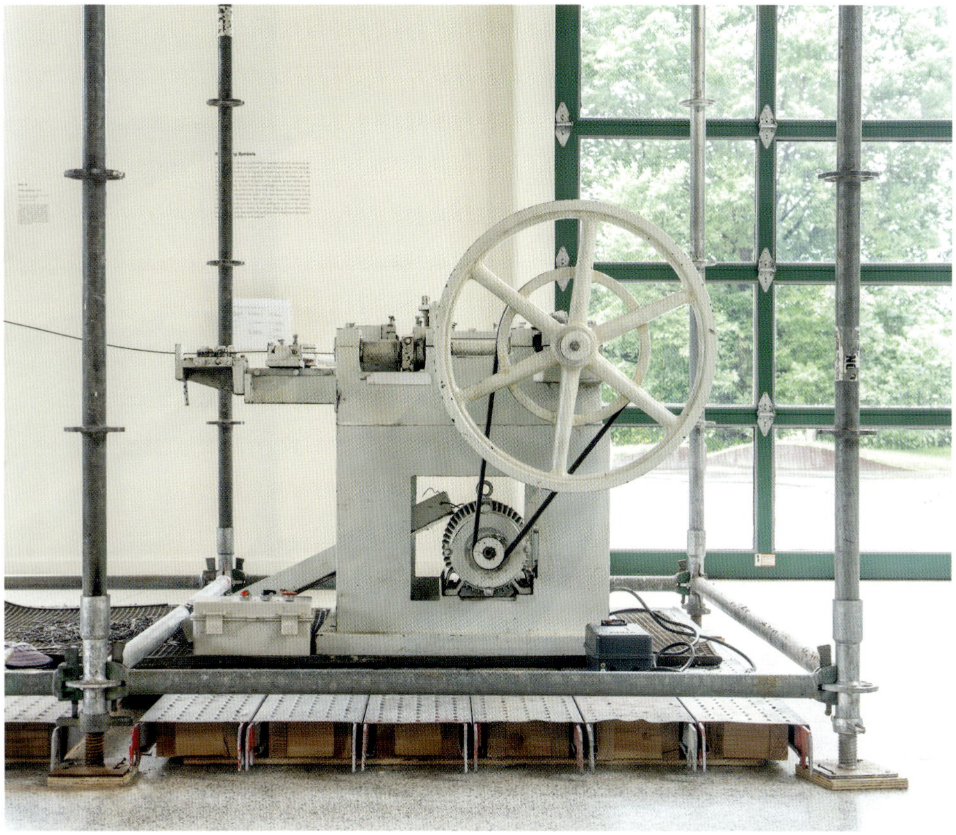

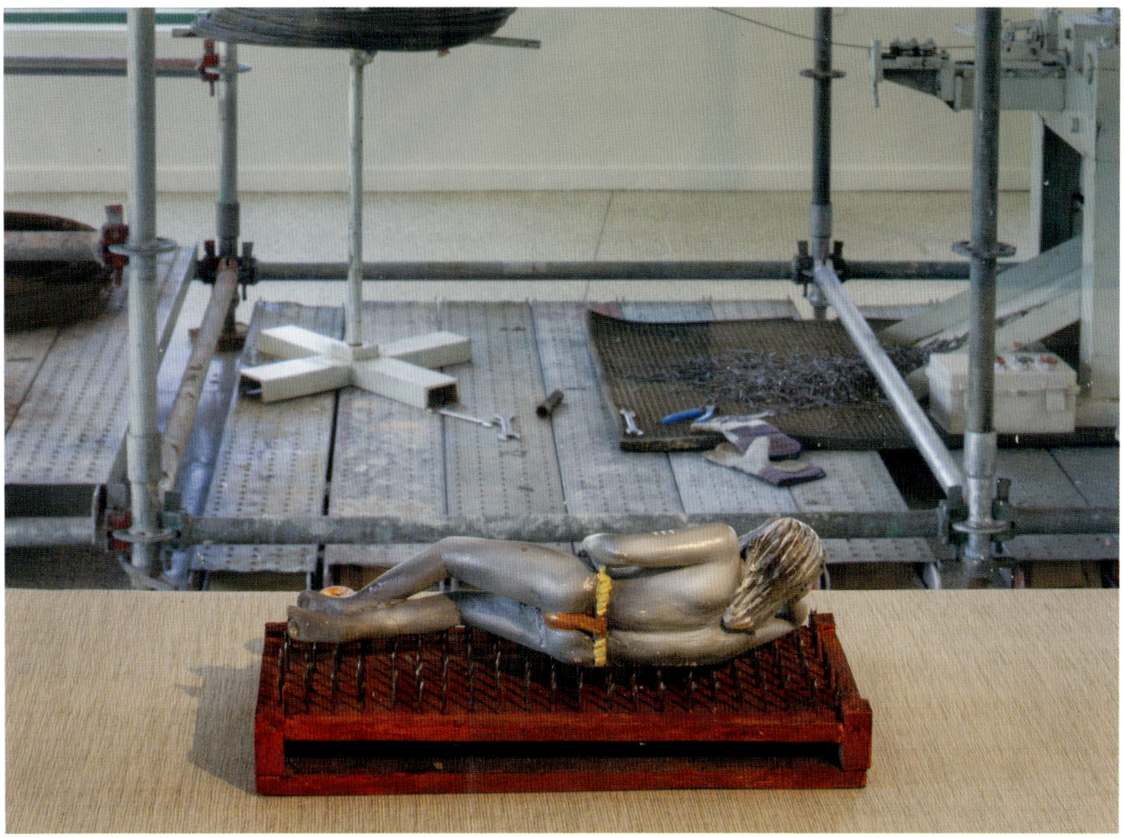

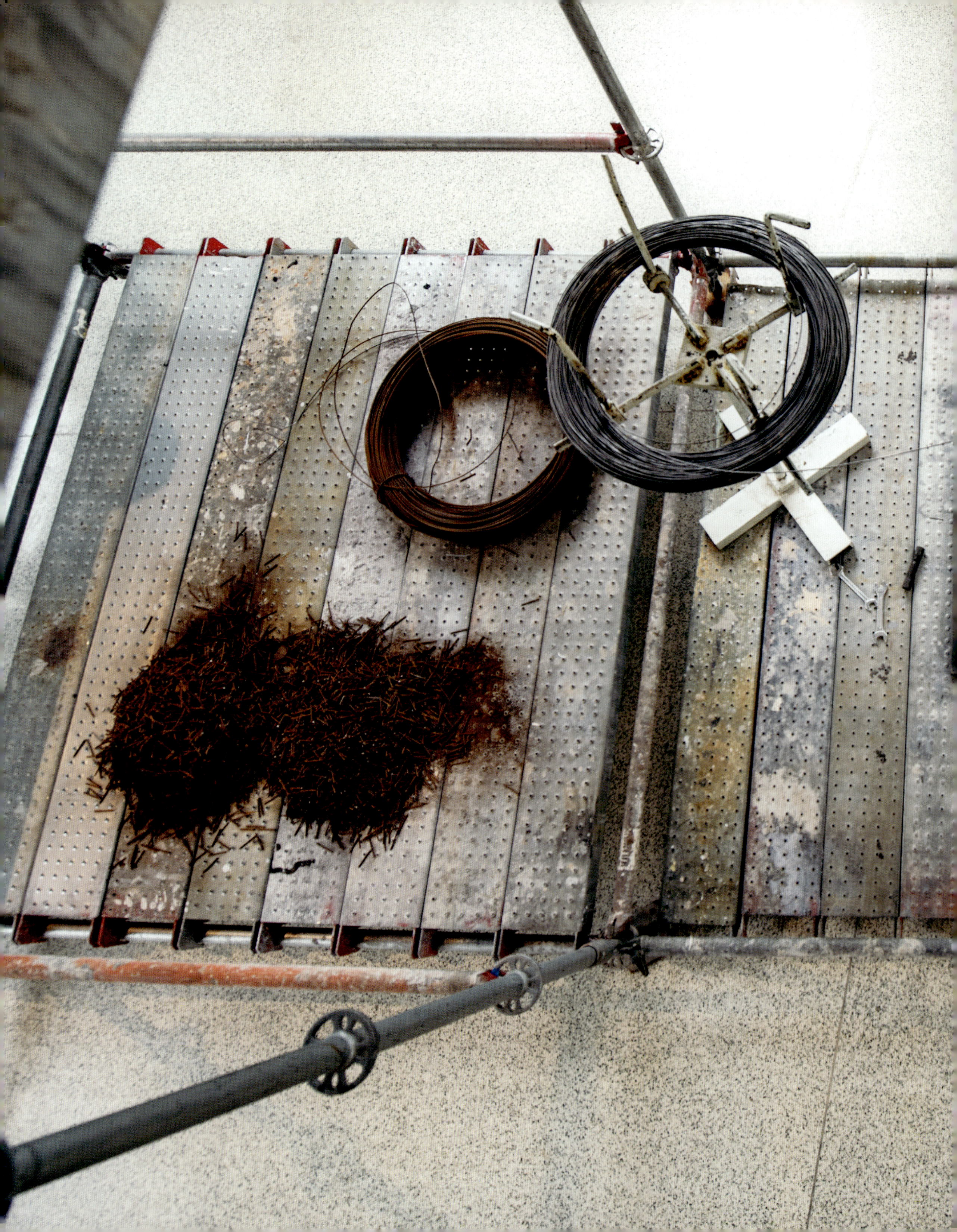

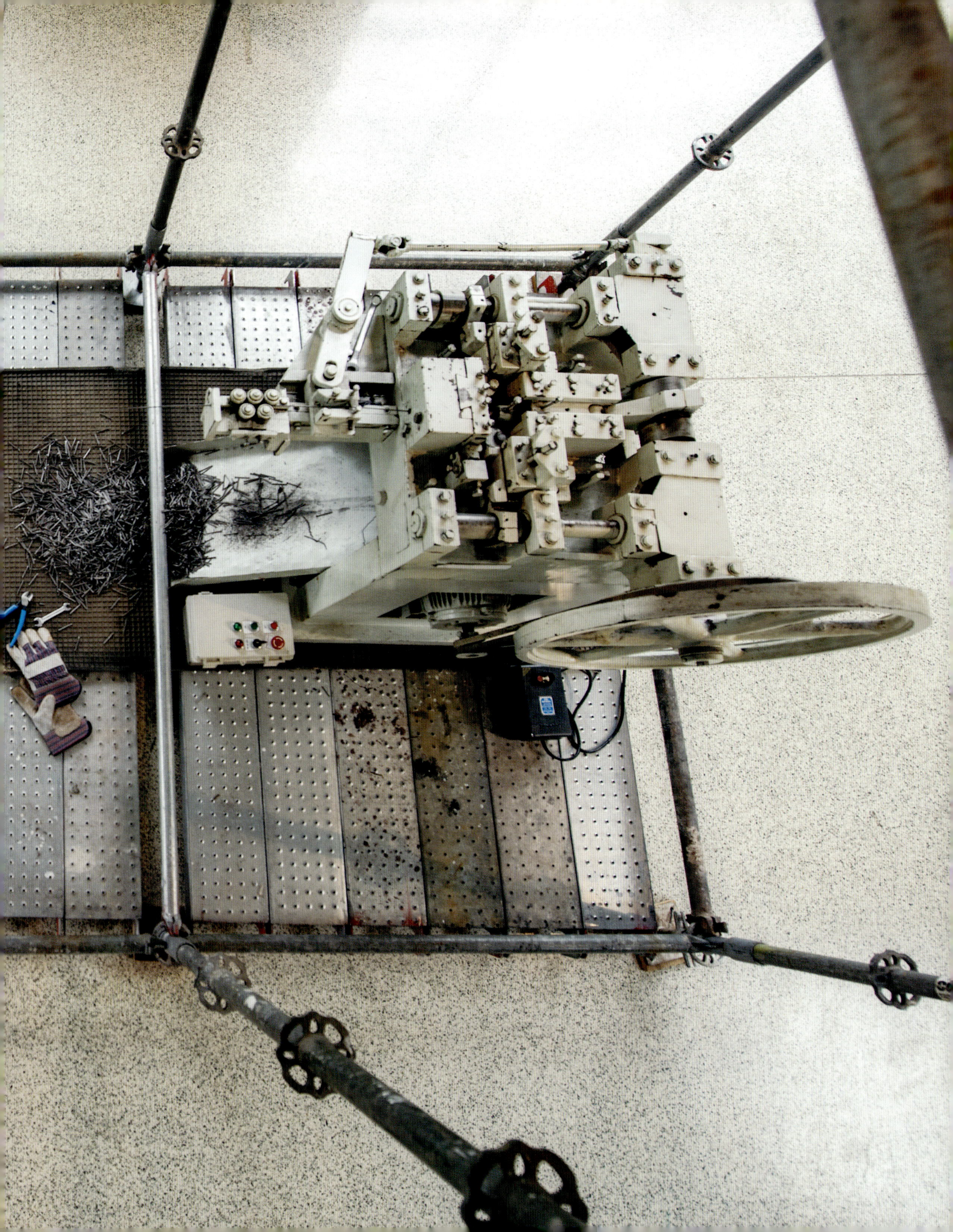

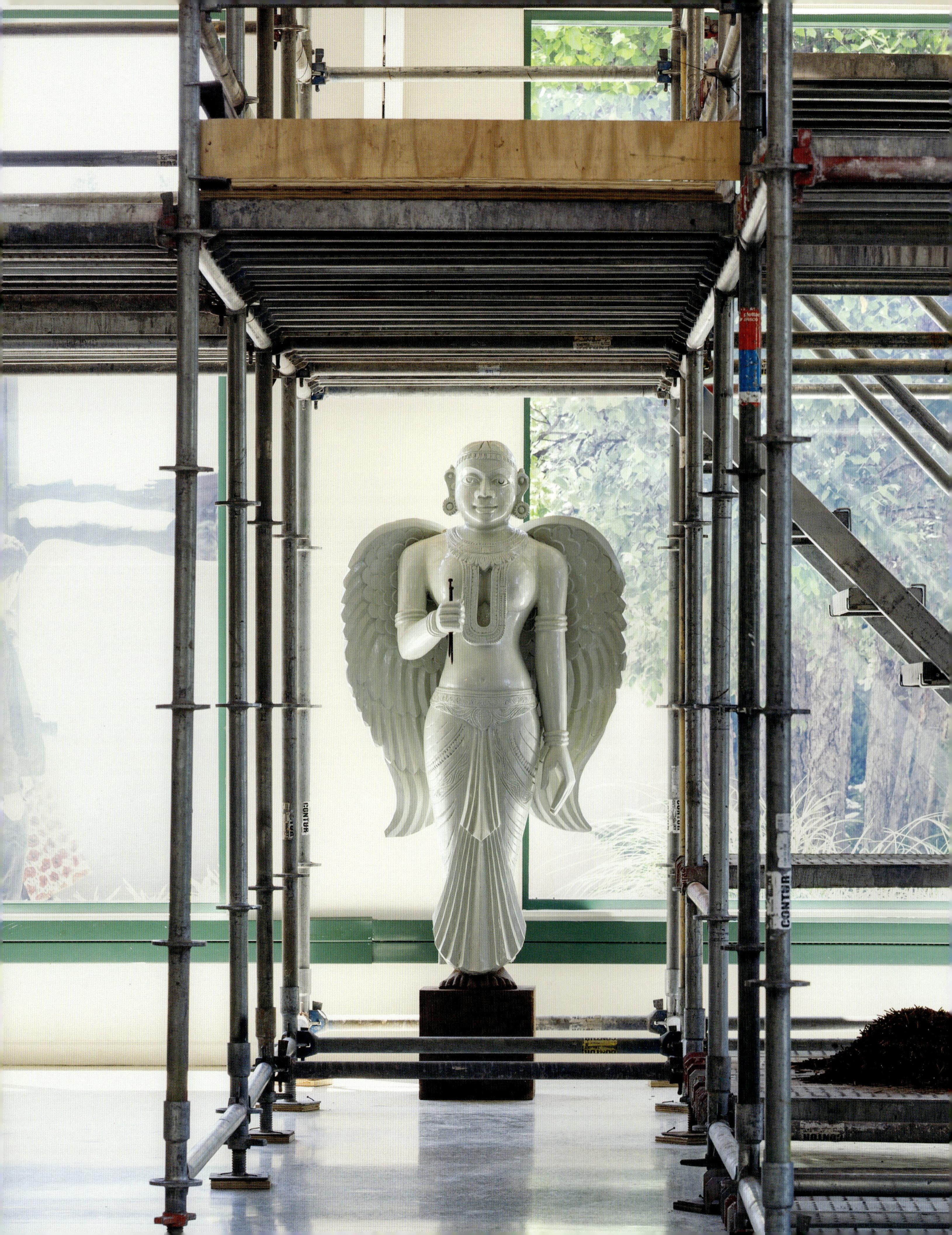
CONTUR

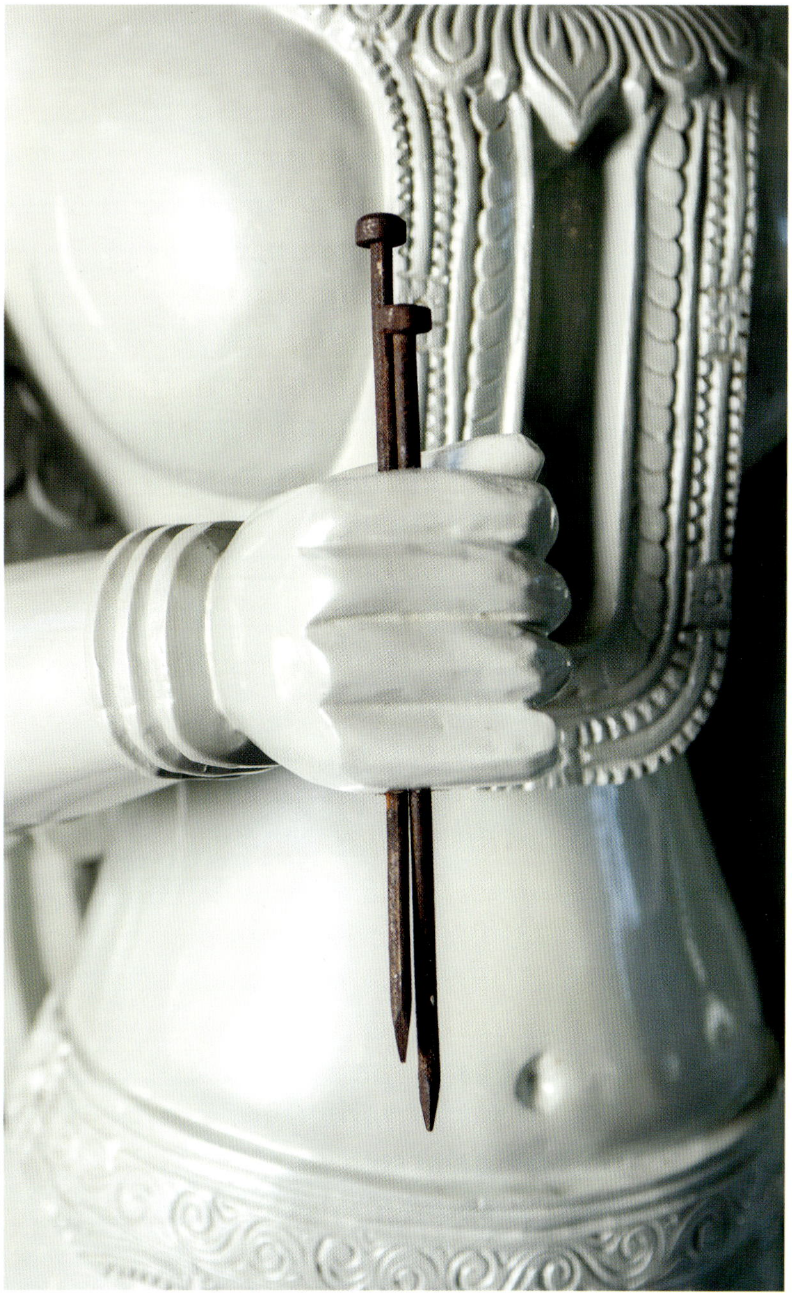

Hatha Yoga, 2012 (cat. 27)

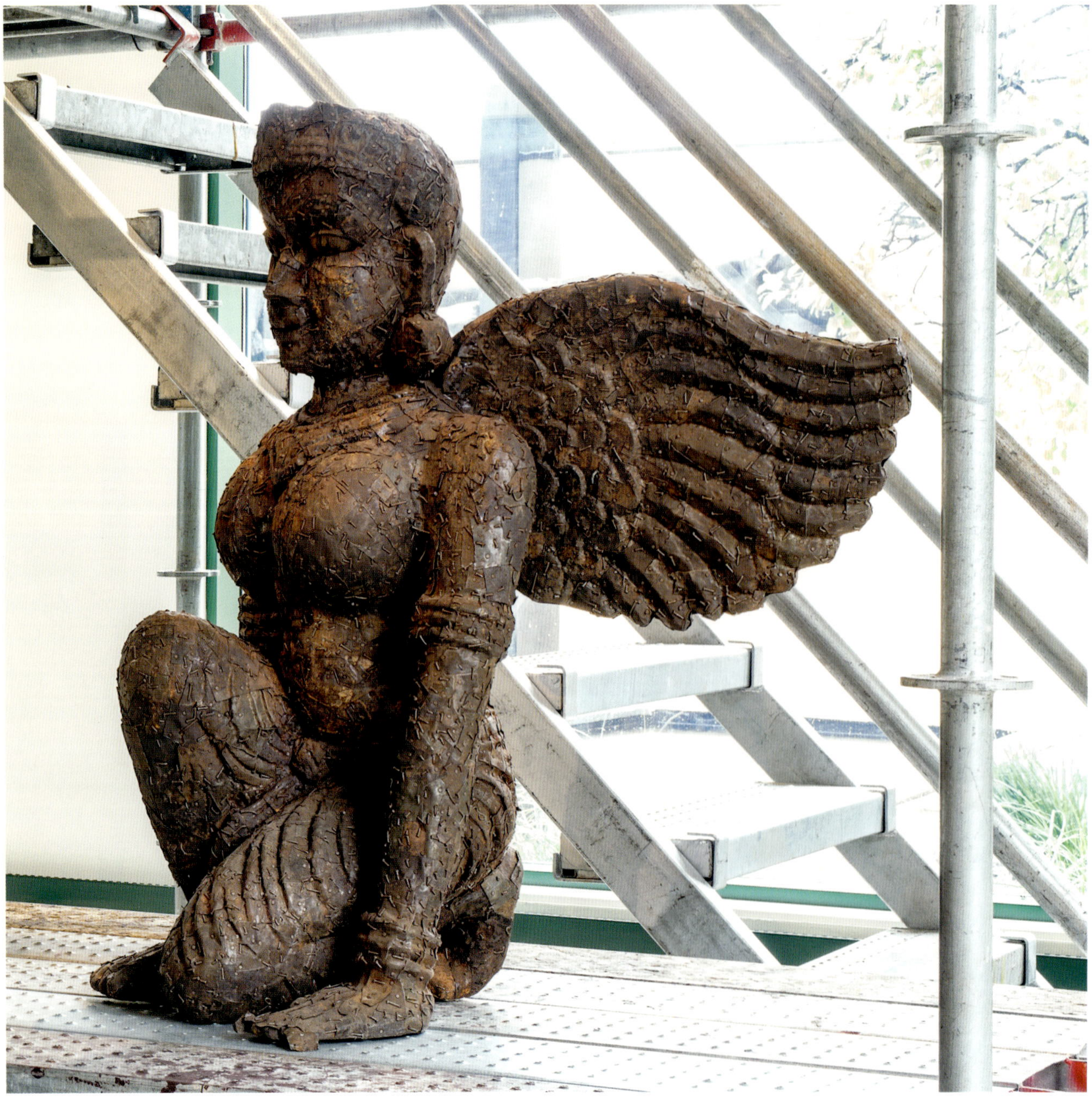

 Hatha Yoga, 2012 (cat. 27)

Untitled (Elephant), 2008 (cat. 21)

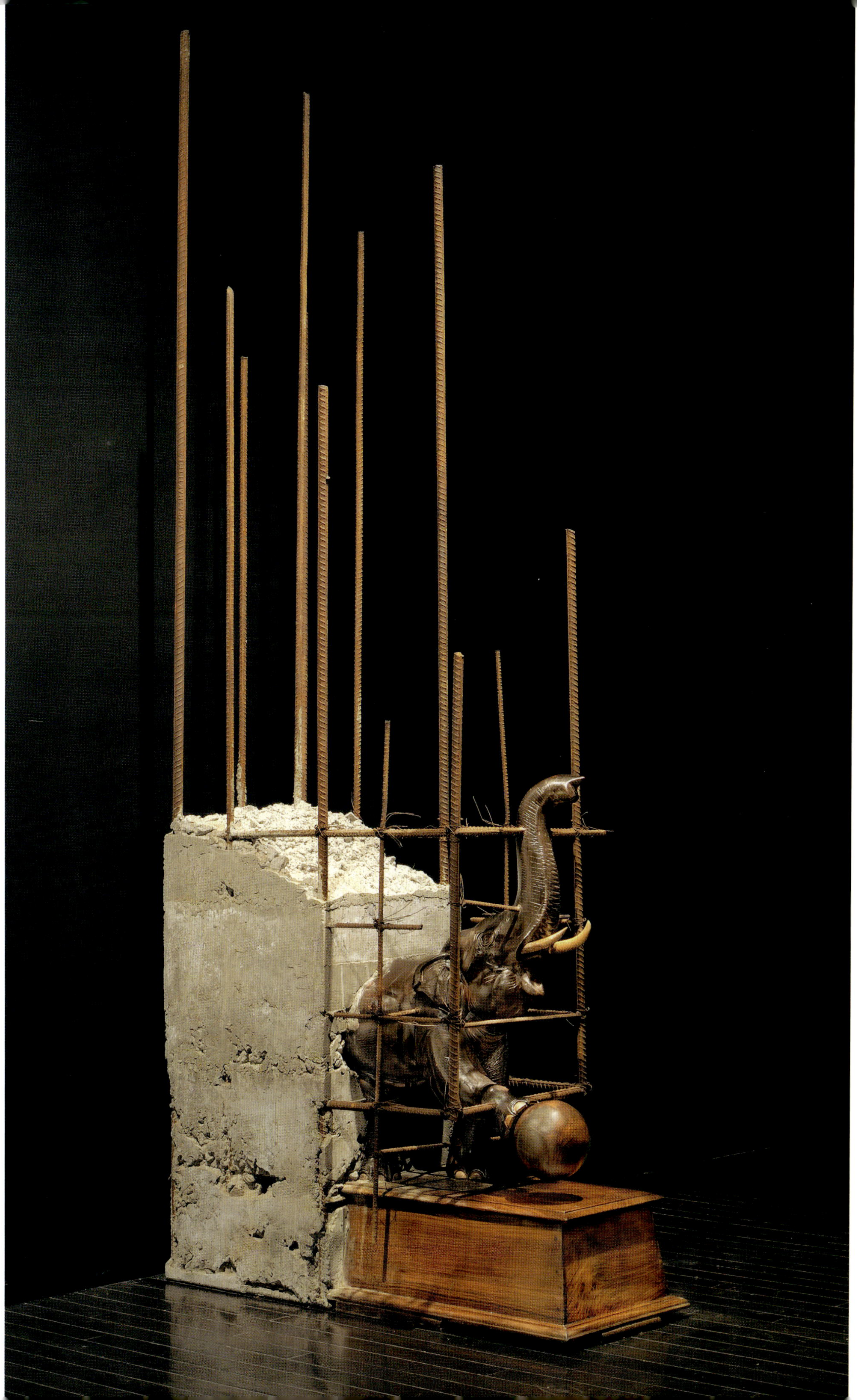

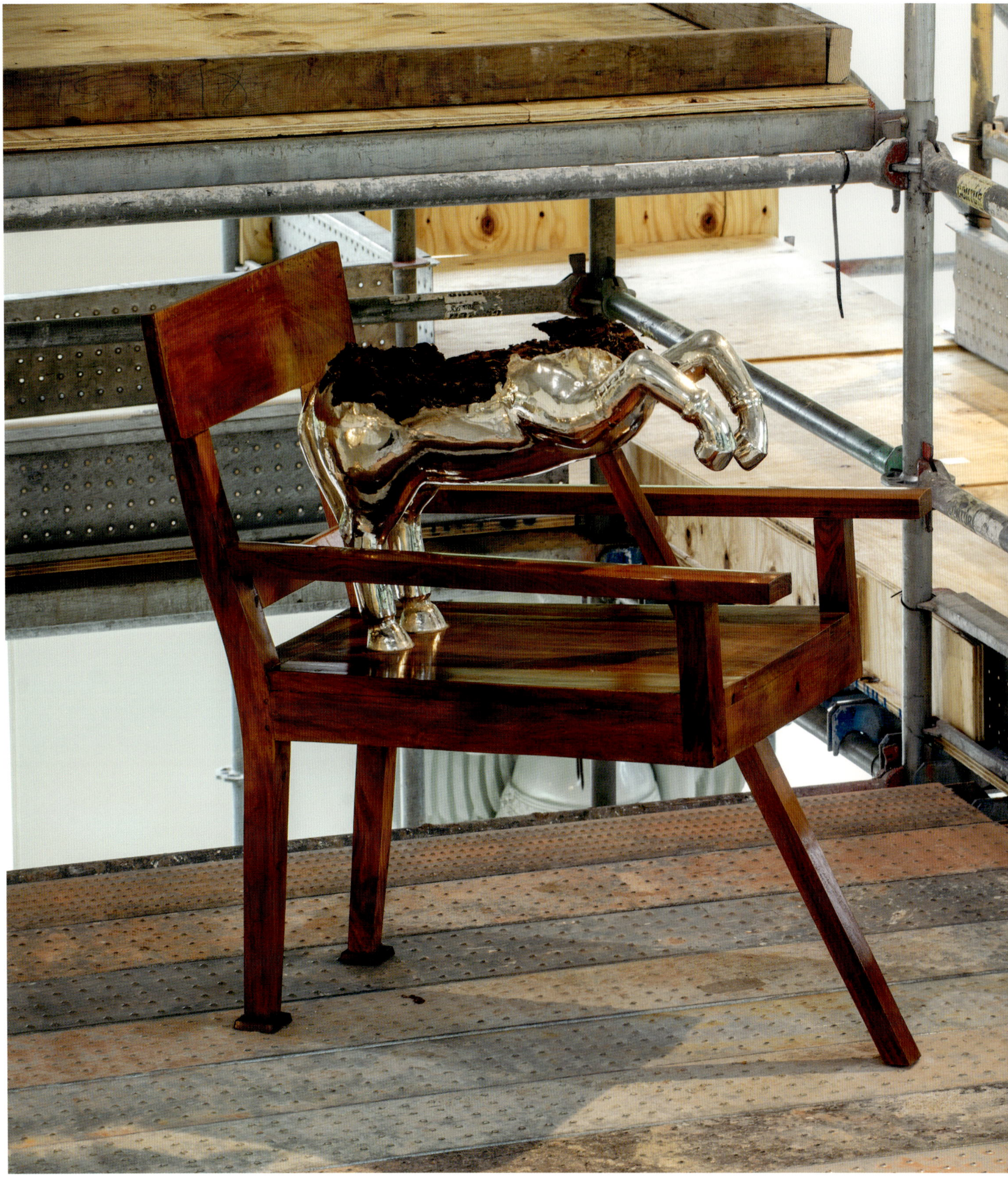

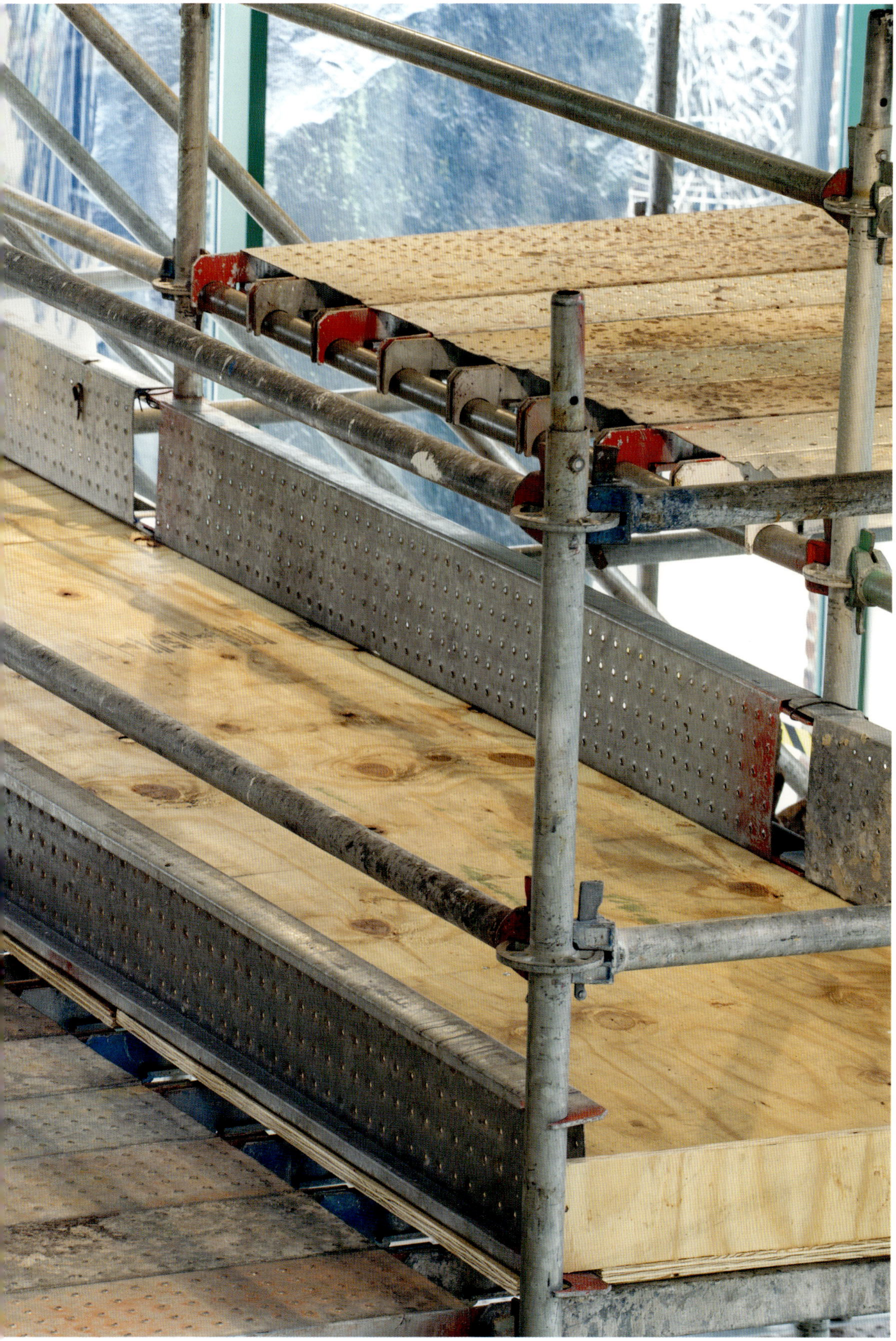

Bulimia 2, 2008 (cat. 22)

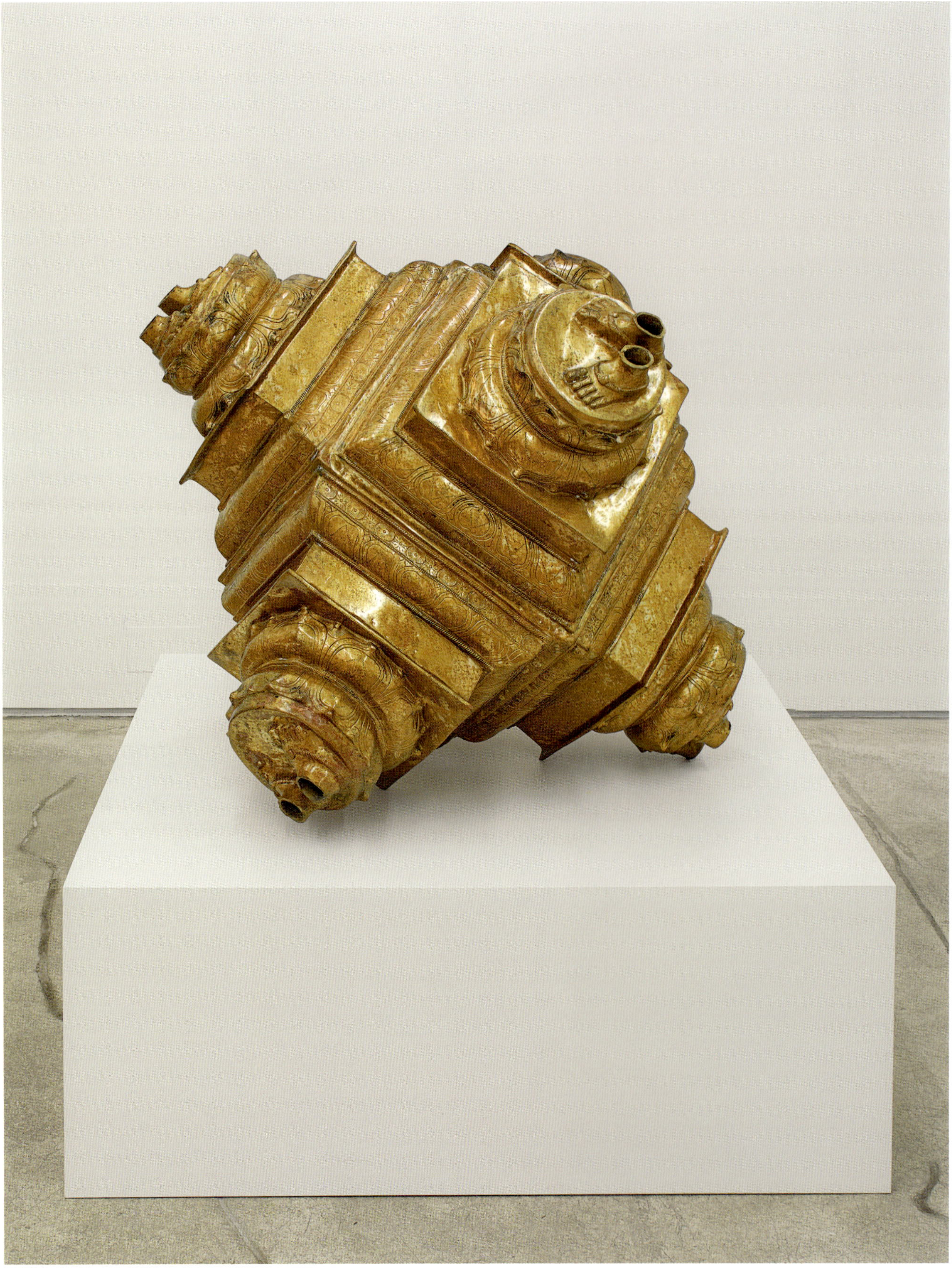

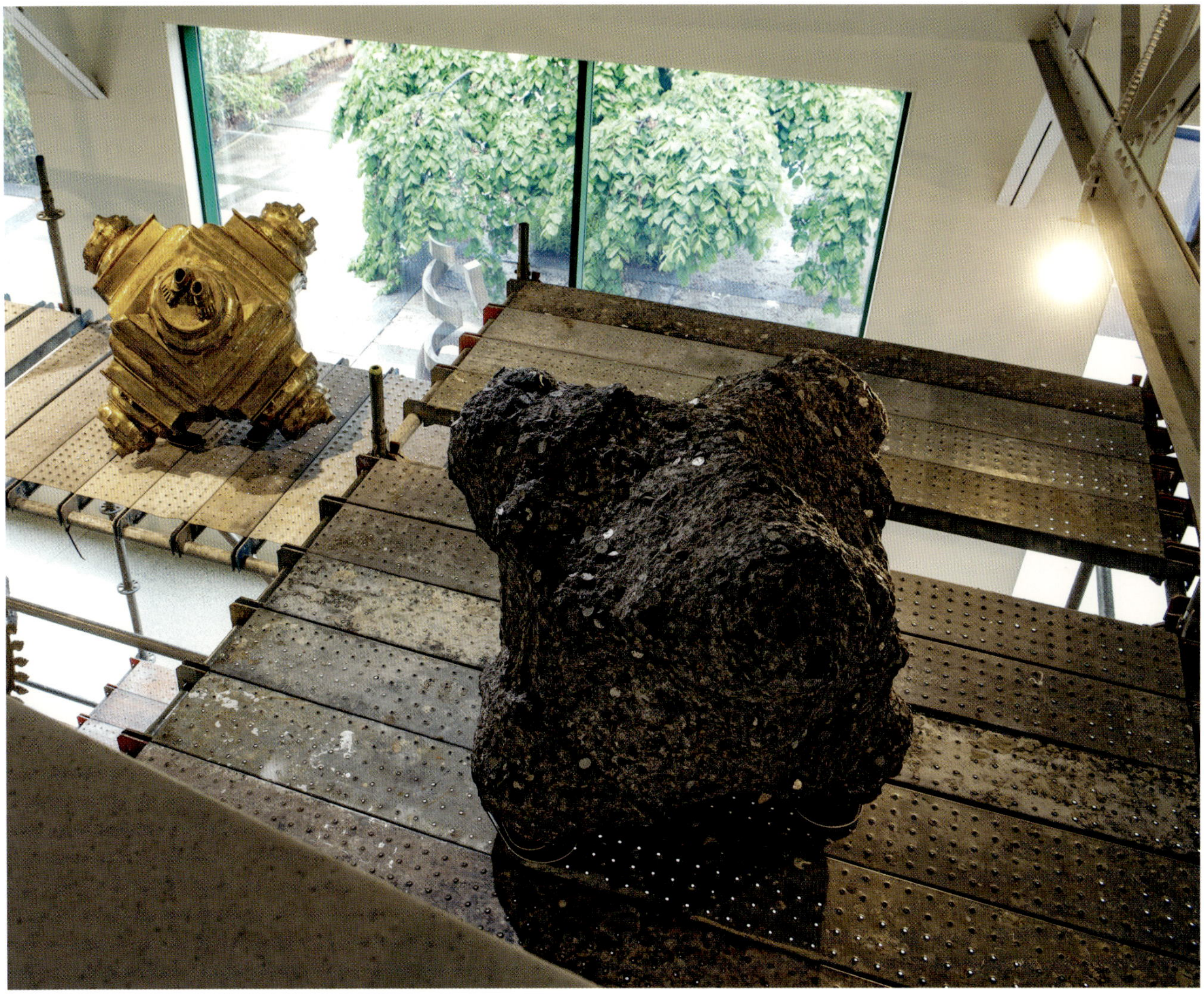

"?", 2011 (cat. 24) ***Pedestal on Pedestal***, 2012 (cat. 26)

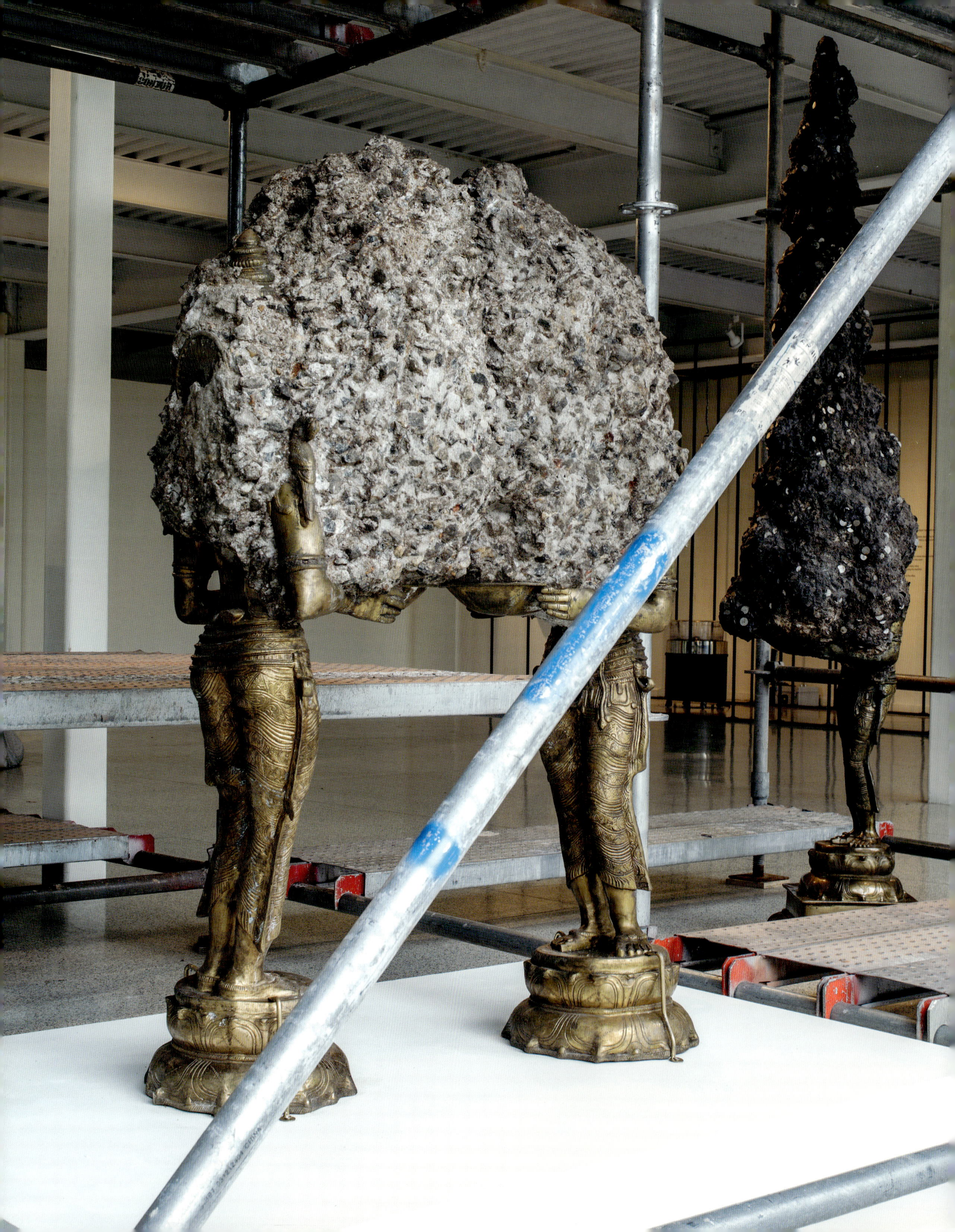

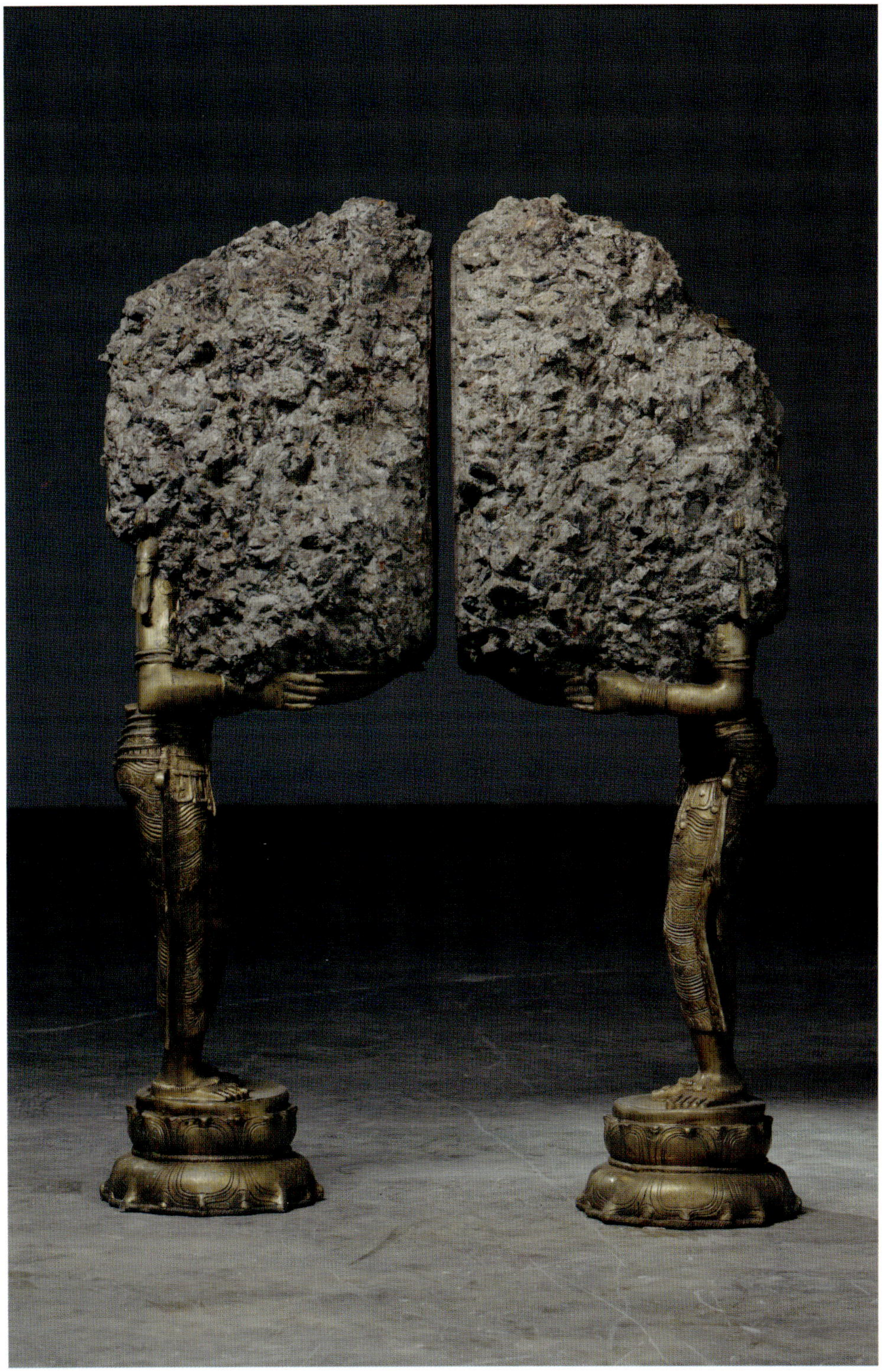

Lamp (Deepa Laxmi), 2010 (cat. 23)

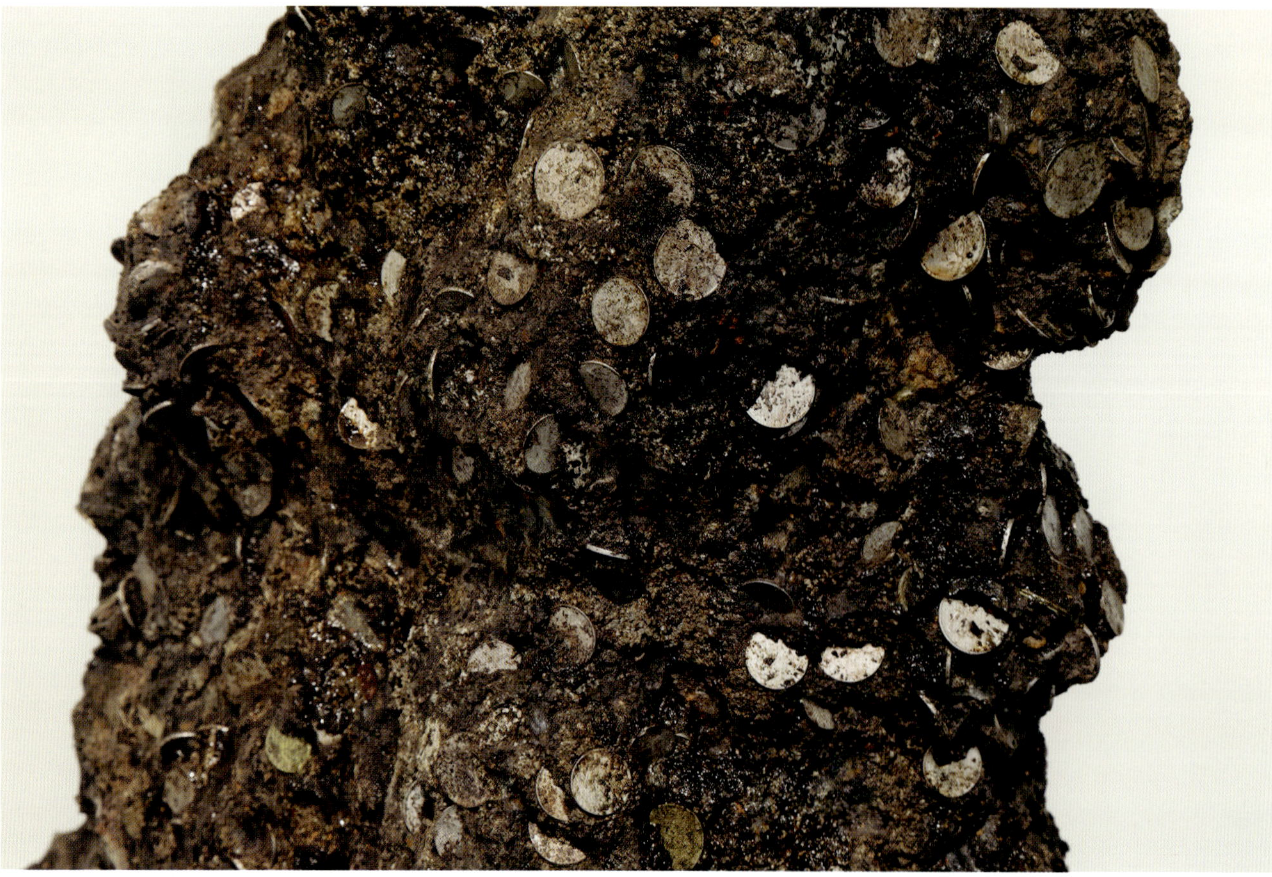

 Victory Pillar, 2012 (cat. 28)

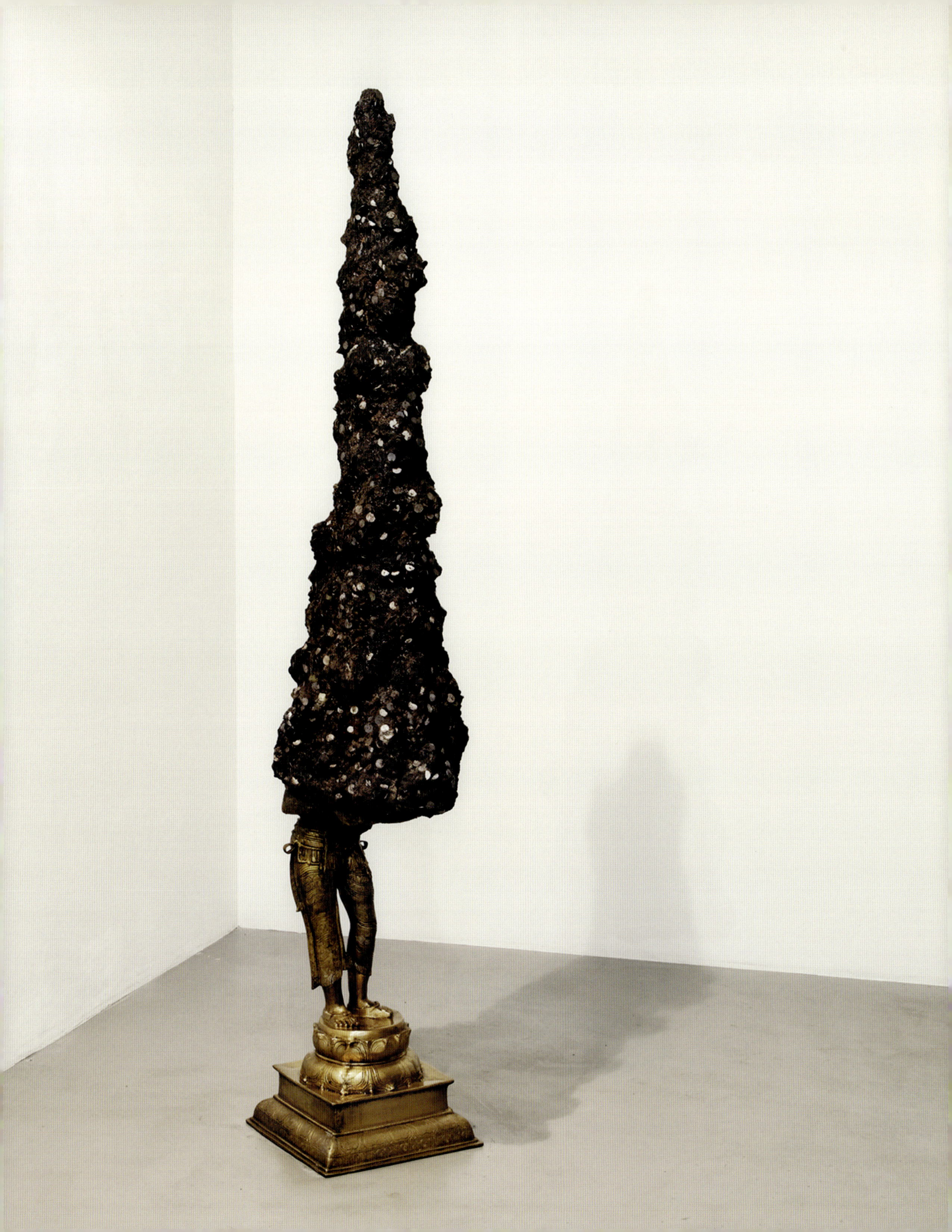

 Unicode, 2011 (cat. 25)

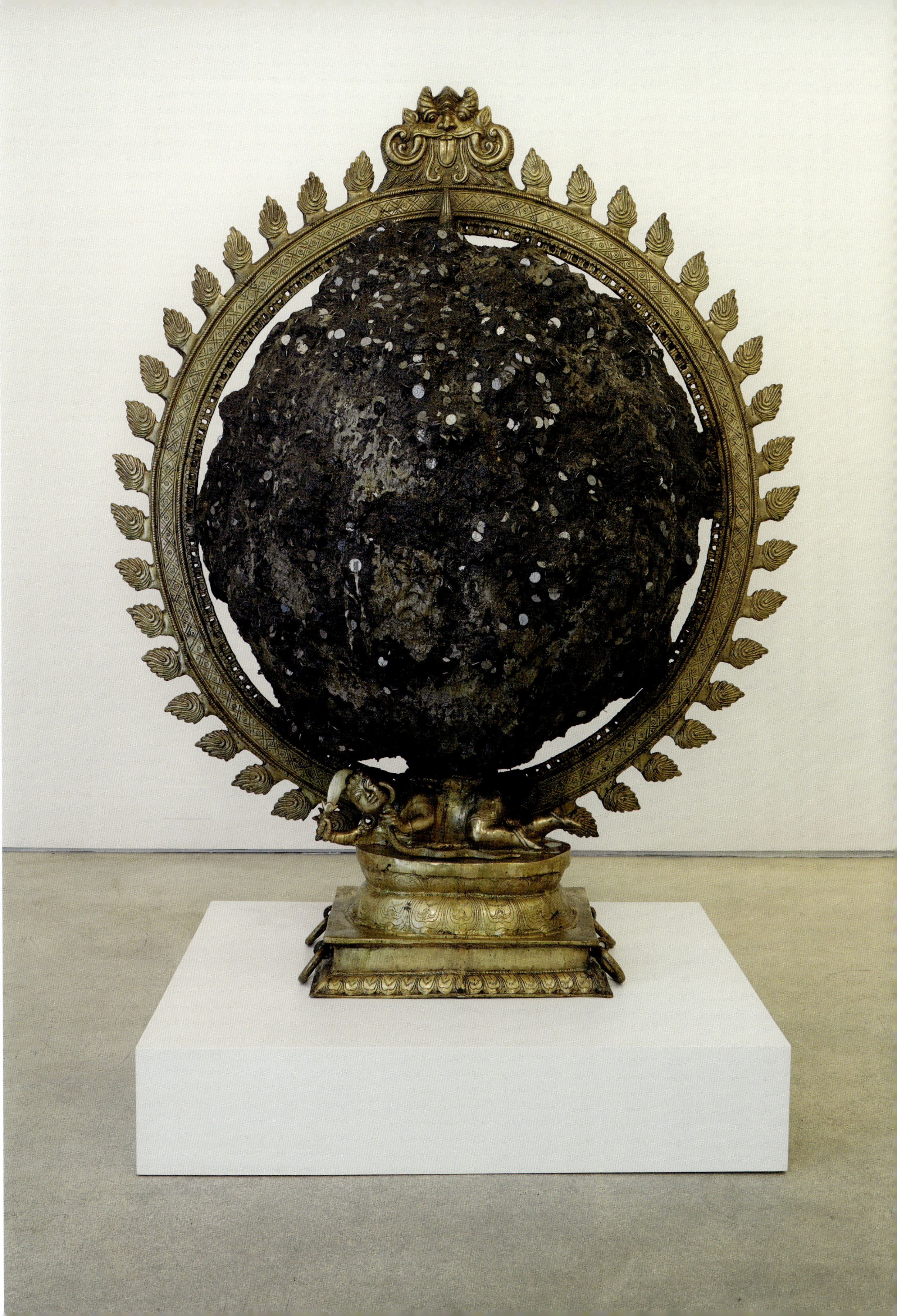

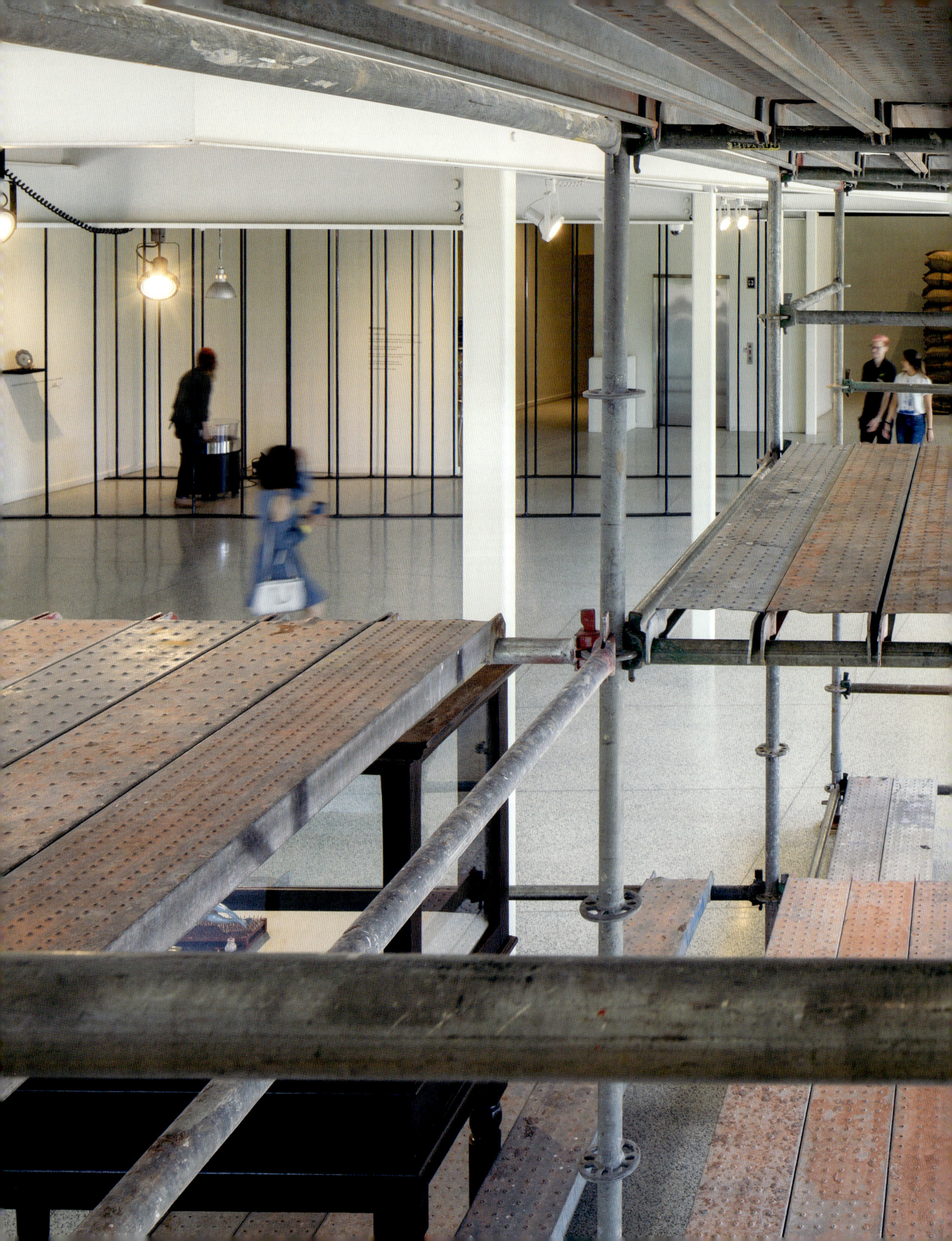

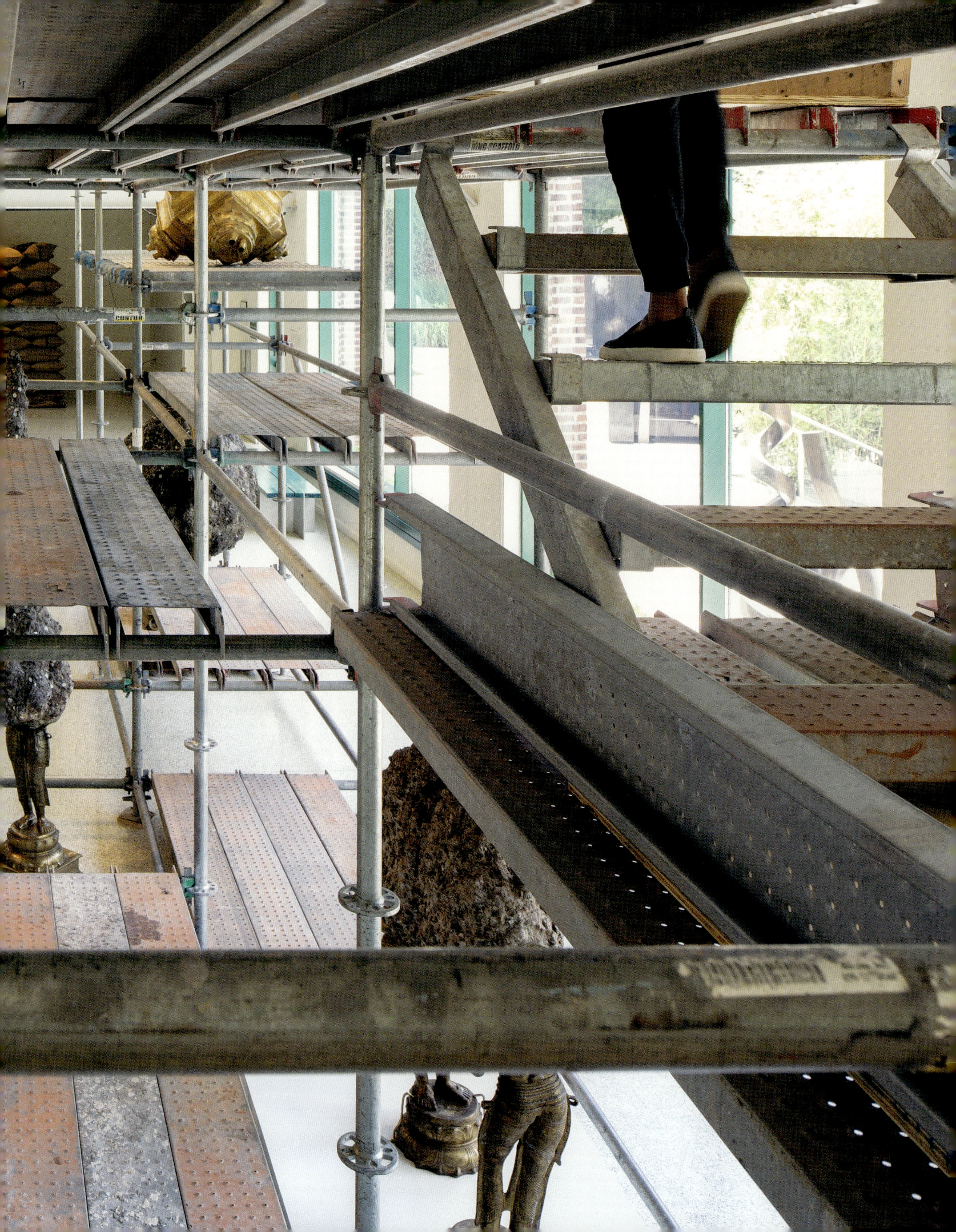
RING SCAFFOLD
CONTUR

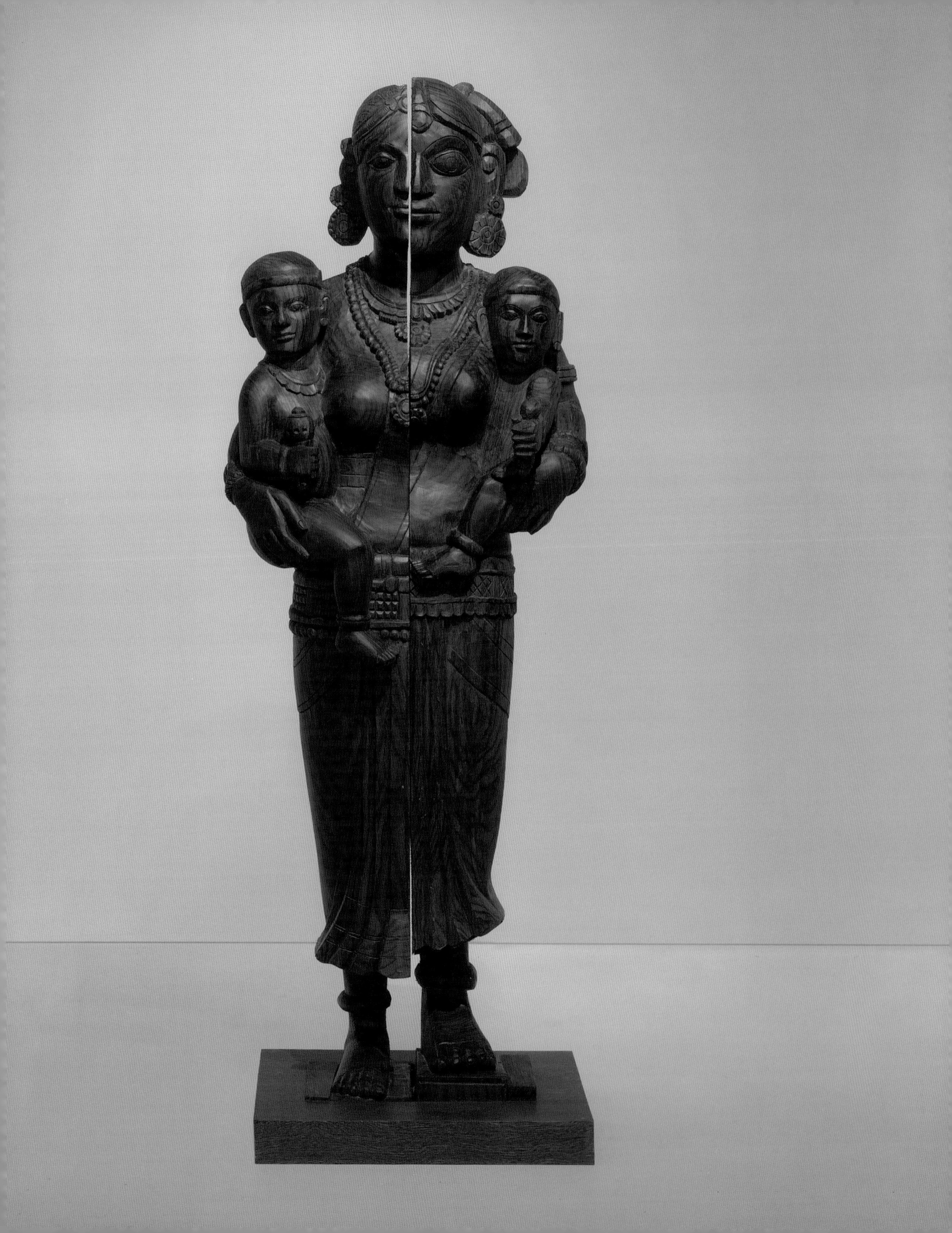

Excavating Obsolescence — The Art of Tallur L.N.

Chaitanya Sambrani

Ever since Tallur L.N. made his professional debut in the late 1990s, his practice has remained unapologetically opportunistic. His approach to the history of art and material culture is determinedly eclectic, paying equal attention to the classical and the coarse. The refinement of fine art seems to offer him as many marvels as do the makeshift aesthetics of everyday improvisation. He trawls media flotsam to harvest outlandish ideas, (pseudo-)scientific theories, rumors and hoaxes, commentaries on economic processes, and technological advances. Medical glossaries, market analyses, anecdotes about iconic designs and disputes over intellectual property, spiritual formulae and moral tales, internet memes, reports about technological disasters and environmental degradation—all these and more are fodder for his omnivorous imagination. If the current historical moment can be characterized as one of unprecedentedly rapid obsolescence and extinction, it may be that Tallur is among the most enthusiastic "first responders" digging through the debris.

Tallur's professional life has been characterized by a series of migrations. His early career proceeded along a somewhat unusual route. Hailing from the small-town environs of Koteswara (population 21,000) on the westward-facing coast of Karnataka in southern India, he moved inland to the erstwhile princely capital of Mysore to study painting for his bachelor's degree at the Chamarajendra Academy of Visual Art. He next moved to Baroda, intending to undertake postgraduate study at the prestigious Faculty of Fine Arts.[1] Failing to secure admission into the MA in painting, Tallur spent two years studying museology instead before going on to Leeds, United Kingdom, on a Commonwealth Scholarship, for another master's degree in visual art.

Since 2006 he has divided his time between his ancestral home in Tallur, near Koteswara, and Daegu, South Korea, his wife's family home.[2] This peregrination—Koteswara-Mysore-Baroda-Leeds-Daegu—interspersed with frequent sojourns in Seoul, New York, Beijing, New Delhi, Bombay, and now Hamilton, New Jersey—has made for a sharpened sense of being in the world. At either terminus, whether in small-town South India or the industrial urbanity of South Korea, Tallur encounters a relatively homogenous monoculture (as compared to say, Bombay or New York) where the sheer otherness of his *other* life serves to recast the familiar as strange in a constant double take. This serial displacement has been essential to Tallur's art; the ongoing stimulation and discomfort it brings has made it possible for him to focus on the substratum of the uncanny beneath the thin veneer of everyday normalcy.

Though they began with disappointment, his student years in Baroda were vital. He traversed the taxidermy cabinets and dark corridors of the museology department while conducting aspirational experiments with assemblage

Colonial Sisters, 2008
(detail; see fig. 8)

that borrowed from the more macabre dimensions of natural history, as well as from modernist experiments with the surreal and the absurd. The results of this intellectual and epistemological hybridity are visible across Tallur's oeuvre over the two decades since his first solo exhibition in 1999. He has developed a methodology that is deliberately scattershot, purposefully hybrid, capitalizing equally on the commonplace and the epiphanic, "interfering" with conventional semantics to produce willfully heterodox meanings.

Tallur's abiding curiosity about Indian philosophical and aesthetic traditions makes it possible to view his works as semantic collisions designed to produce unforeseen consequences in the manner of *dhvani* (sound, resonance) theory, a key element of Sanskrit aesthetics propounded by Ānandavardhana in the ninth century CE and refined by his disciple Abhinavagupta (born c. 1000 CE).[3] The central premise of Ānandavardhana's theory of *dhvani* is that the highest measure of achievement in (literary) art is the production of suggestive meaning (*vyañjanā*) that is distinct from and superior to mere denotation (*abhidhā*) or connotation (*lakṣhaṇā*). The *dhvani* theory of aesthetic experience (*rasa*) privileges the artist's ability to evoke unspoken meanings above the virtues of naming things or implying their presence through causal logic. Thus, Tallur engineers an arrangement of charred stumps covering a pseudo-antique bronze of Shiva Nataraja in cosmic dance surrounded by a nimbus of fire, encasing the god in a globe of carbonaceous residue as he dances the universe through cycles of becoming and dissolution. *Obituary Note* (2013; cat. 9) suggests its meanings by way of *sphoṭa* (detonation, explosion), a rush of recognition wherein the viewer understands that it is neither the celestial dance of Nataraja nor the charcoal in itself that the artist means to prioritize, but that something entirely different and more complex than the ingredients is being suggested. Much in the manner of the optical phenomenon after which this exhibition is titled, the coming together of different "wavelengths" of signification produces amplification or condensation in patterns that cannot be discerned in the initial signs by themselves.

During his student years in Leeds, Tallur began experimenting with the possibilities of material manipulations, even as his earlier investigations into the absurd and the surreal started being realized. It was also in England that he began to develop his particular perspective on the global, peppered with fragments of local cultures that surfaced persistently in the form of the outlandish, the incongruous, and the subversive. Cultural displacement conjoined with immersion in a cosmopolitan art environment has been instrumental in the sharpening of Tallur's stake in the contemporary. He relishes the conceptualist strategy of aloofness and distance, warily circling emotional investment in his subject, while offering the audience a series of deferrals that simultaneously tantalize and confound—not least because of their apparent exoticness. Premised as it is in alienation, the experience of modernity generates an abundance of absurdity, a rich vein explored by several generations of artists for over a century now. Tallur's preferred *modus operandi* for the generation of *dhvani* seems to consist in an amplification of absurdity, applied with equal generosity to the quotidian and the momentous. And while such amplification may be a worthwhile end in itself, it is the union of this highlighting with strategies

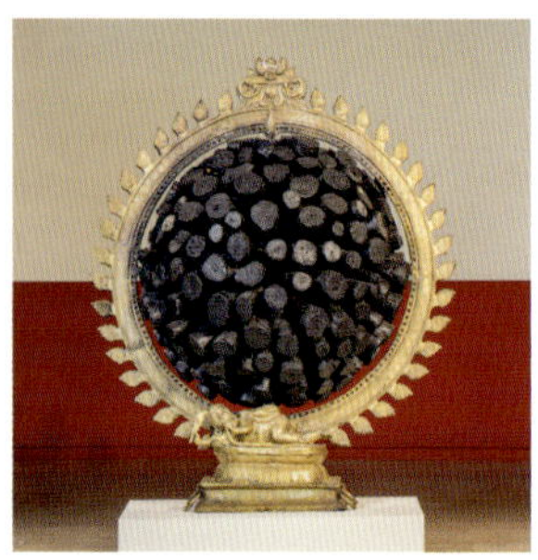

Obituary Note, 2013 (cat. 9)

of subversion that leads to the interventionist edge in Tallur's work.

The large-scale inflatables with which Tallur emerged as a significant practitioner originated from his student years in Leeds. *Made in England: A Temple Design for India* (2002; fig. 7) is a signal work here, a sublimation of his migratory existence and a statement of a political position in the globalizing world from the naïve yet knowing eyes of the interloper who speaks what Indonesian curator Jim Supangkat characterized as "art with an accent."[4] This six-meter-high inflatable mimicked at once the form of a *Saivite* temple from South India and an overblown image of trembling, tumescent male genitalia. The metaphor was compounded in that viewers could physically enter and exit the womb-dark interior, just spacious enough to hold one adult comfortably, through a red-lined slit between two of its upright air chambers, which convincingly approximated an experience of reentering and re-exiting the womb in a parody of born-again religiosity. Squeezing through this meager entrance, carrying one of the provided flashlights in hand, the visitor/supplicant was offered no glimpse of the divine. The black interior smelled of plastic and featured mass-produced fluorescent stickers instead of potent divinity.

Another comment was implicit in the transportable nature of this edifice, made in England but destined for India. Tallur had observed multinational corporations performing acts of appeasement when setting up factories. While acquiring land to set up industries that benefited from India's bountiful supply of cheap labor, corporations would sponsor the construction of community facilities to secure goodwill among people whose lands had been repurposed from agriculture to manufacturing. Tongue firmly in cheek, Tallur offered this collapsible temple as a one-stop solution for multinationals wanting to set up shop in India. To continue with Supangkat's metaphor, Tallur's heavily accented speech is nonetheless alert to a continuing contestation over sites and modes of production that the replacement of mercantile imperialism by free-market multinationalism has not effaced. Remember that the nationalist struggle in India, especially the Gandhian ideology *swadeshi*, championed the locally manufactured handmade against mass-produced imports. Tallur's painstakingly handmade import mockingly offered to facilitate localized mass production.

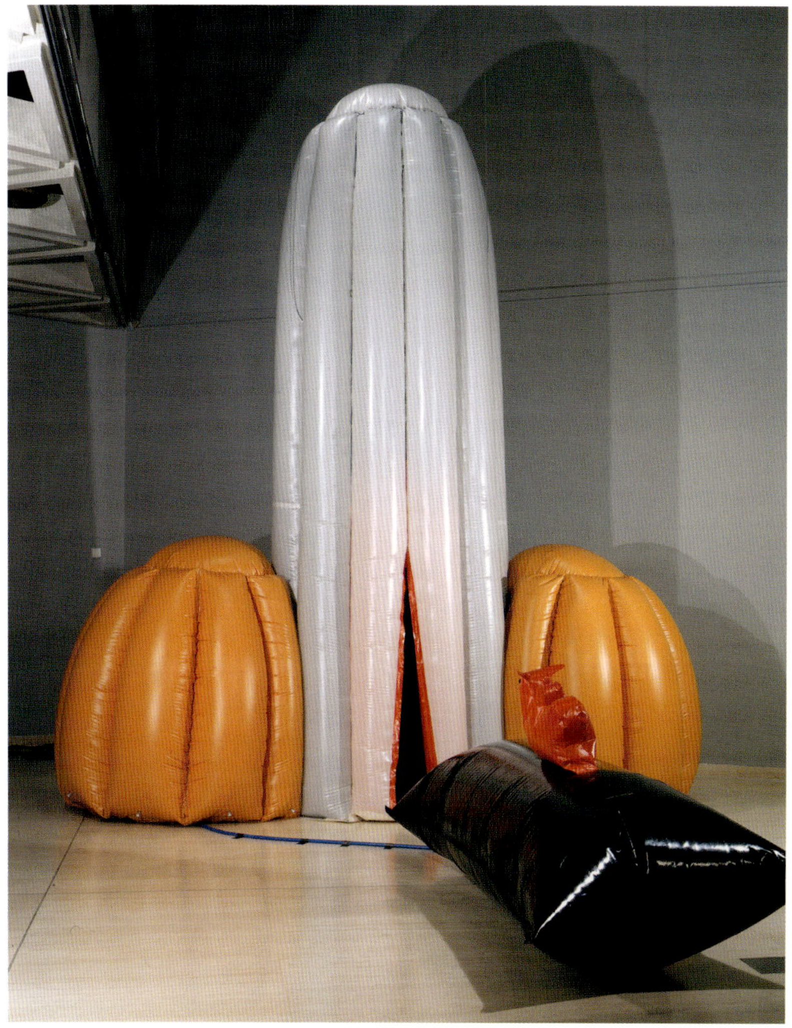

Fig. 7
Made in England: A Temple Design for India, 2002
PVA coated fabric, blower
236 × 118 × 118 inches
Collection of Anupam Poddar

Panic Room (2006; cat. 3) provides another experience of engulfment, augmented in that the viewer activates the work after stepping into its enclosure. The work signals a market phenomenon that particularly affects rural agrarian societies in poorer parts of the world: its inflatable envelope of jute bags is based on newspaper reportage of engineered food shortages and speculative profiteering. The drive toward profit produces scarcity amid plenty, people going hungry while sacks of food are piled high. The title, of course, refers to a kind of enclosure that occurs primarily in prosperous communities. Playing on the prevalence of such fortified refuges against domestic invasion among the affluent, Tallur isolates the participant through spatial and olfactory immersion in an inflated hoard of food grain. It is a sly gesture toward the world's imperiled resources, and to the specters of dispossession and despair that haunt India's dreams of rapid economic growth (notwithstanding the jingoistic posturing that has, of late, found favor in government policy).

An Archaeology of Obsolescence

Tallur writes:

> The computer market changes so fast that a newly produced computer becomes obsolete by the time it reaches its end user. . . . These junks are either being used as land fills [*sic*] or incinerated or being sent to poor third world countries [where] environmental recycling and disposal standards are often non-existent.[5]

Tallur returns again and again to rummage through the remnants of older worlds that appear as palimpsests under the new. In peeling open the seemingly secure layers of modernization and international linkages, he hints at an abiding archaeology of obsolescence that characterizes the contemporary. Tallur harnesses another trope of contemporary society and its teleological pursuit of modernization: that of things succeeding each other into obsolescence ever more rapidly, accompanied by constant reinvention as a corollary. Reinvention does not mean renewal, however, and the leftovers of progress—the discards of yesterday—continue to spirit in and out of today and tomorrow, especially in the rapid and often violent processes of transformation in rural India.

Tallur's excavations at the interstices of the premodern and the postmodern reveal startling juxtapositions, much in the manner of the "marvelous chance encounters" prized so highly by the Surrealist avant-garde in Europe at the end of the first quarter of the twentieth century.[6] The revolutionary implications of the Surrealist project seem to find continual echoes and inheritors in recent art, especially in non-Euro-American contexts. The negation of conventions such as bourgeois morality and cultivated aesthetic taste, together with the freedom of associative couplings, makes it possible for artists like Tallur to muster their peculiar range of experience and aspiration to unusual and surprising ends while essaying the role of the naïve interloper, exempt from the strictures of genteel behavior and social graces.

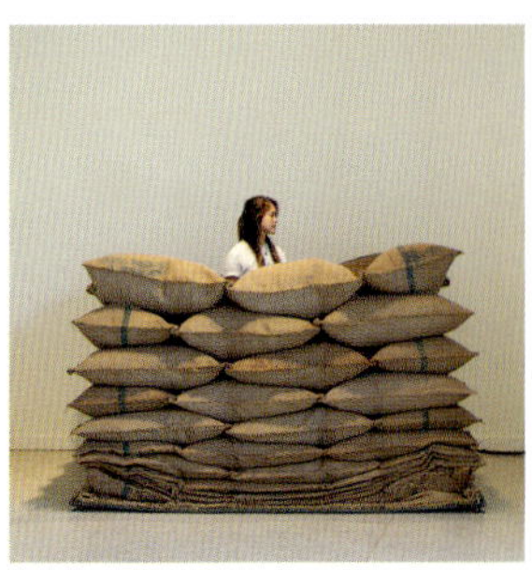

Panic Room, 2006 (cat. 3)

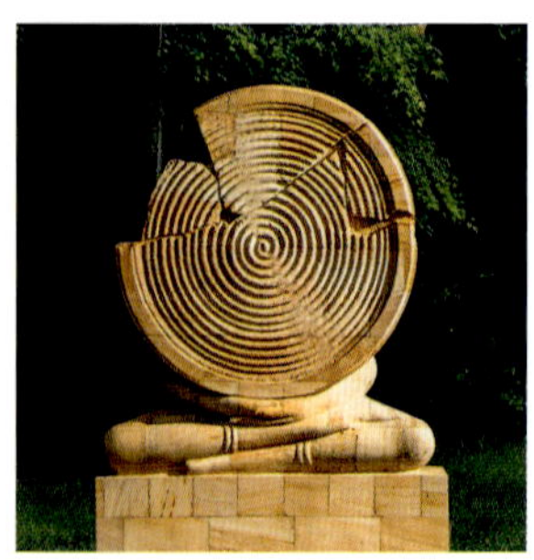

Tolerance, 2019 (cat. 15)

Obsolescence has an important visual corollary in absence (or at least, partly erased presence). Many of Tallur's works seem to be meditations on absence and erasure, as is the case with the figure of the meditating Buddha in *Tolerance* (2019; cat. 15), or with earlier sculptures that feature remnants or traces of the walking figure of Mahatma Gandhi: *Eraser Pro* (2012; cat. 8) and *Iron Age* (2013; cat. 10). In *Alzheimer's* (2006; cat. 4) and *Bulimia 2* (2008; cat. 22) Tallur reprises processes of decay and consecration, making use of termite-eroded figures resembling *bhoota* deities, embedding or overlaying them with silver as though to restore a measure of life and protection to icons that have outlived their usefulness.[7] These works are elaborations on the assisted readymade, though their cultural meanings and the amount of labor applied to the found objects make the comparison limited. The prancing horse in *Bulimia 2* is a diseased remnant of civic monuments featuring equestrian heroes, a fragment of a prior representation of energy, speed, and vitality. By encasing it in polished silver and placing it on an a three-legged chair/throne of awkward and dysfunctional design, Tallur plays the role of a mock conservator even as he makes it clear that the restoration of organic or spiritual function to these twice-dead fragments of the past is a cruel and futile labor. Furthermore, he invites the question of whether such restoration is at all worthwhile: the works present a contrarian argument, seeking to reinstate the abandoned past through a substantial change in context. Discarded artifacts of a living faith are transformed through the artist's audacity into objects of contemporary art. Here, as in other places, Tallur charts a trajectory closely skirting the troublesome terrain of primitivism and its relationship to modernism and contemporary art. Does the fact that it is his own ancestral tradition that Tallur uses as raw material for his conceptualist experimentation place this endeavor in the realm of an affirmative reclamation of tradition? I suspect the answer is not so simple; it is complicated by Tallur's assumption of the position of intimate stranger, both in his rural hometown and in the metropolitan art circles of Bombay, Seoul, and New York.

Translation as Loss, and as Gain

Indian traditions are characterized by complex accretions of impulses and influences. Despite the tendency to see traditions as a singular envelope, they remain a site of vexation due to their mobilization for various political projects, including that of nation building in the context of colonization. In recent decades, the rise of fundamentalist politics has seen a monolithic fabrication of tradition being invoked in the service of a purported Hindu cultural hegemony. The vertically disjointed and fragmented appearance of

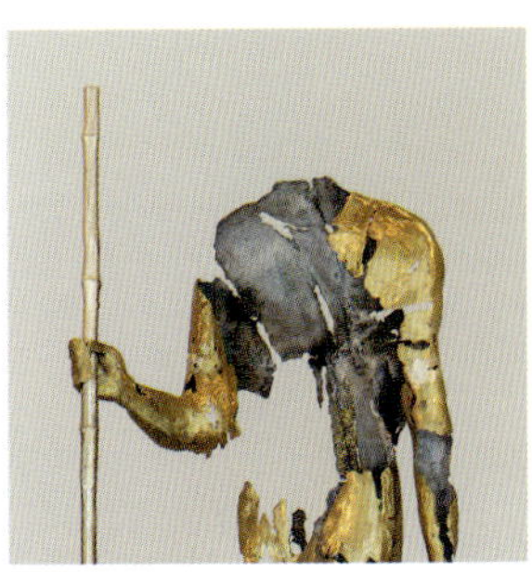

Eraser Pro, 2012 (cat. 8)

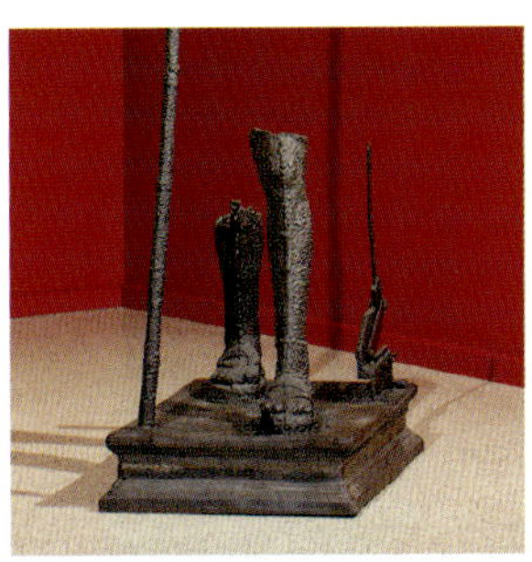

Iron Age, 2013 (cat. 10)

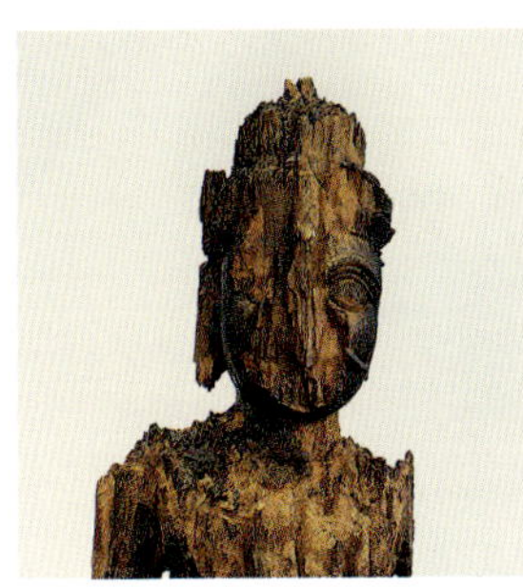

Alzheimer's, 2006 (cat. 4)

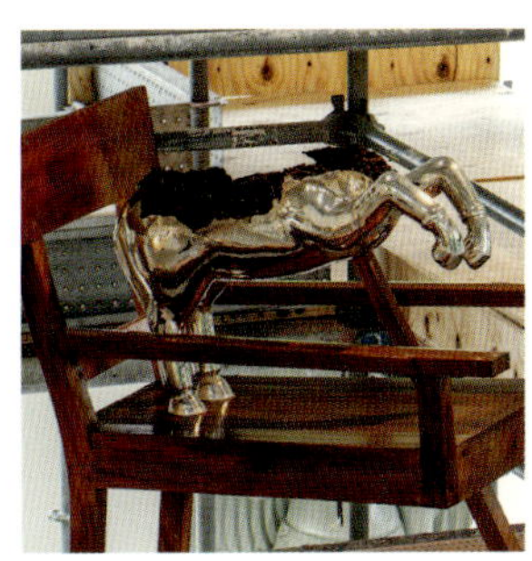

Bulimia 2, 2008 (cat. 22)

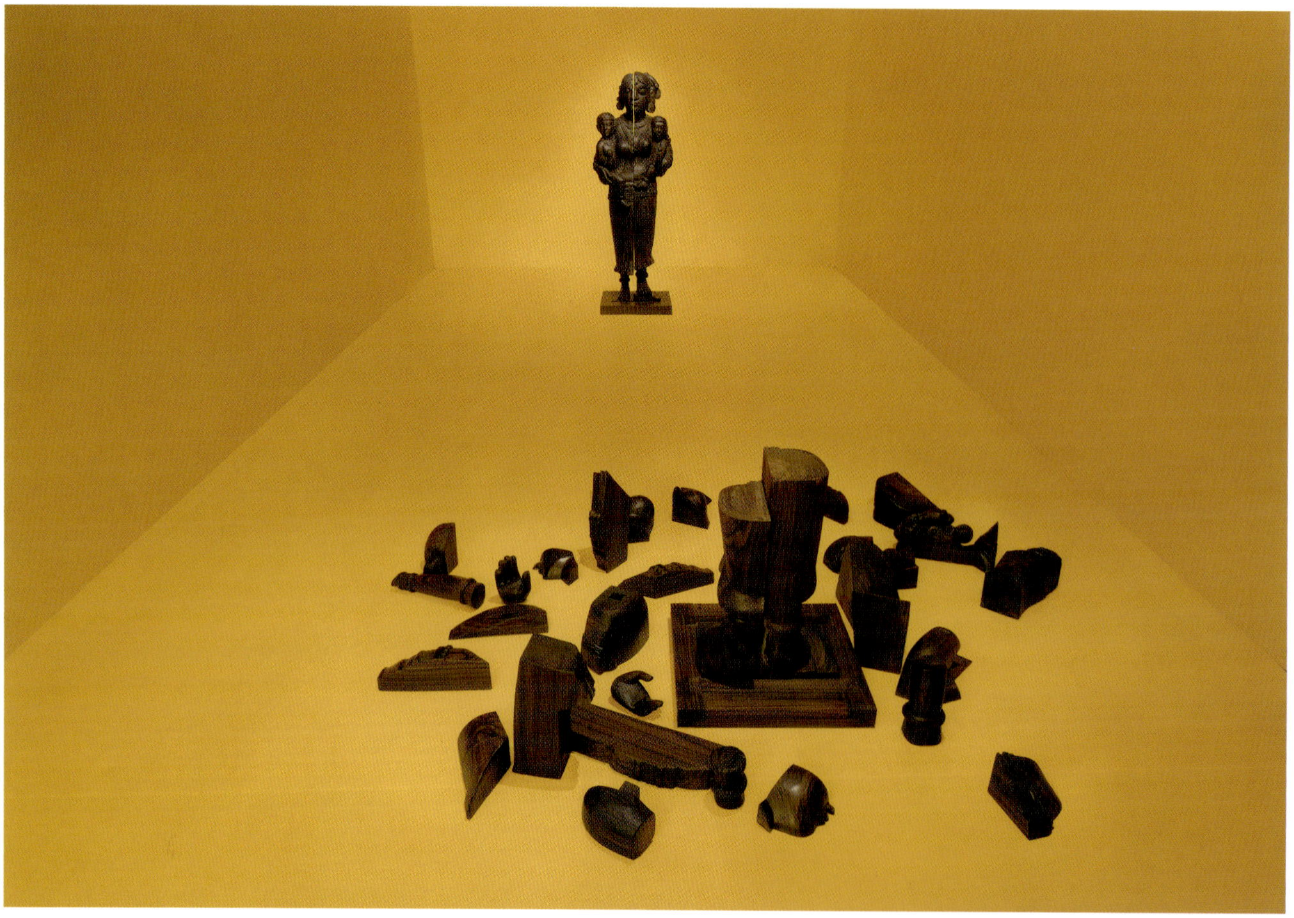

Fig. 8
Colonial Sisters, 2008
rosewood
62 × 62 × 20 inches (30 individual pieces of varying sizes)
Collection of M+ Museum, Hong Kong

Colonial Sisters (2008; fig. 8) highlighted the constructed nature of tradition, underscoring its internal inconsistencies. Tallur has regularly employed skilled craftspeople from his district in executing sculptural work. Often, the artisans he chooses belong to distinct traditions and bring with them different skills with materials and figurative idioms. Within the Indian context, their respective skills are usually cast in a hierarchical relationship to each other, subordinate to the overarching notion of classical art manifest in a Hindu-Buddhist canon. One half of *Colonial Sisters* offered up a split reconstruction of the same formulaic figure as interpreted by a traditionally trained sculptor, on the viewer's left, and by a folk artist, on the viewer's right, presenting a bilateral asymmetry that in its visual misalignment parallels the tension between versions of what is termed tradition in the Indian context. The division of labor highlighted connections as well as disconnections across divergent streams within Indian tradition, using the motif of a mother/goddess figure with a child on each hip. Alongside this split figure, Tallur presented a second, literally deconstructed sculpture in the manner of a three-dimensional puzzle. First exhibited in New York, the work toyed with the expectations of the gallery-going audience, schooled not to touch works of art, by offering the beguiling invitation to play with building blocks, to try their hand at reconstructing the sculpture. The work stands in for several acts of translation, from the ancient classical to the contemporary traditional and folk, and ultimately to Tallur's own conceptualist intent in presenting the work to an international audience.

In other works, such as *Untitled (Elephant)* (2008; cat. 21), *Lamp (Deepa Laxmi)* (2011; cat. 23), and *Victory Pillar* (2012; cat. 28), artifacts of a recent, though fast-disappearing past persist within the construction of the present, a material reassertion of the coexistence of multiple layers of history in contemporary India. During the first decade of what can be called postmodernity in Indian art, the teacher, artist, and poet Gulammohammed Sheikh (born 1937) argued against the teleological strictures of progress and ontological priority. Sheikh offered the postcolonial artist a way out of the historical bind of always playing a chronologically posterior role in the grand narrative of modernist endeavor. "Living in India," he wrote, "means living simultaneously in several cultures and times. . . . The past exists as a living entity alongside the present, each illuminating and sustaining the other."[8] Three decades later, Tallur's work presents this enduring simultaneity of dissimilar situations as having become uncomfortable and abrasive rather than "illuminating and sustaining." The optimism of coexistence implied in Sheikh's writing has been replaced by a lumpen struggle for survival.

In *Untitled (Elephant)*, the polished wooden figure of a playful elephant kicking a ball, trunk held aloft—recalling the figures of animals and composite creatures carved into the base of pillars in Hindu temples in southern India—emerges from an armature of iron and a concrete pillar; in *Lamp (Deepa Laxmi)* and *Victory Pillar*, female figures of divine attendants holding ceremonial lamps are enveloped in cancerous masses of cement and other materials. Will the elephant break through the concrete and steel to reassert its primal energy? Or is its animation in the process of being swallowed by the obliterating encroachment of reinforced concrete? Will the lamp corrode the cement with its heat and soot to reclaim its position in the (old) order of things, where lighting the lamp symbolizes beginnings, or will it be engulfed and snuffed out by the irrepressible energies of development?

Memorials to Erasure

Much of Tallur's work presents commentaries on the increasingly rapid processes of obsolescence that characterize the modern world, and the physical, spiritual, and intellectual violence that accompanies these. In a pointed reference to recent political developments in India and elsewhere in the world, *Tolerance* presents this violence in a *dhvani*-evoking form. The shattered halo of the Buddha figure has grown to engulf the head and torso, its radiance transformed into a coiled maze with only its inward terminus

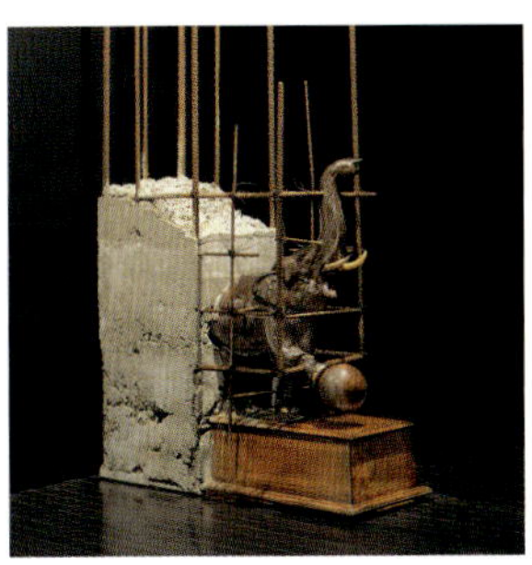

Untitled (Elephant), 2008 (cat. 21)

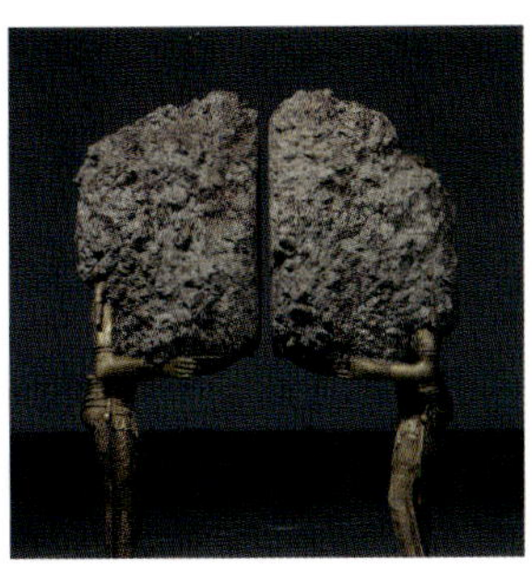

Lamp (Deepa Laxmi), 2010 (cat. 23)

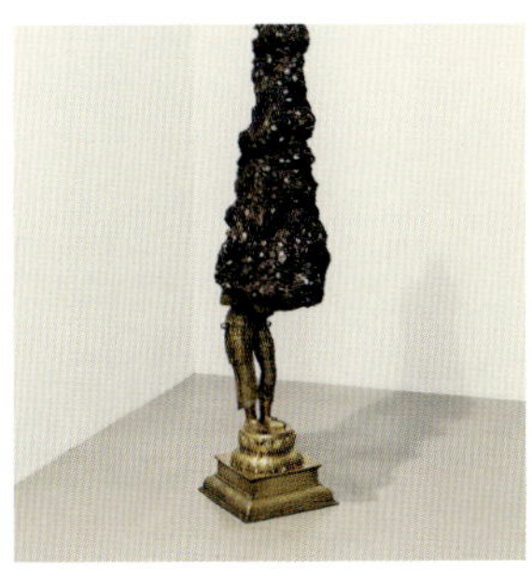

Victory Pillar, 2012 (cat. 28)

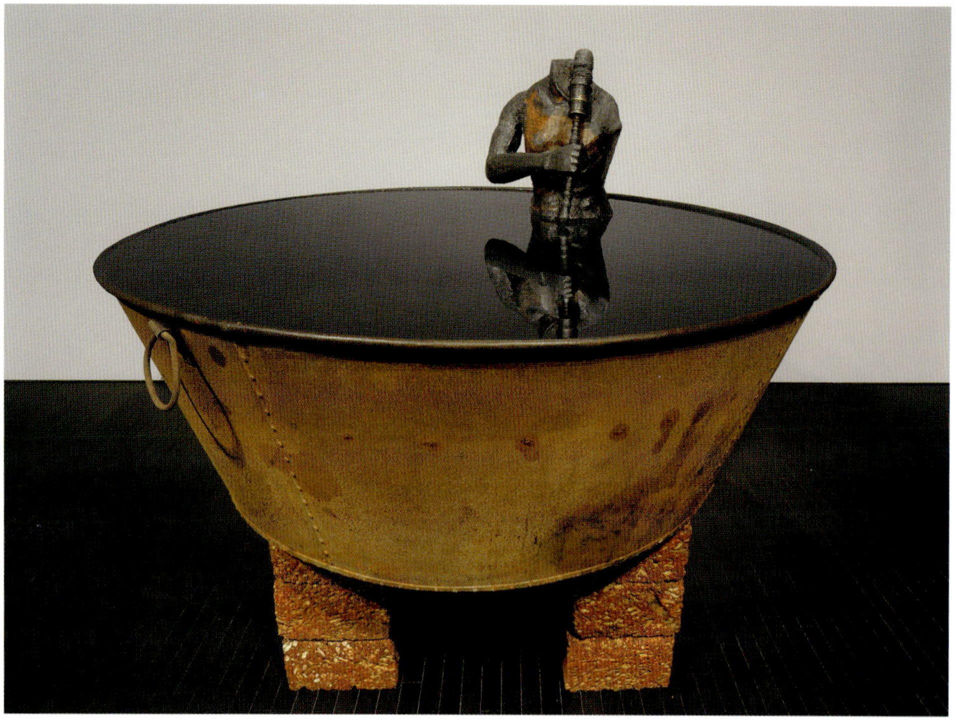

Fig. 9
e=mc², 2008
large iron vessel, oil, laterite stone, wood, silicon
64 × 77 × 64 inches
Collection of the artist

Fig. 10
Untitled, 2007
inflatable bed, silicon, latex rubber, medical cot, and forceps
108 × 110 × 63 inches
Collection of Saatchi Gallery

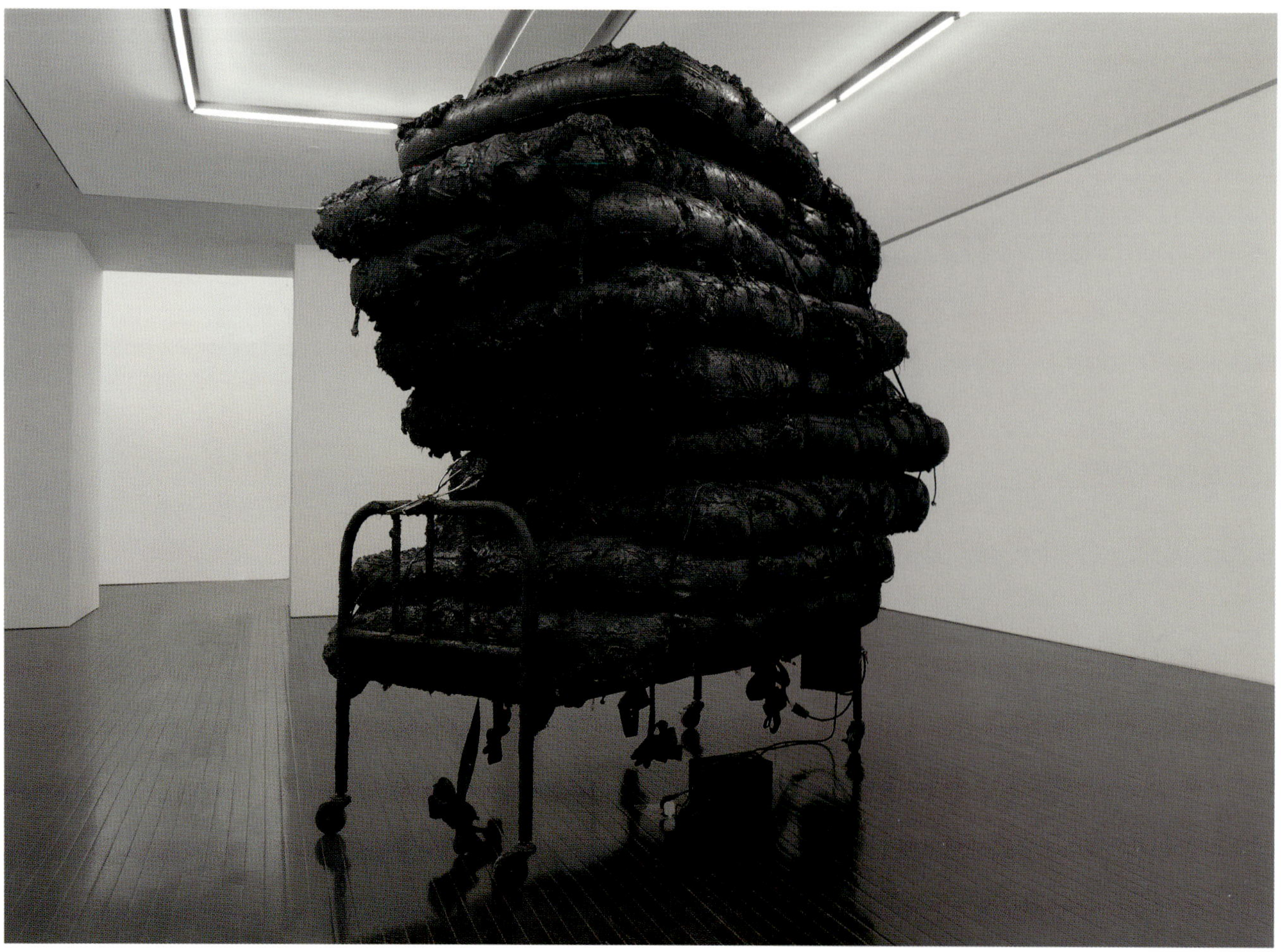

discernible: an impending supernova / black hole. In *e=mc²* (2008; fig. 9), a soldier-like headless male figure stands half submerged in a bath of spent oil. The one remaining arm of this charred warrior clutches an extinguished torch, as though a charnel-house remnant of a past battle. Residues of conflict are presented as spectacle for the audience, but there is the added discomfiture of not knowing what battle is being referenced. Iraq is, of course, the first answer, with its continuing tragedy of human suffering and political injustice fueled by contests for the world's shrinking oil reserves. Further references could be made to the vast number of headless statues in museums, each one testifying to the aftermath of conquest where victors symbolically behead or topple the effigies of their opponents. To complicate matters further, Tallur chose to erect this tableau on the foundation of an iron vessel used for making jaggery (unrefined sugar, an essential ingredient in traditional food and medicine) by boiling sugar cane juice—a rural, small-scale industry that has become practically extinct with the dominance of factory production in recent decades. The Einsteinian title relating the production of energy to a destruction of matter presents the last piece of the puzzle; the seemingly inexorable forces of physics provide an uneasy analogue to historical transformation and a state of permanent conflict.

Scientific progress and technological nightmares appear to be conjoined twins in Tallur's work. He is drawn to mechanical contraptions that creak and rattle, wheeze and groan. *Untitled* (2007; fig. 10), with its towering pile of inflatable mattresses accompanied by surgical forceps on a hospital bed, is thoroughly disquieting in its invocation of a teetering mound of scorched bodies. Tallur declines to name the disaster via a title, preferring perhaps to gesture toward brutalization as an existential state in our times. Nor is this a brutalization born solely of war and riot. The ghastly phenomenon of farmers' suicides in India triggered by the replacement of food crops with cash crops using genetically modified seeds has claimed the lives of tens of thousands of male breadwinners and consequently condemned their families to even greater suffering.[9] Tallur had previously made a more direct comment on this through *Hangover* (2006; fig. 11), where a six-foot-tall effigy of coconut husks and clay was suspended from the rafters.

In a similarly harrowing vein that harnesses the interactivity of many of his

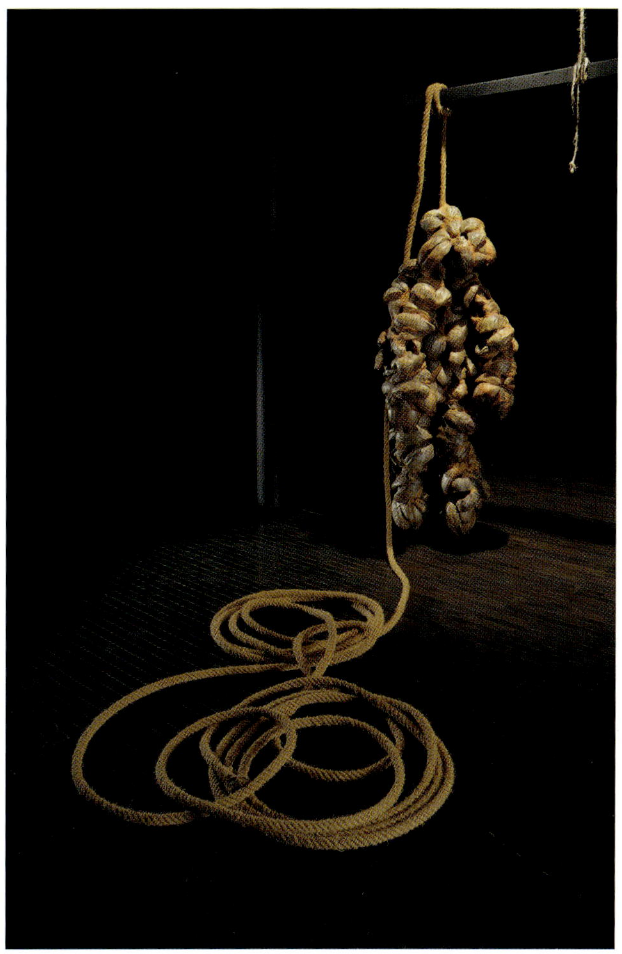

Fig. 11
Hangover, 2006
dried coconut cover, coir rope, clay
71 × 32 × 28 inches
Collection of the artist

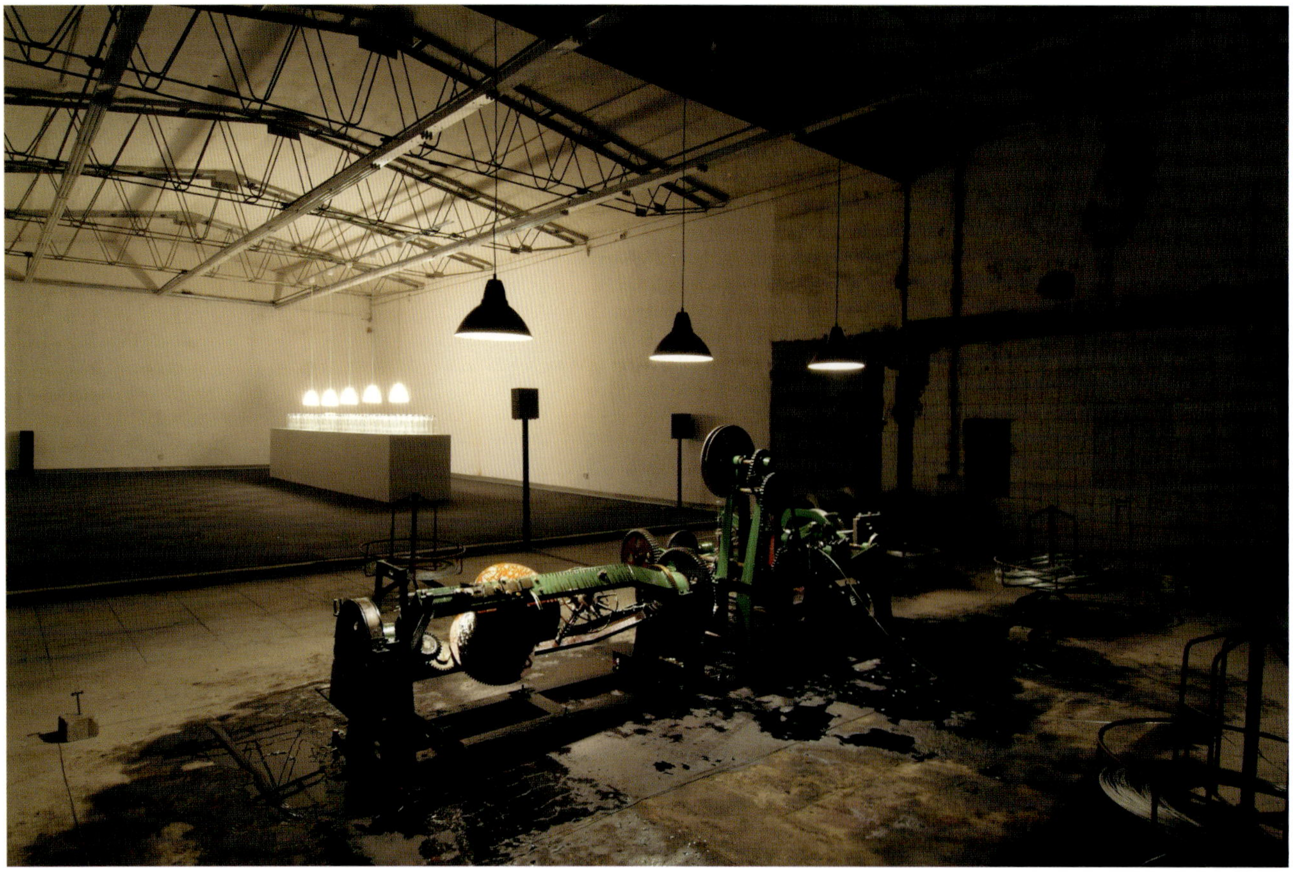

works, Tallur revisited in 2009 an earlier (2005) project that features the production of barbed wire.[10] *Souvenir Maker: Designed in America, Conceptualized in India, Made in China, Sponsored by Korea. Yes . . . we are conditioned to think under flags* (fig. 12) features a barbed wire–making machine that the viewer/participant can turn on for thirty seconds at a time. The machine's operation is accompanied by an instrumental soundtrack of national anthems. Alongside the machine, finished samples of gold-plated barbed wire are on display in narrow glass jars uncannily similar to those used for storing food in kitchens or specimens in museums and laboratories. Making the viewer into participant is a well-trodden trope of contemporary art. Here, the barbed wire–fashioning viewer-participant is implicated in the production of nationhood through acts of boundary marking, recalling Benedict Anderson's thesis on the nature of nations as imagined communities, "imagined as both inherently limited and sovereign."[11] As Anderson further argues, the nation is characterized by an assumption of deep, horizontal comradeship, which persists in spite of the presence of inequality and violence. The *Souvenir Maker* participant/buyer who produces a little piece of precious barbed wire and takes it home in a display jar is, ipso facto, recreating the judicially sanctioned precept of private property, as well as the conceit of the nation as a discrete community with limited membership and inviolable sovereignty. In *Bon Appetite*, a 2007 artist's book produced after the work's first iteration, Tallur supplied readers with a discussion of historical disputes over the patenting of machines

Fig. 12
Souvenir Maker: Designed in America, Conceptualized in India, Made in China, Sponsored by Korea. Yes . . . we are conditioned to think under flags (China version), 2005
barbed wire–making machine, gold-coated barbed wire, national anthems of 26 countries, glass jars
dimension variable (site specific)
Collection of the artist

used for producing barbed wire. He even reproduced a copy of his own application to the Patent Cooperation Treaty seeking a patent to be issued for his *Souvenir Maker*.[12] Significantly, this discussion of patent disputes relating to the now-ubiquitous device for property control and national security traces the origins of twisted-wire barriers to the later nineteenth century (1863–74), a time of capitalist consolidation as well as imperial expansion in large parts of the world.

During the first decade of the present century, Tallur embarked on a series of works dealing with the monetary and cultural values implicit in currency and icons. Taking mass-produced coins and slightly less common icons that demand reverence, Tallur started subjecting them to the abrasive scrutiny of his mechanical devices. With its improvised machinery, the interactive work *Apocalypse* (2010; cat. 5) polishes coins into devaluation in the pursuit of civilization, rendering them into certified "clean" money that is manifestly useless. In the process, claims of national sovereignty implicit in the coinage are made irrelevant, and ultimately transferable, as every coin can be made to be like every other regardless of the issuing authority. Meanwhile, *Enlightenment Machine (Beta Version 3.0)* (2019; cat. 16) offers participatory access to transcultural erasure, inviting the audience to contribute to effacing features from iconic religious, cultural, or political symbols. As a transnational artist operating between countries and across cultures, Tallur has developed a special perspective on intercultural communication. His work points to the links between fear and desire in capitalist societies; it laughs equally at the desire for prosperity and wholeness—for the veneer of civilization—and at the fear of erasure that attends these desires.

Resolutely catholic in references and materials, Tallur's work is characterized by investigations and recuperations amid a varied field of debris left behind in the triumphal wake of "the storm of progress," to invoke Walter Benjamin's meditations on history.[13] Like a purveyor of illicit goods on the black market, Tallur solicits our attention to his phantasms, these irruptions of perversity that the purportedly rational arrangements of the nation-state and global capitalism would like us to forget. If it is at all possible to contemplate in contemporary art a counter discourse to these totalities, then Tallur's work would suggest that it manifests as ghosts-in-the-machine, *bhootas* who refuse to die away, bugs that defy programming, and irregularities that refuse erasure.

"Time and Space died yesterday. We already live in the absolute, because we have created eternal, omnipresent speed," proclaimed Filippo Tommaso Marinetti in the *Manifesto of Futurism* in 1909.[14] More than a century later, Tallur's work reaffirms the death of future-driven progress. The future is already obsolete. Marinetti's "eternal, omnipresent speed" has assumed thoroughly dystopian, even mindless dimensions propelling the world headlong into a chaotic intermingling of conditions where the vernacular and the international join in uneasy marriages, and where epiphanies can only be stumbled upon among endlessly accumulating piles of debris.

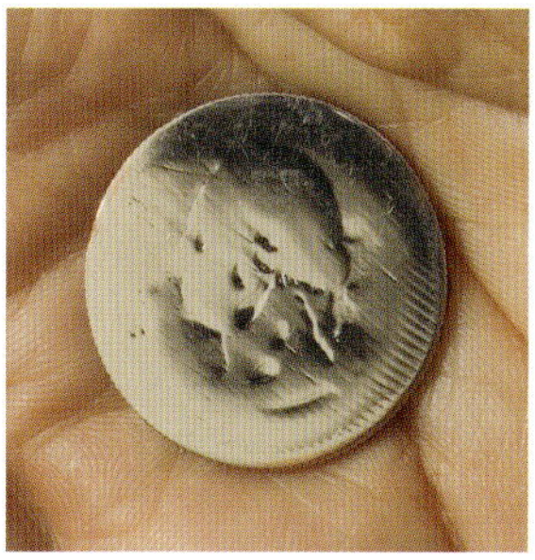

Apocalypse, 2010 (cat. 5)

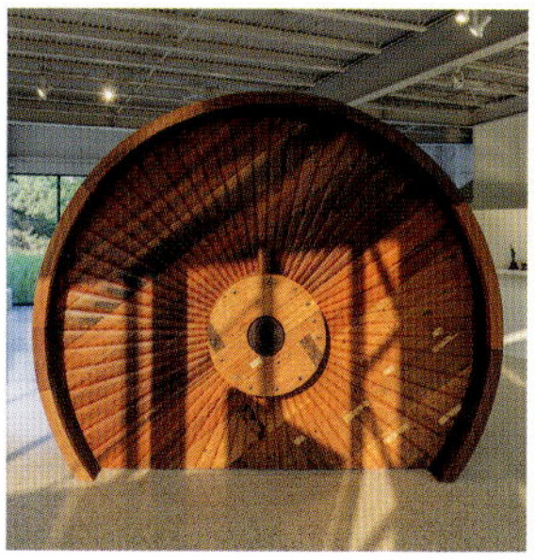

Enlightenment Machine (Beta Version 3.0), 2019 (cat. 16)

Notes

1. Established as a distinctively post-Independence institution in 1950 as part of the Maharaja Sayajirao University of Baroda, the Faculty of Fine Arts remained the preeminent art school in India well into the 1990s.

2. The artist's family name is the same as the name of his ancestral village, a practice common in parts of southern India, as well as in other parts of Asia.

3. Among the extensive literature on Ānandavardhana's *Dhvanyāloka* and Abhinavagupta's subsequent commentary, see Patrick Colm Hogan, "Toward a Cognitive Science of Poetics: Ānandavardhana, Abhinavagupta and the Theory of Literature," *College Literature* 23, no. 1 (February 1996): 164–78; and G. T. Deshpande, *Abhinavagupta* (New Delhi: Sahitya Akademi, 1995), especially chapter 5, "Abhinavagupta's Theory of Aesthetics (II)."

4. Jim Supangkat, "Art with an Accent," in *CP Open Biennale 2003: Interpellation* (Jakarta: CP Foundation, 2003), 20–28.

5. Tallur L.N., *Bon Appetite* (Seoul: Arario Seoul, 2007), 78.

6. André Breton, in his "First Manifesto of Surrealism" (1924), invokes the marvelous as being the ultimate form of beauty: "Let us not mince words: the marvelous is always beautiful, anything marvelous is beautiful, in fact only the marvelous is beautiful." The marvelous for Breton and the Surrealists is epitomized in the description of beauty by the French Uruguayan poet Comte de Lautréamont (Isidore Ducasse, 1846–1870) in his *Les Chants de Maldoror*: "As beautiful as the chance encounter between a sewing machine and an umbrella on a dissecting table." André Breton, "First Manifesto of Surrealism," in *Art in Theory, 1900–2000: An Anthology of Changing Ideas*, edited by Charles Harrison and Paul Wood (Malden, MA: Blackwell, 2003), 450, 453.

7. The cult of *bhoota* (meaning ghost, but also past or bygone time) and *preta* (corpse, undead) deities is prevalent in parts of coastal Karnataka. These demigods are considered analogues of living creatures and are imbued with a potency that may be expressed in benevolence or in mischief. Tallur has made use of such animal and human images in several works.

8. Gulammohammed Sheikh, "Among Several Cultures and Times," in *Contemporary Indian Tradition*, ed. Carla Borden (New York: Smithsonian Institution, 1989), 107. Sheikh taught art history and painting at the Faculty of Fine Arts for three decades until 1993, and has remained an important influence on several generations of Indian artists.

9. According to journalist and author P. Sainath, 182,936 Indian farmers took their own lives in the decade 1997–2007, the majority of them in the states of Maharashtra, Madhya Pradesh, Chattisgarh, Andhra Pradesh, and Tallur's native Karnataka. See Sainath, "Neo-liberal Terrorism in India: The Largest Wave of Suicides in History," *Counterpunch*, February 12, 2009, http://www.counterpunch.org/2009/02/12/the-largest-wave-of-suicides-in-history-2/. The deaths are attributed, in part, to the "terminator technology" in the seeds supplied by major multinational corporations. These seeds bear a genetic modification that makes it impossible for farmers to save part of their crop as seed stock for the next planting, obliging them to purchase the expensive seeds every time, compounding a cycle of debt and desperation—especially if the monsoon fails.

10. See Tallur, *Bon Appetite*, 110–19.

11. Benedict Anderson, *Imagined Communities: Reflections on the Origins and Spread of Nationalism* (London: Verso, 1983), 6.

12. Tallur, *Bon Appetite*, 118–19.

13. Walter Benjamin, "Theses on the Philosophy of History," in *Illuminations*, trans. Harry Zohn (London: Fontana, 1992), 245–55.

14. F. T. Marinetti, "The Founding and Manifesto of Futurism" (originally published in *Le Figaro*, Paris, February 20, 1909), in *Documents of 20th Century Art: Futurist Manifestos*, ed. Umbro Apollonio, trans. R. W. Flint et al. (New York: Viking Press, 1973), 19–24.

Plates
—
Exhibition

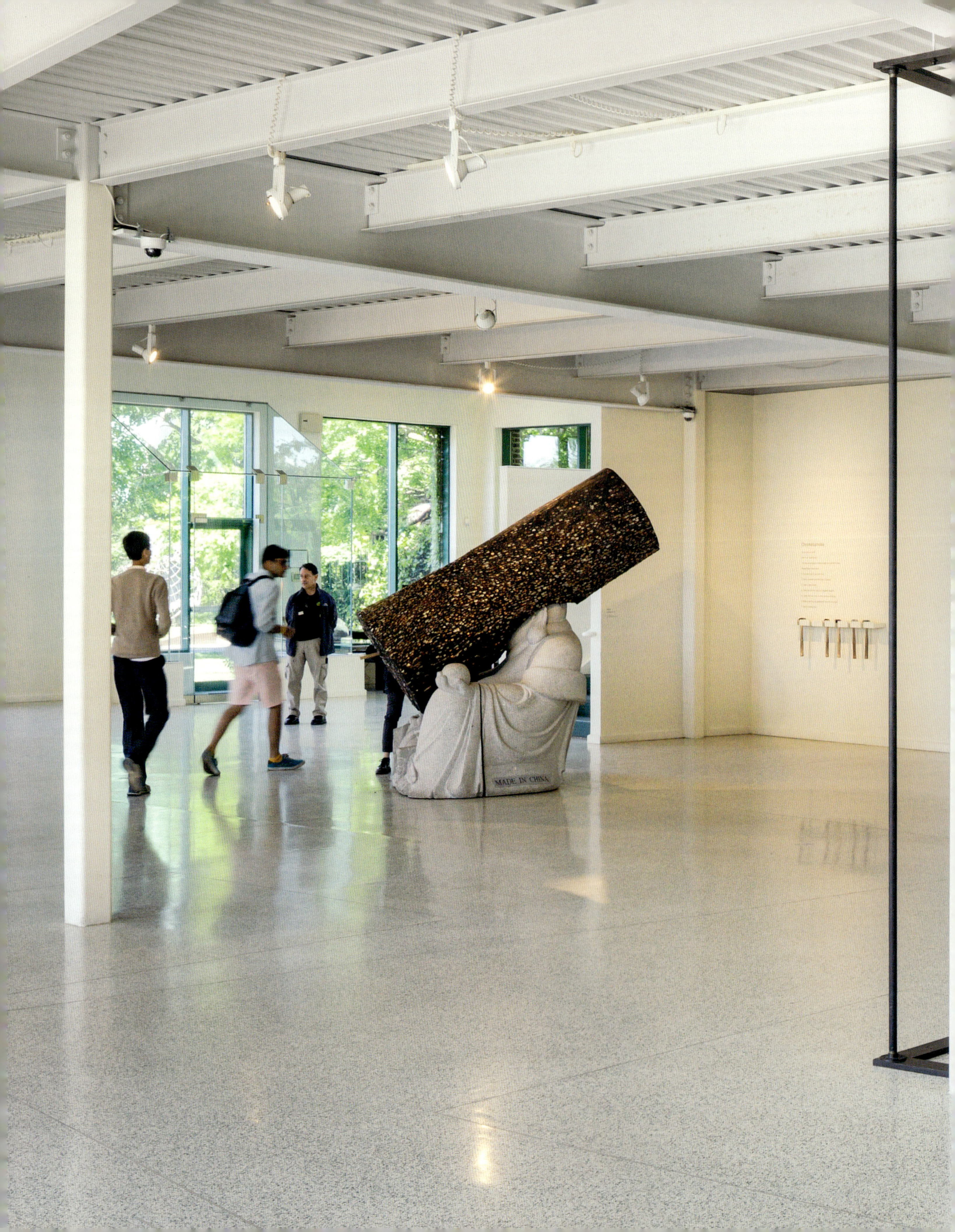
MADE IN CHINA

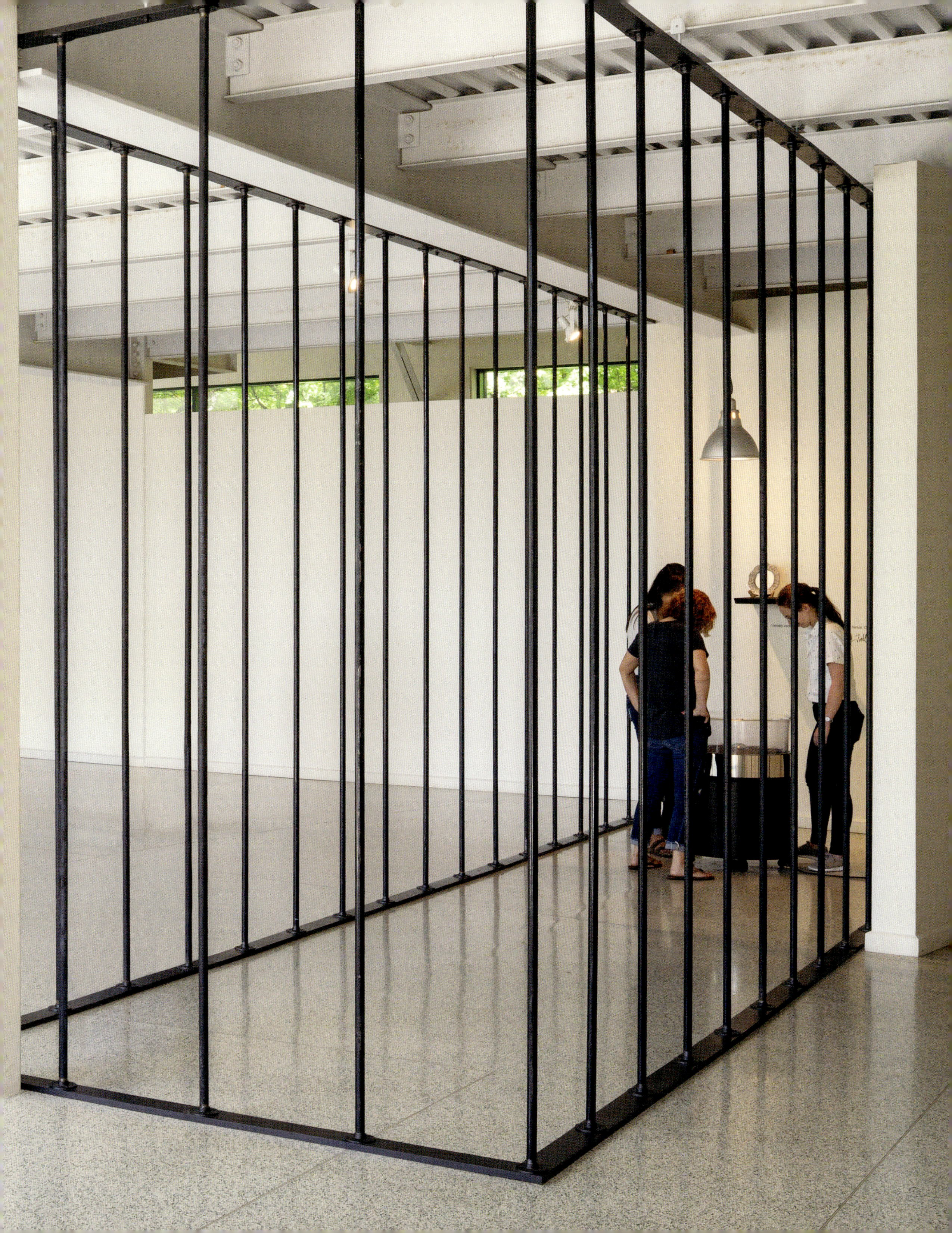

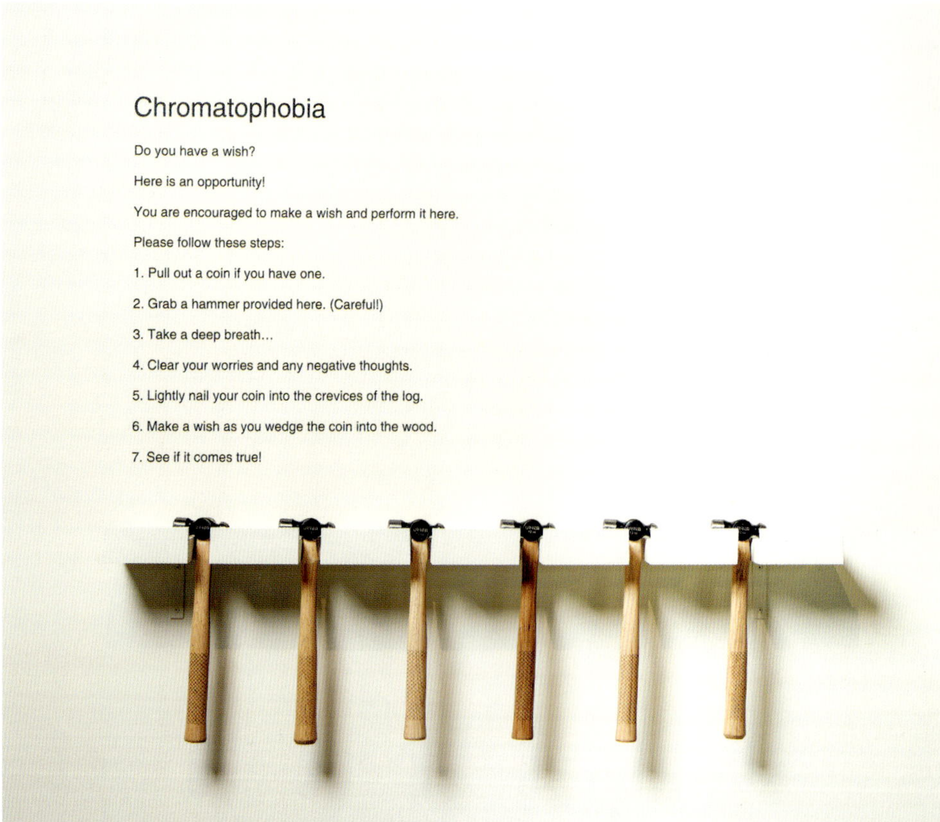

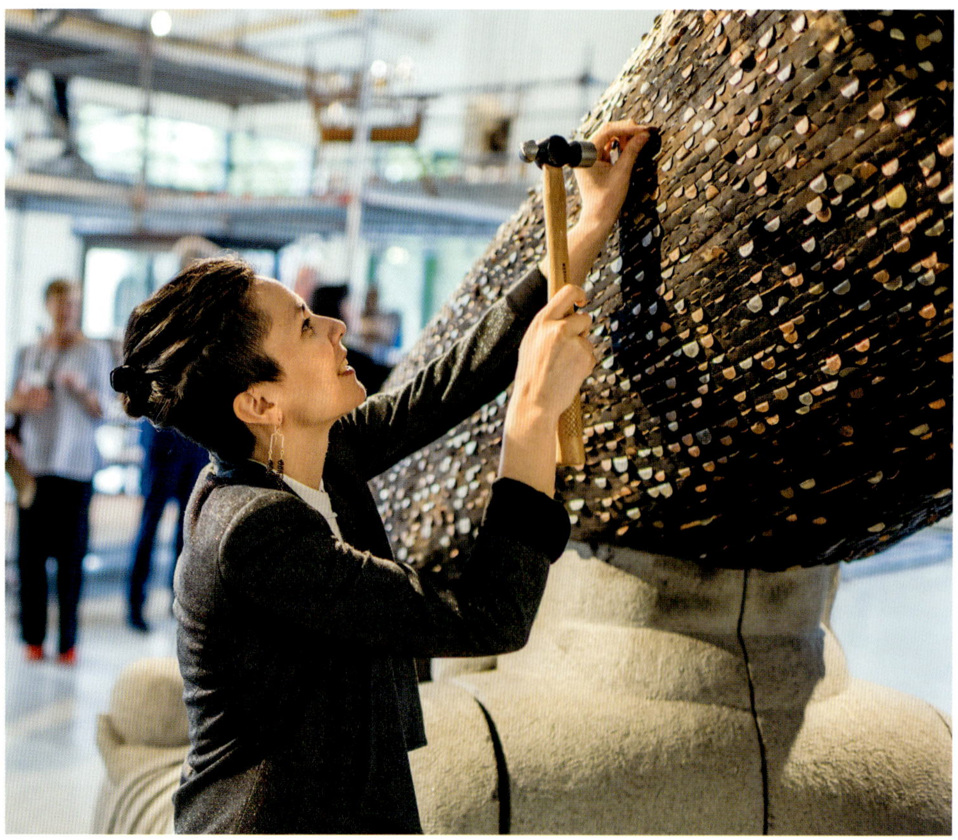

Chromatophobia, 2012
(cat. 7)

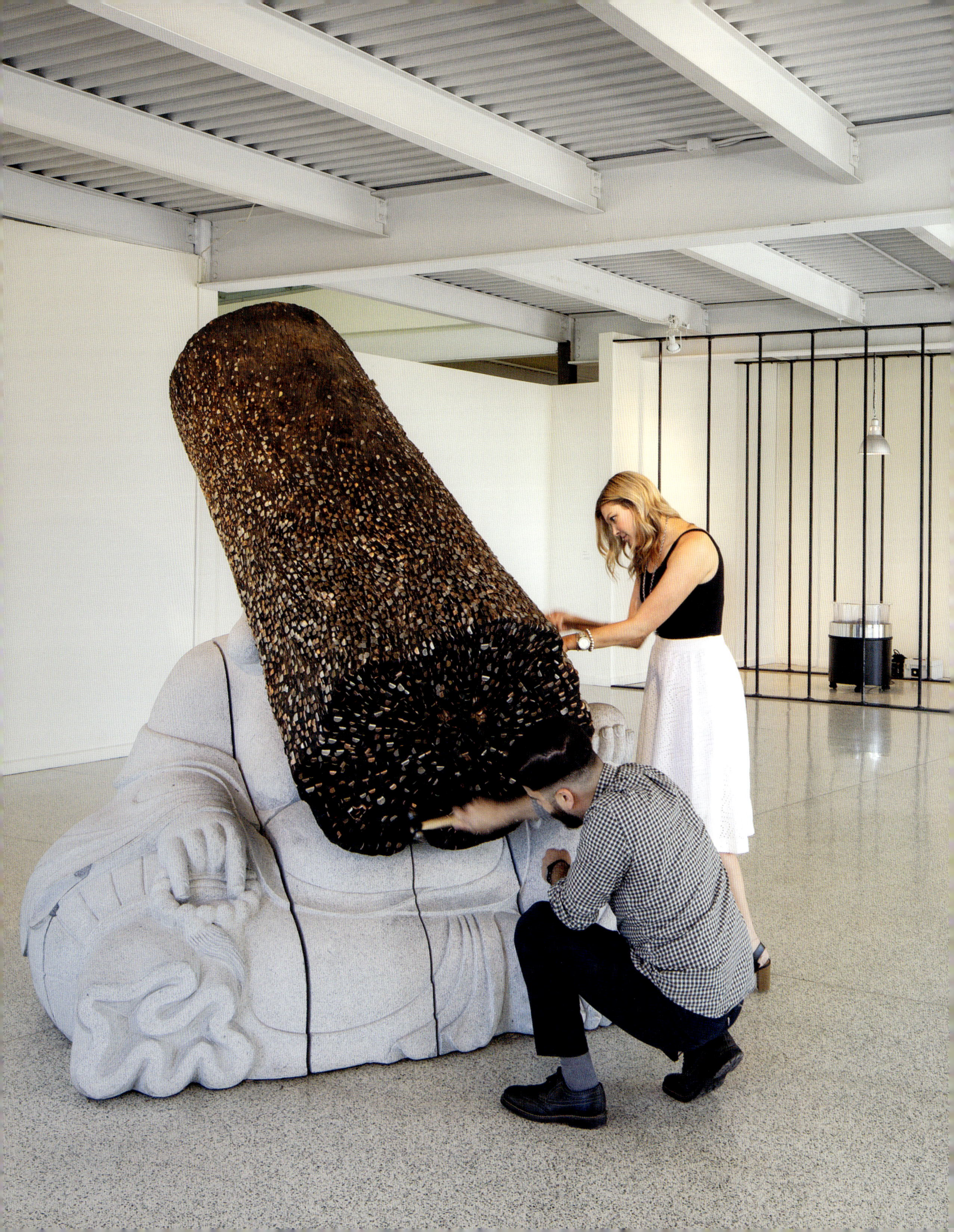

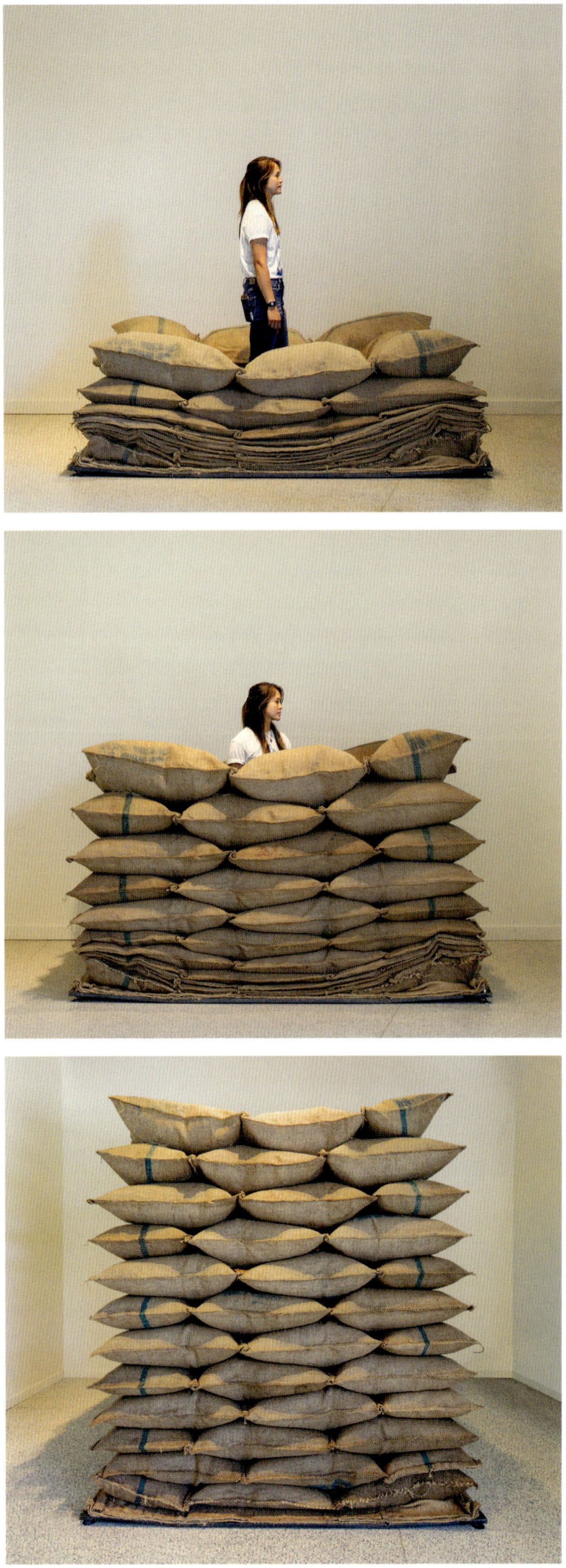

Panic Room, 2006 (cat. 3)

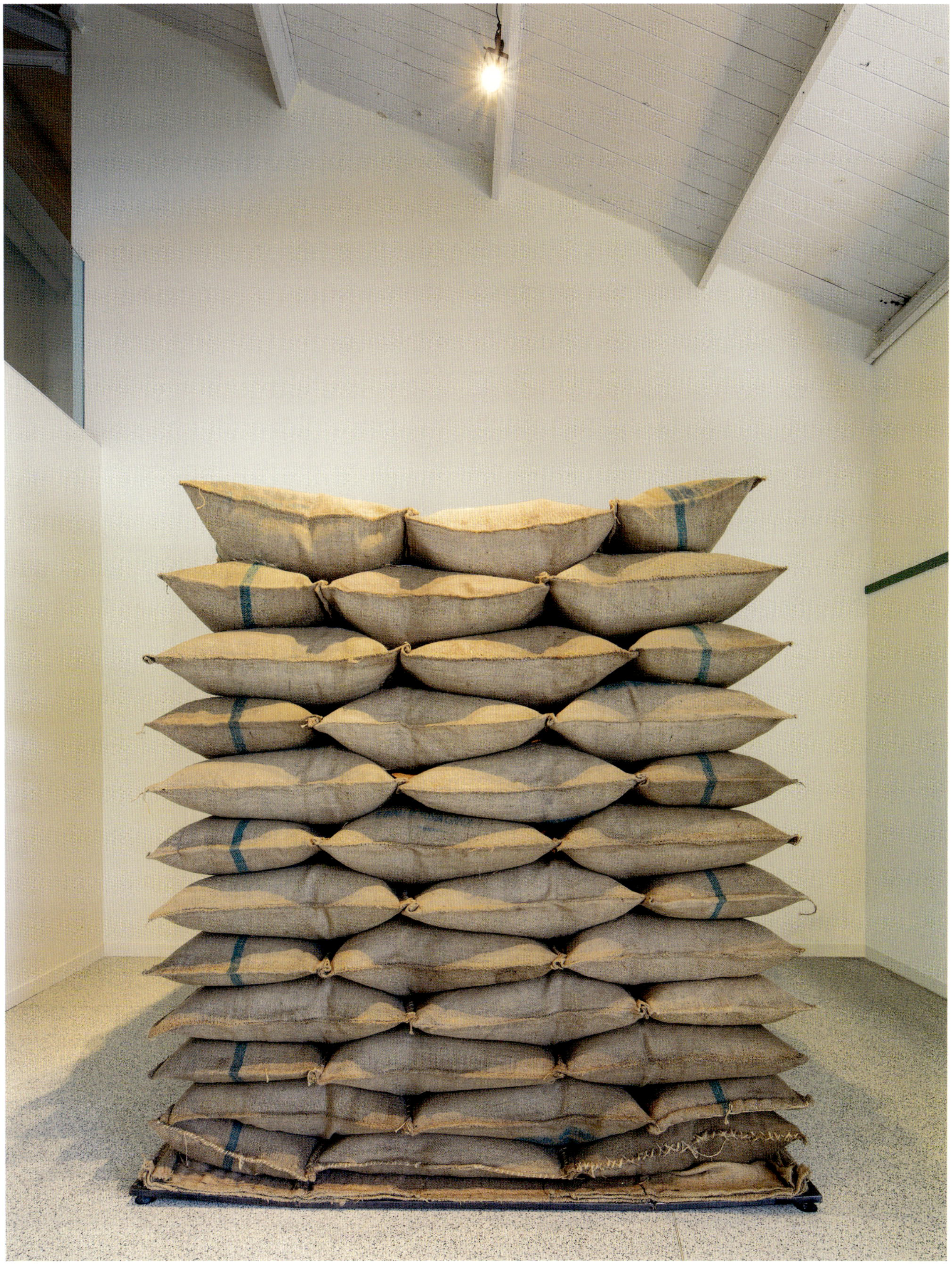

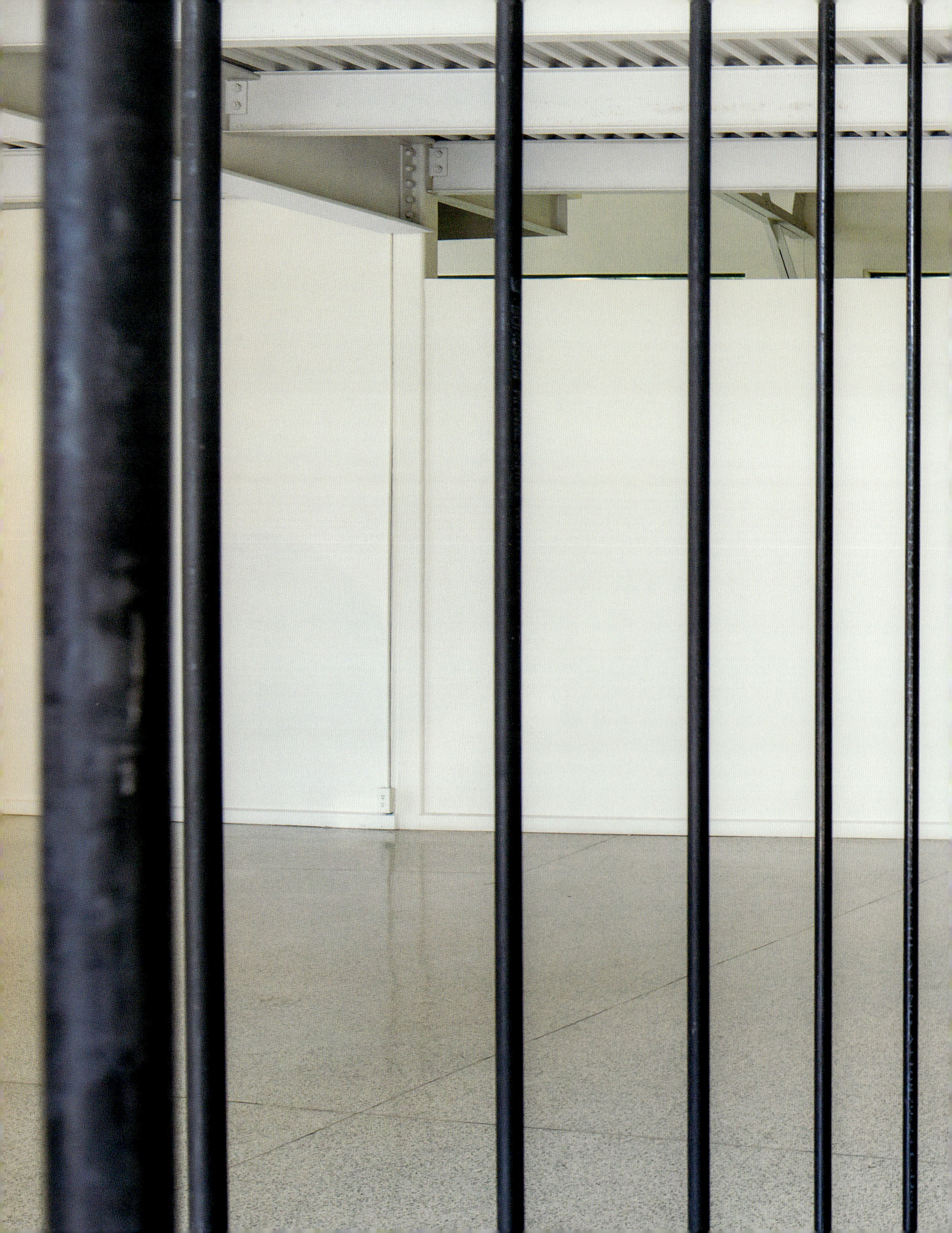

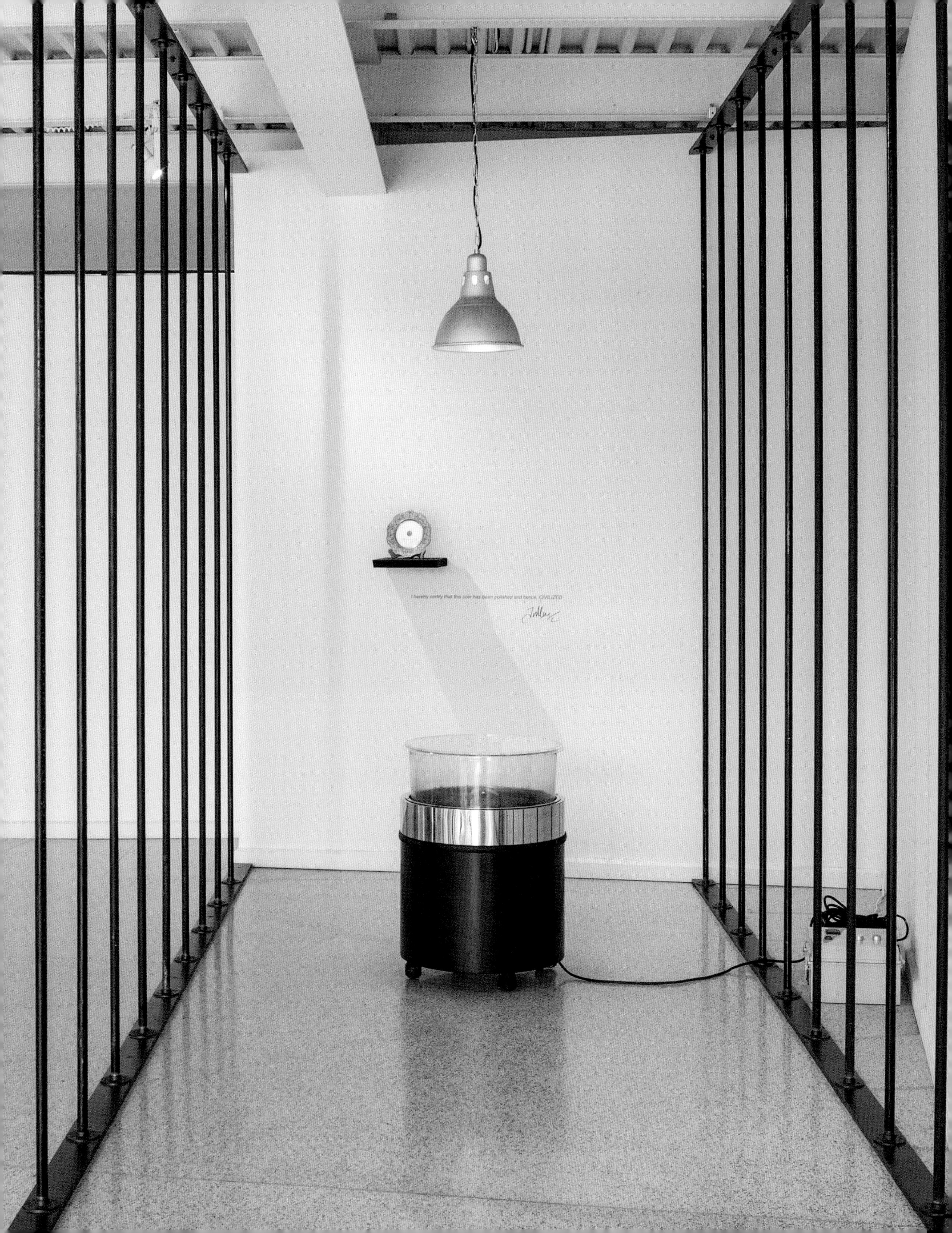
I hereby certify that this coin has been polished and hence, CIVILIZED

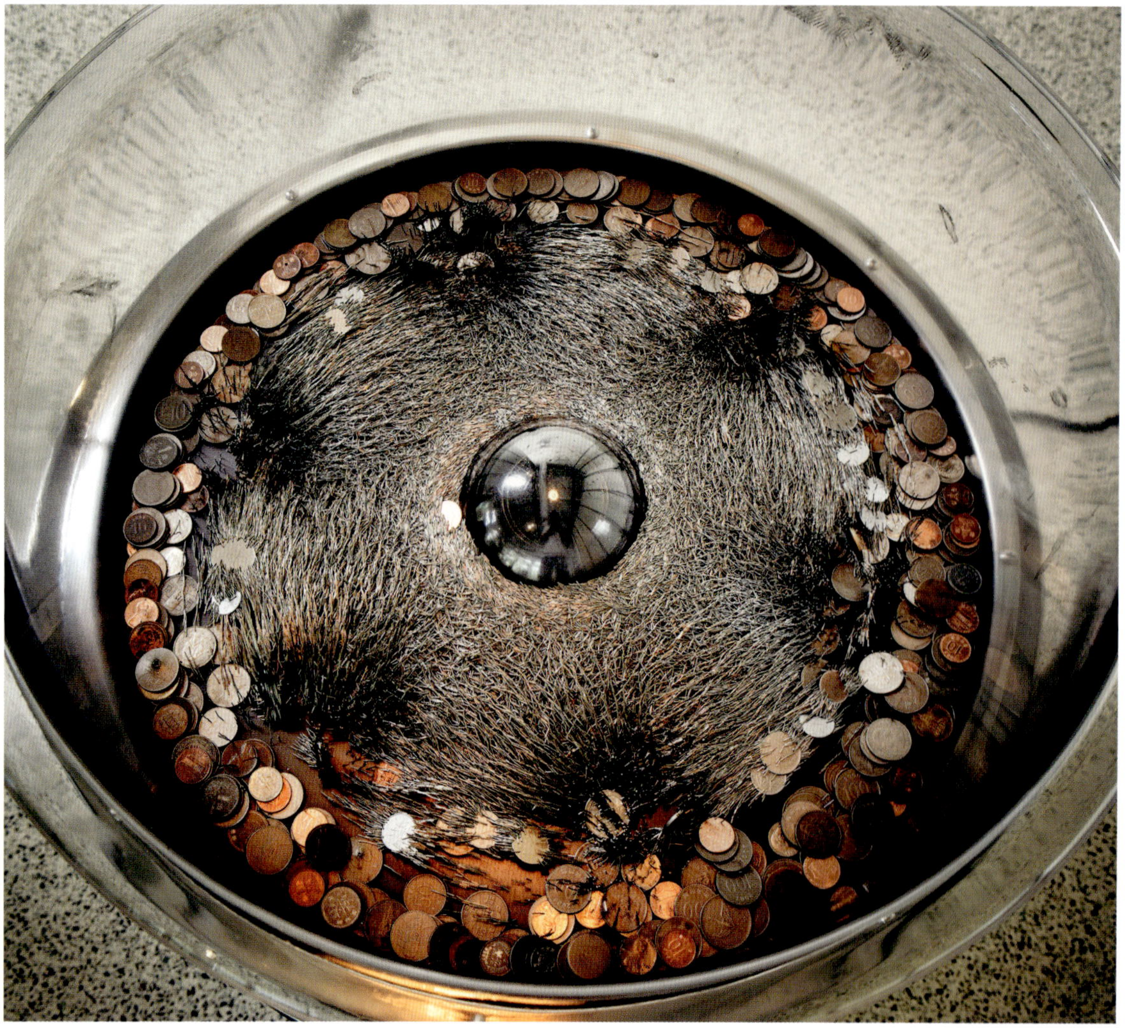

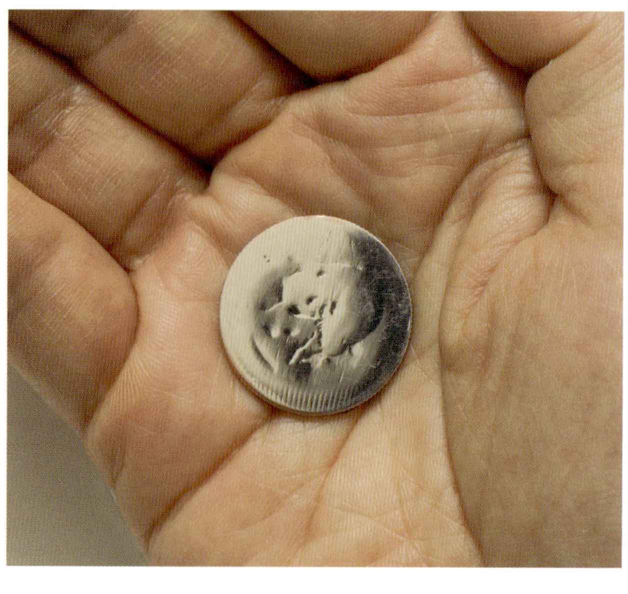

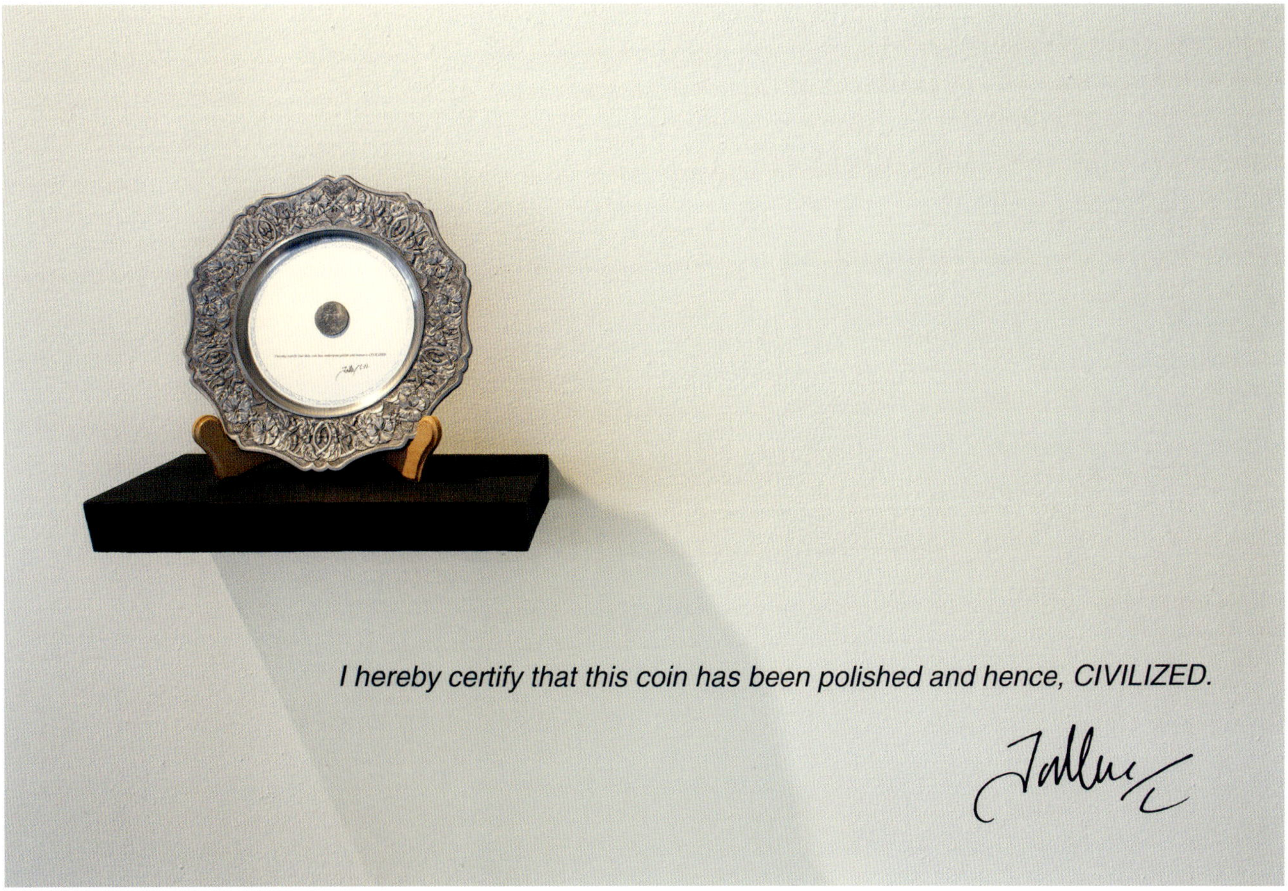

Apocalypse, 2010 (cat. 5)

 0+0=0-0, 2011 (cat. 6)

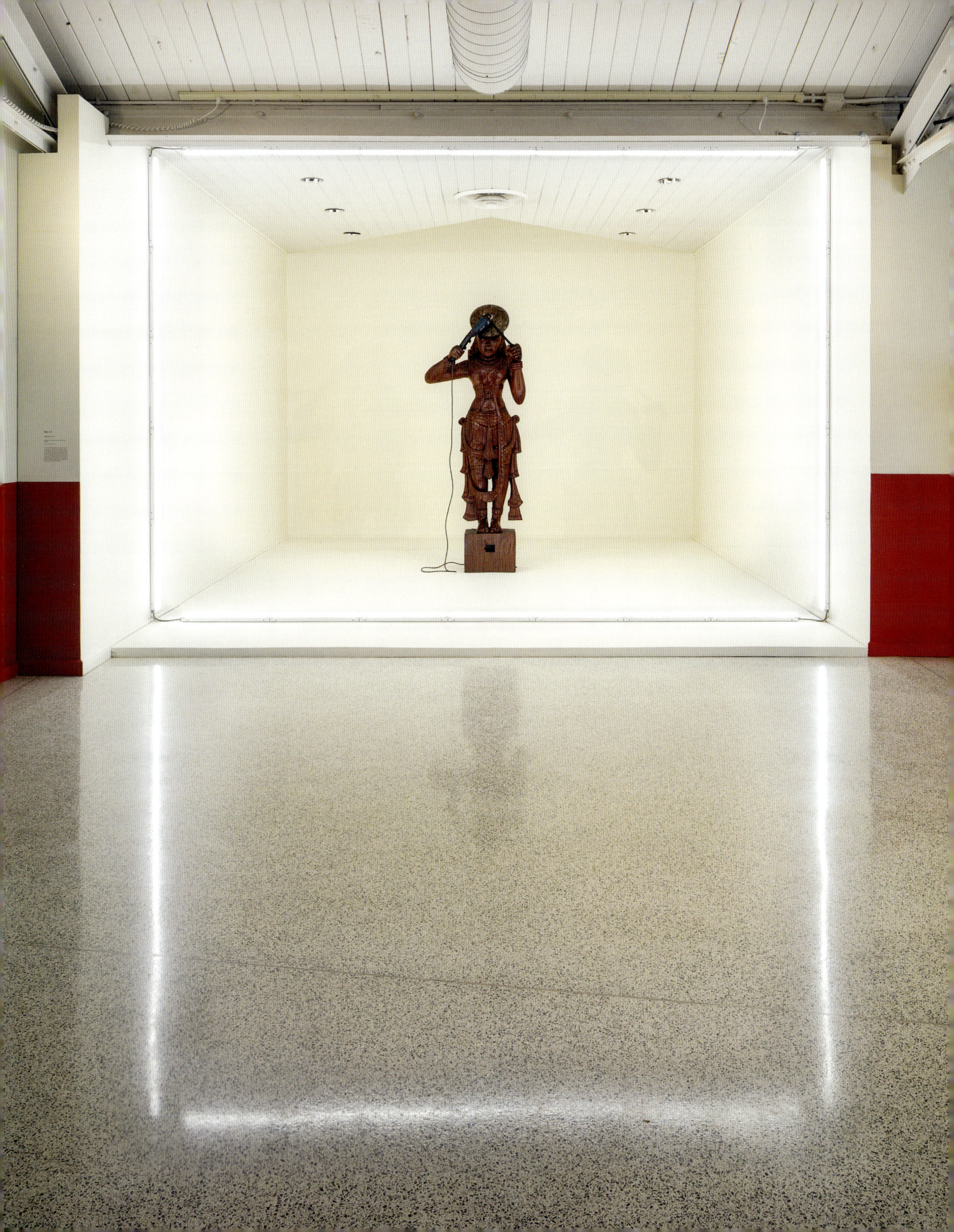

Alzheimer's, 2006 (cat. 4)

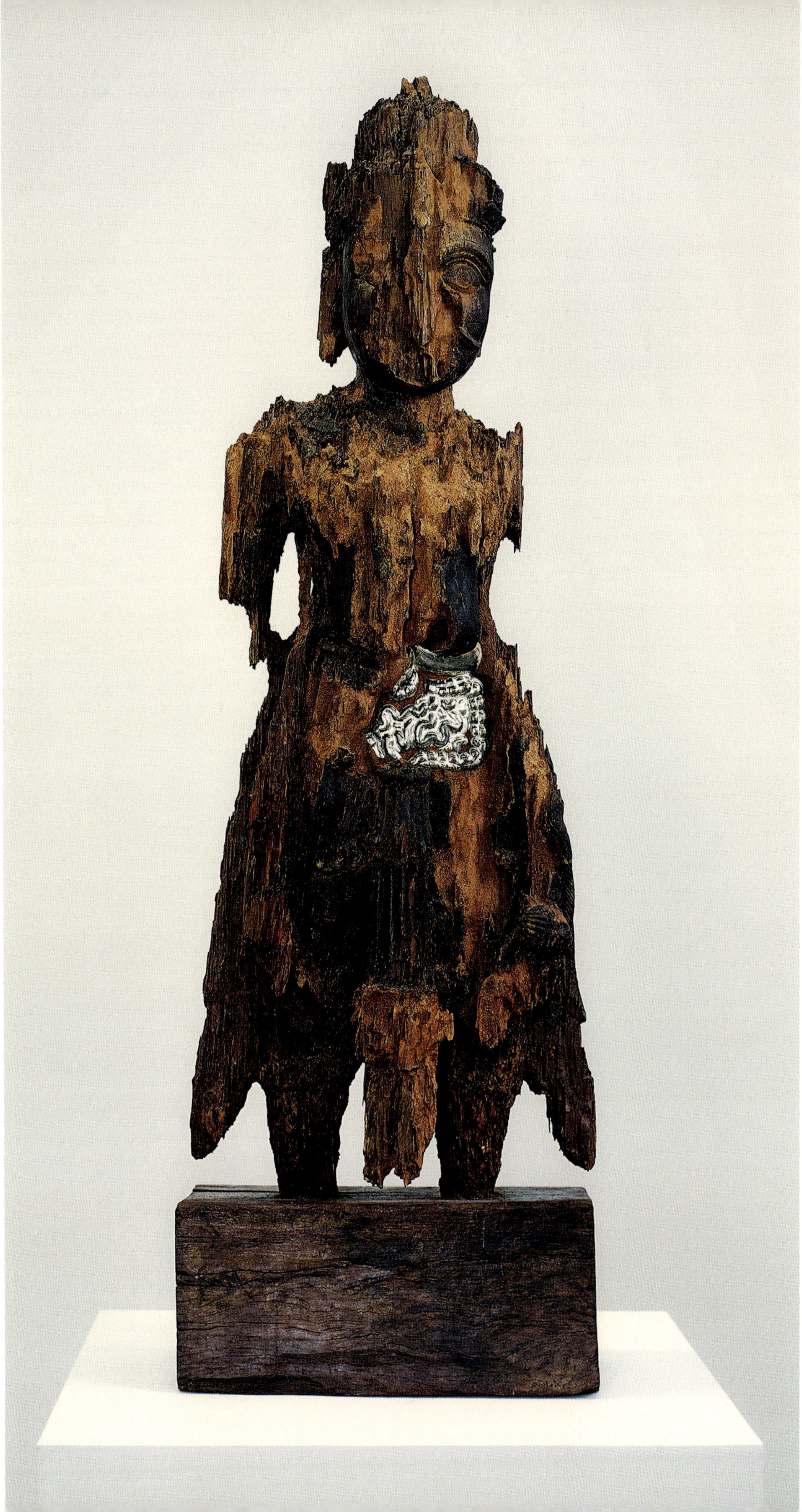

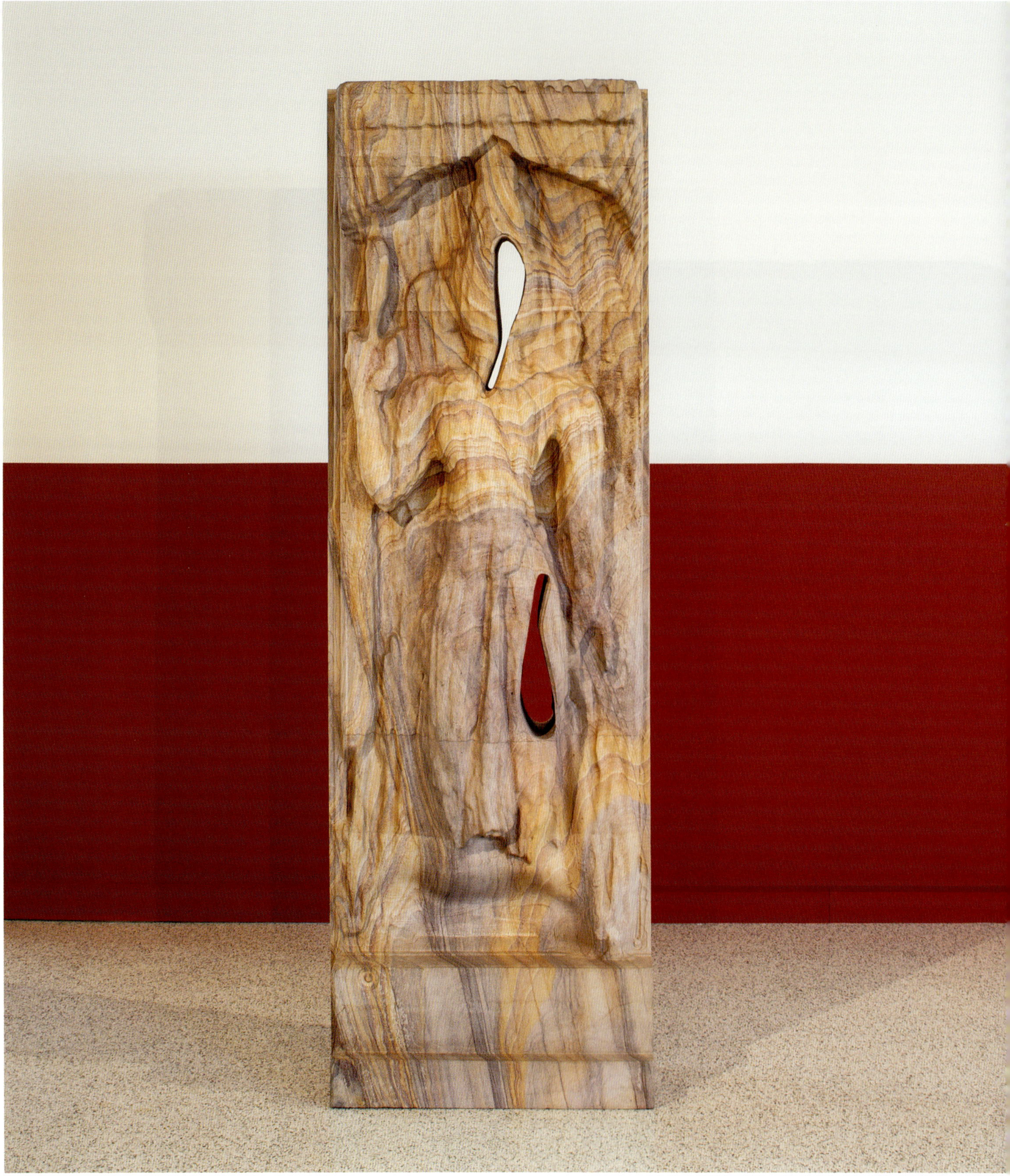

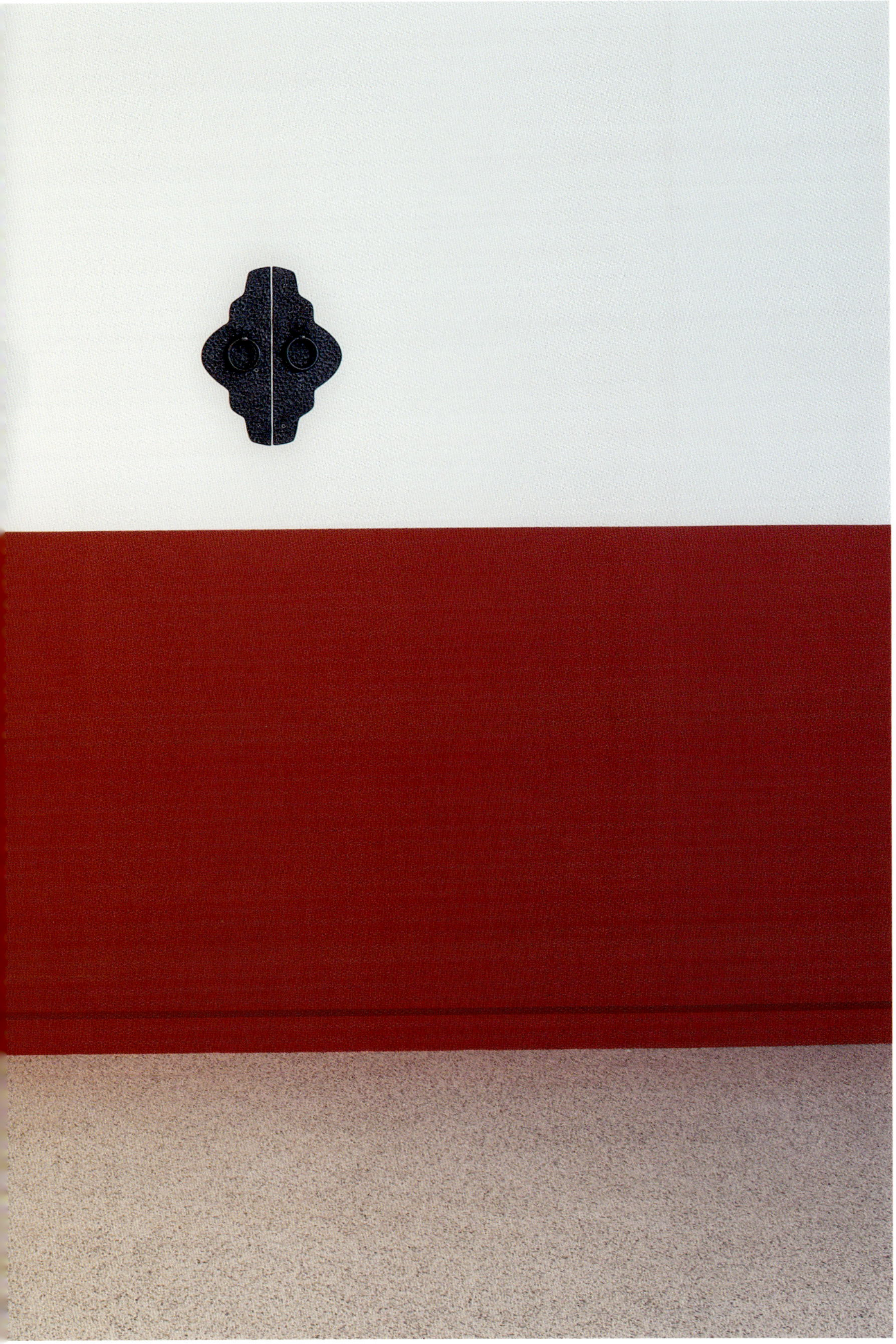

Milled History, 2014 (cat. 12)

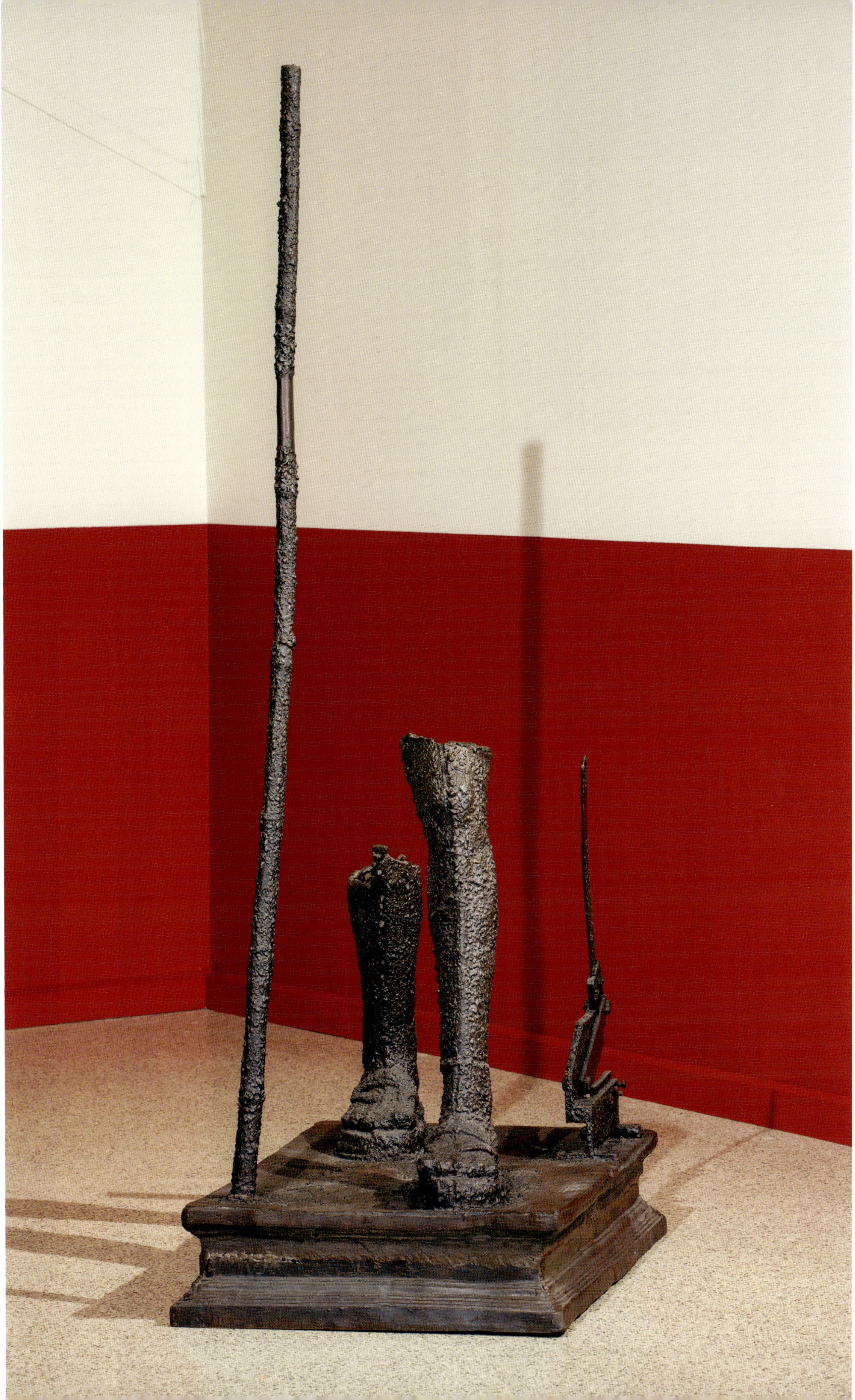

 Obituary Note, 2013 (cat. 9)

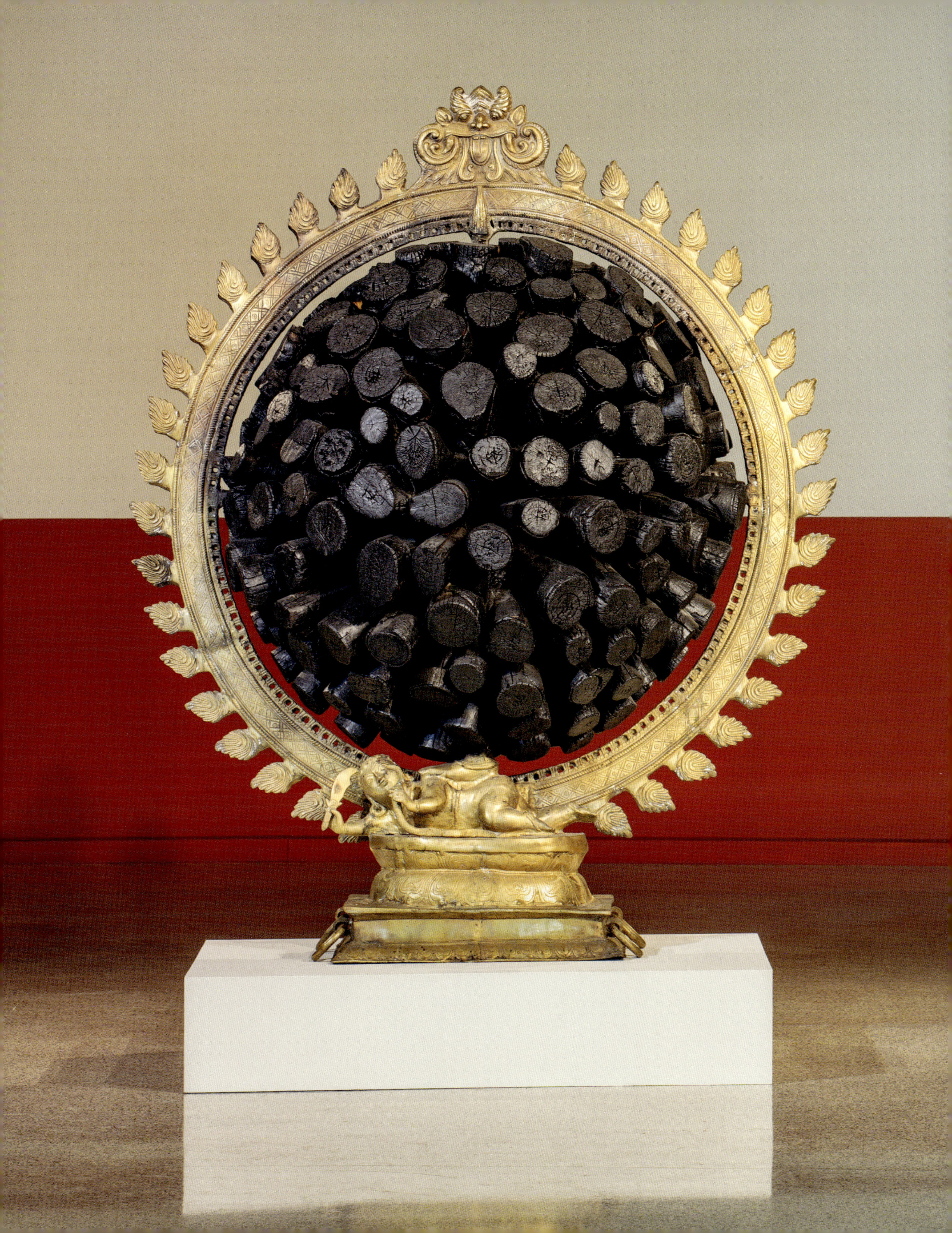

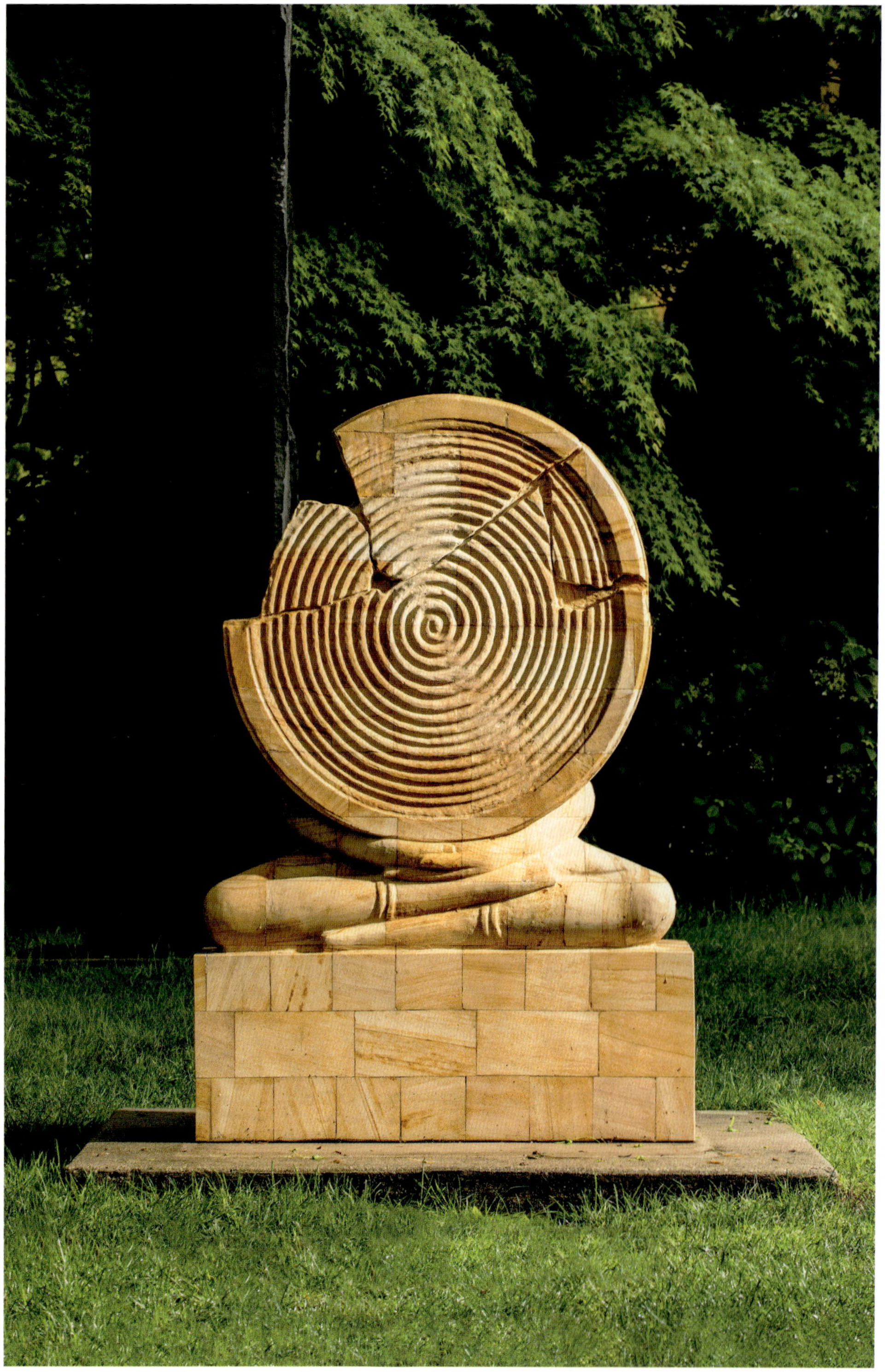

Tolerance, 2019 (cat. 15)

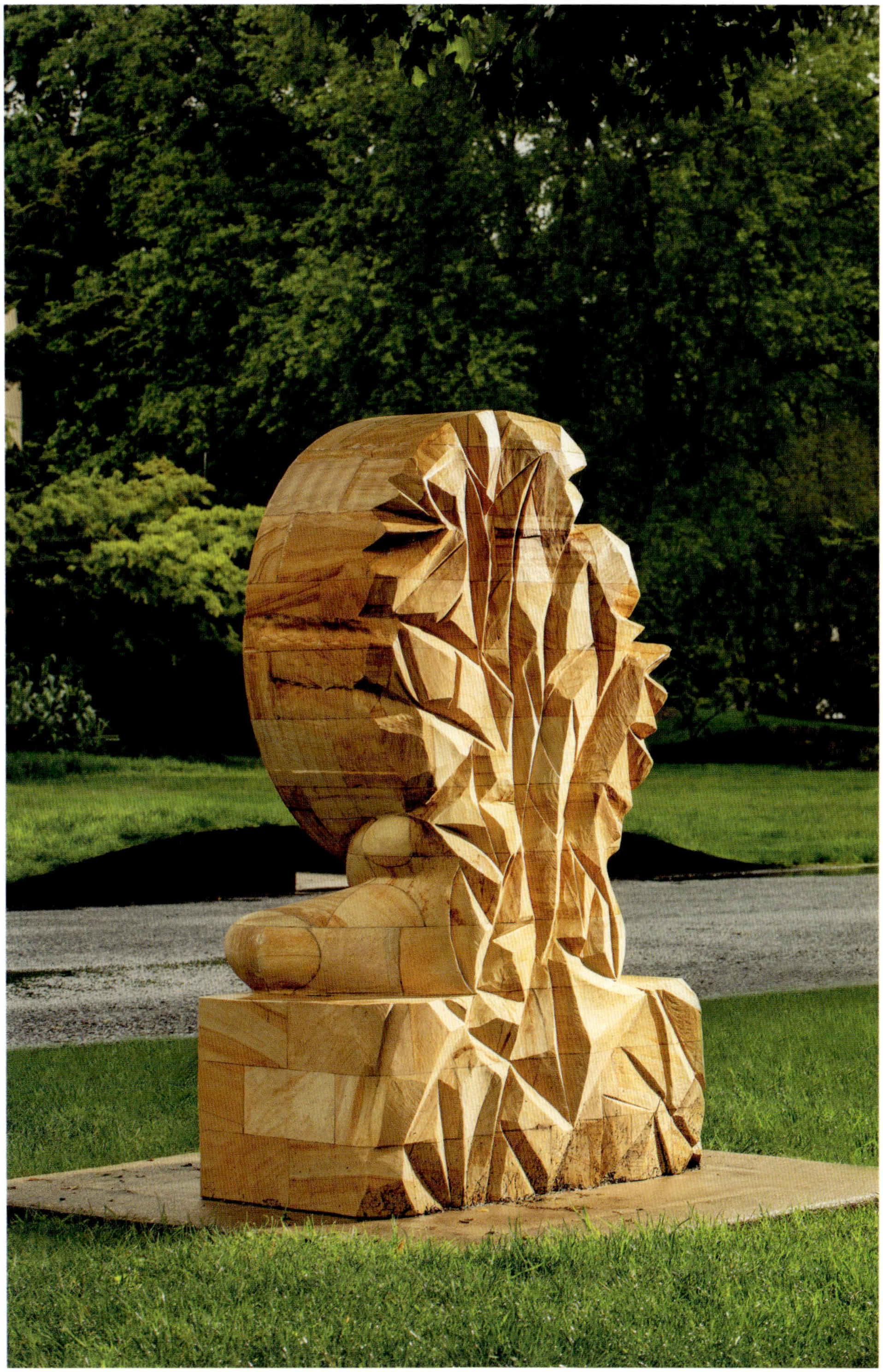

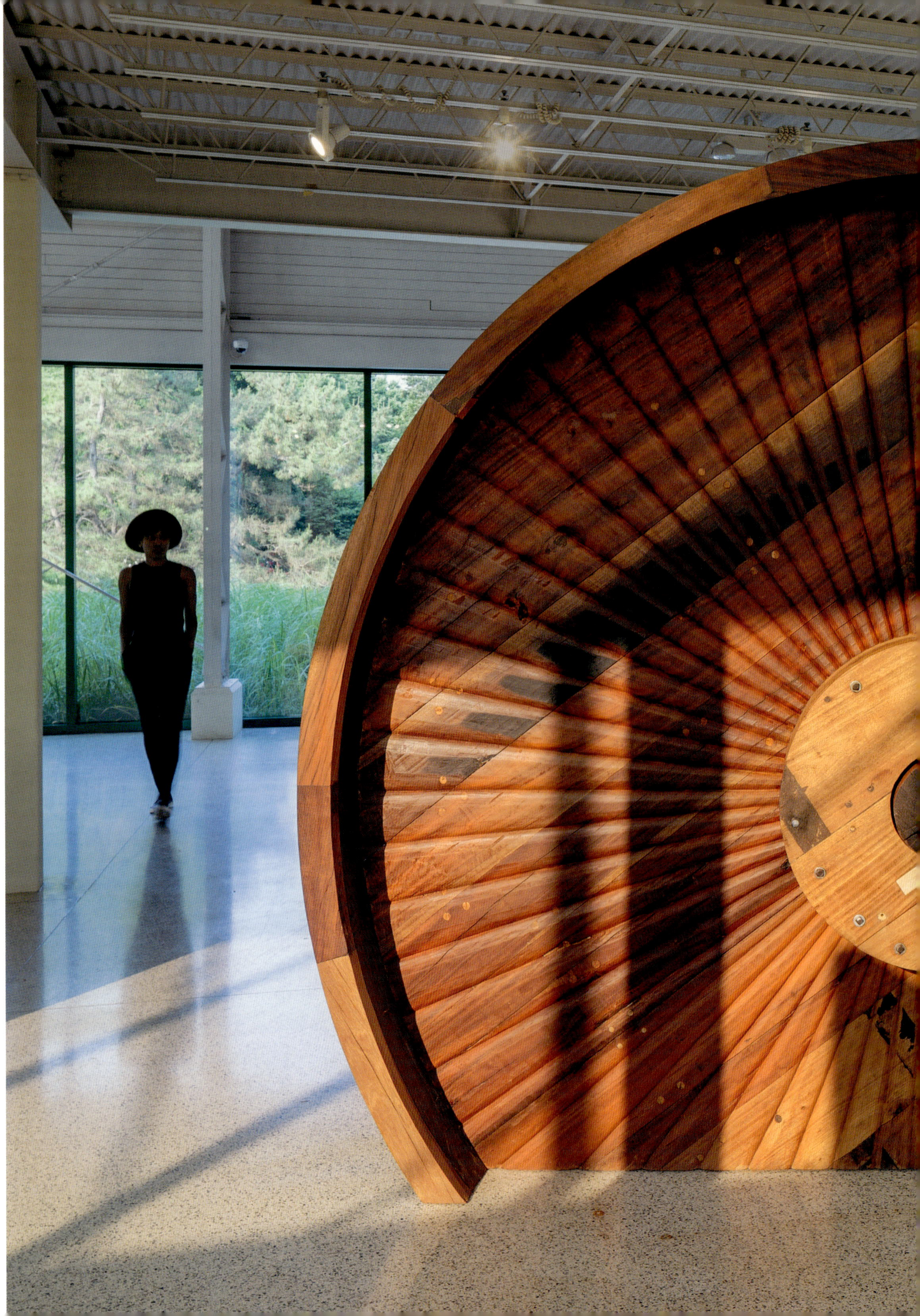

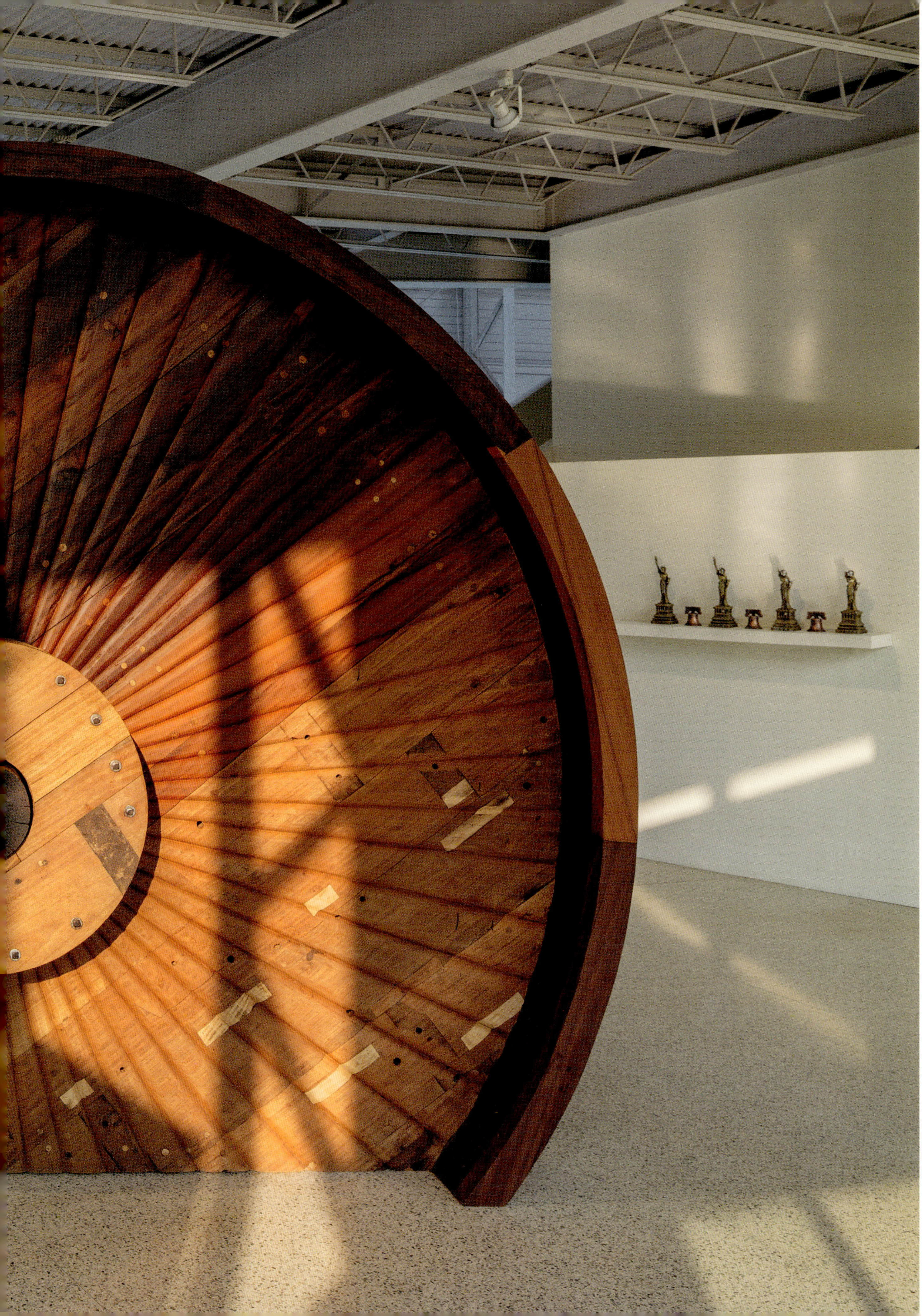

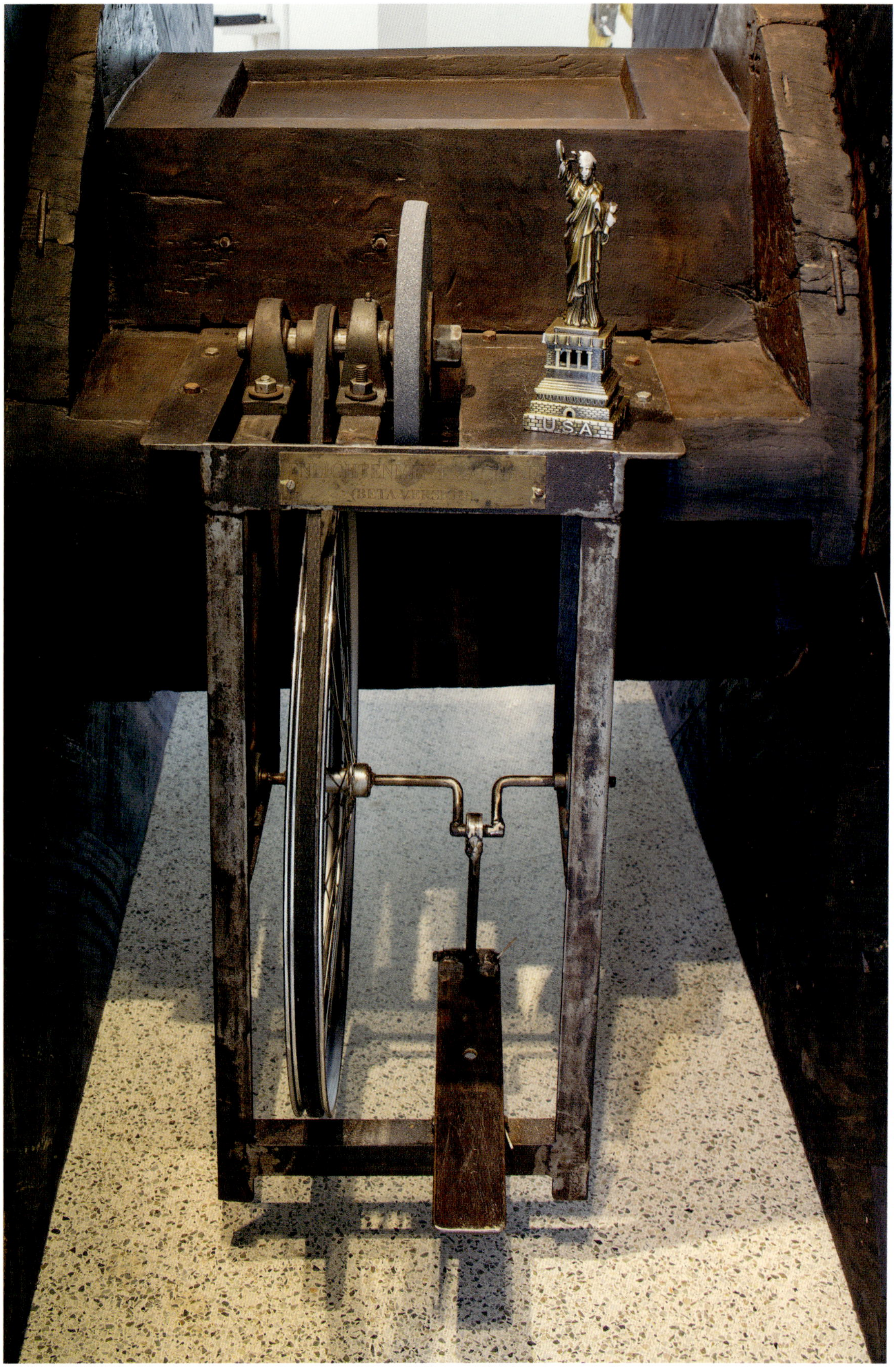
U.S.A.

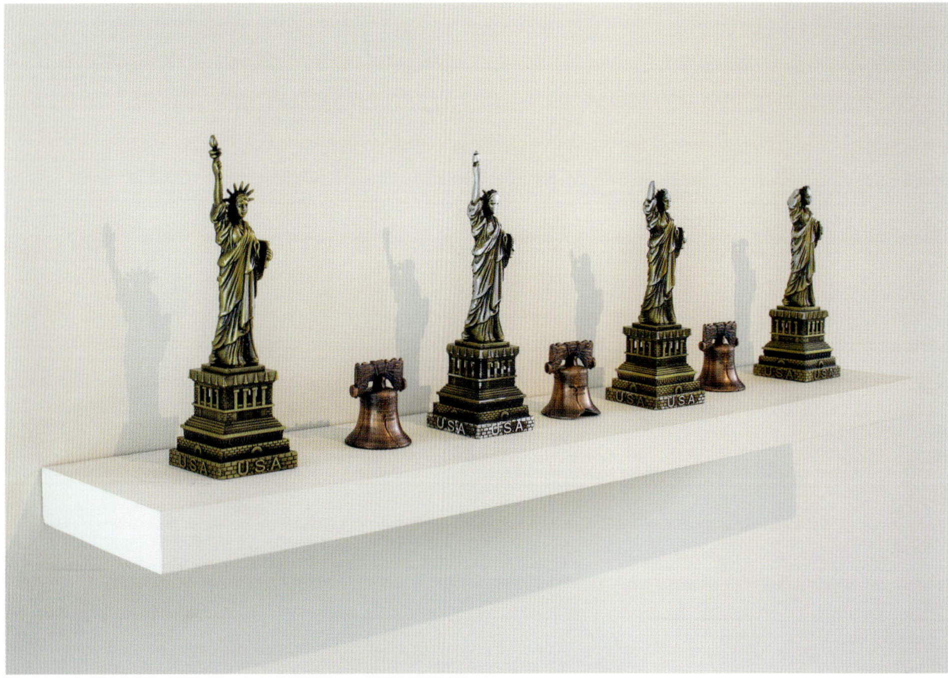

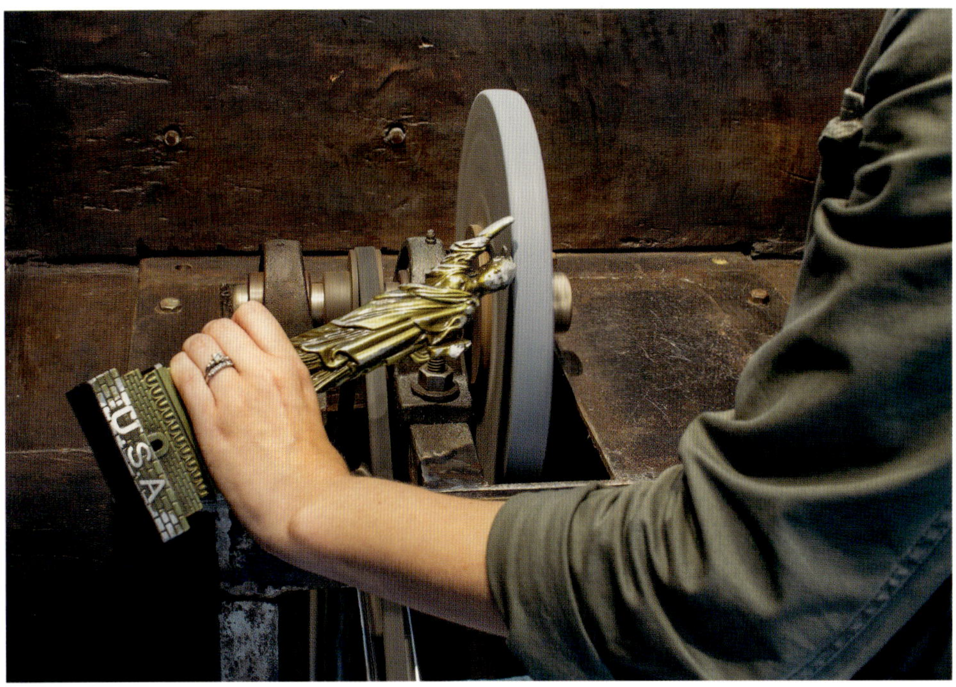

Enlightenment Machine (Beta Version 3.0), 2019 (cat. 16)

 Eraser Pro, 2012 (cat. 8)

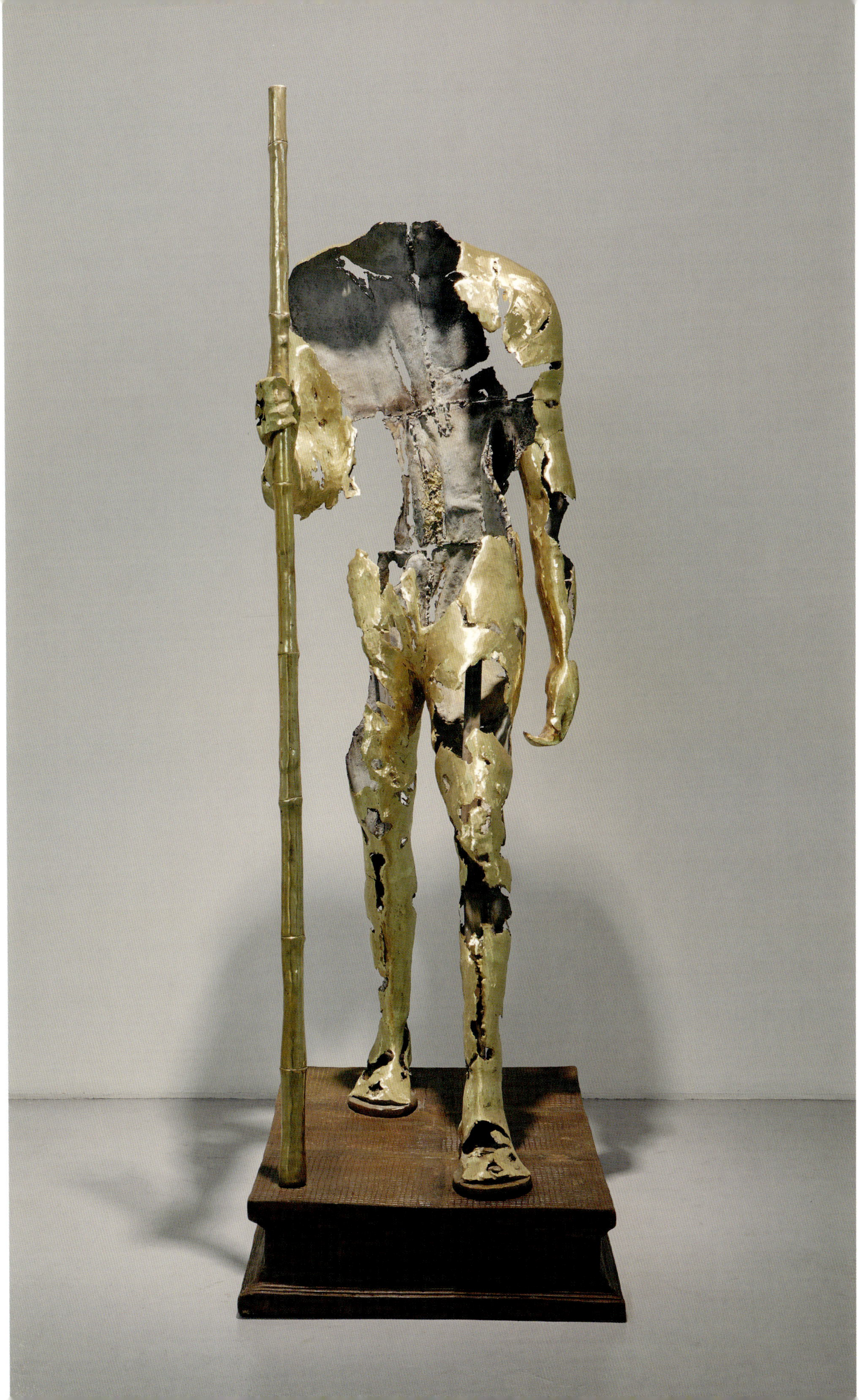

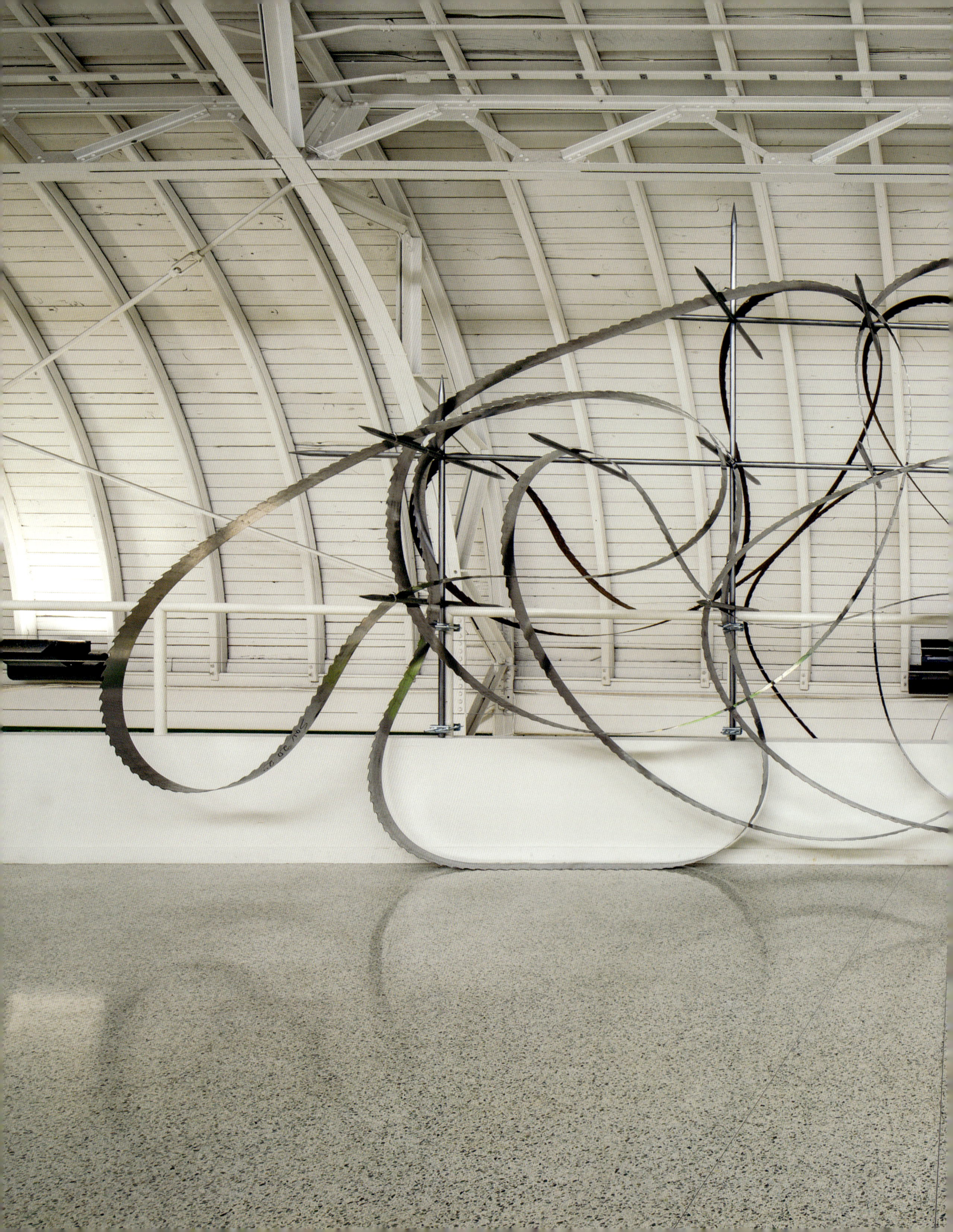

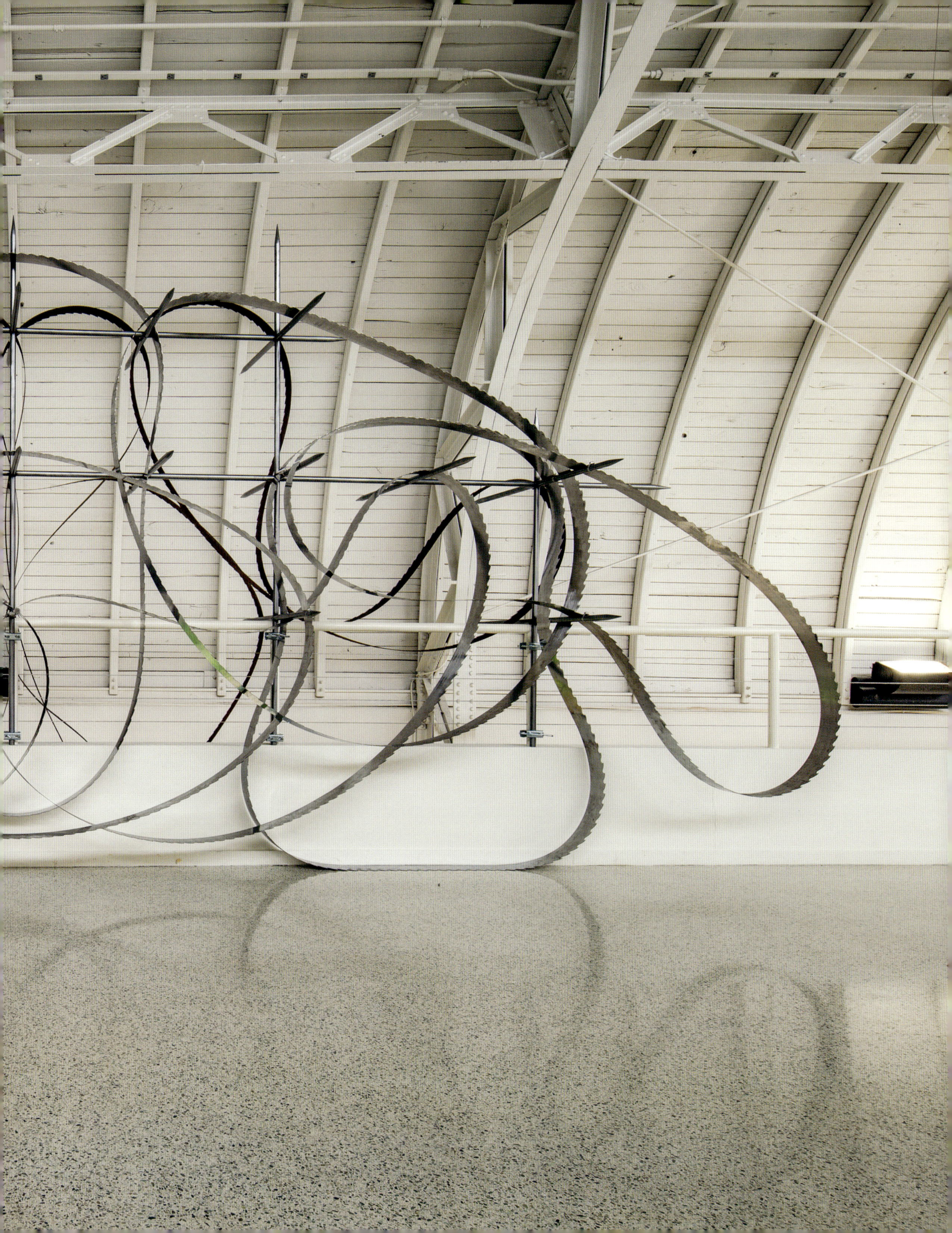

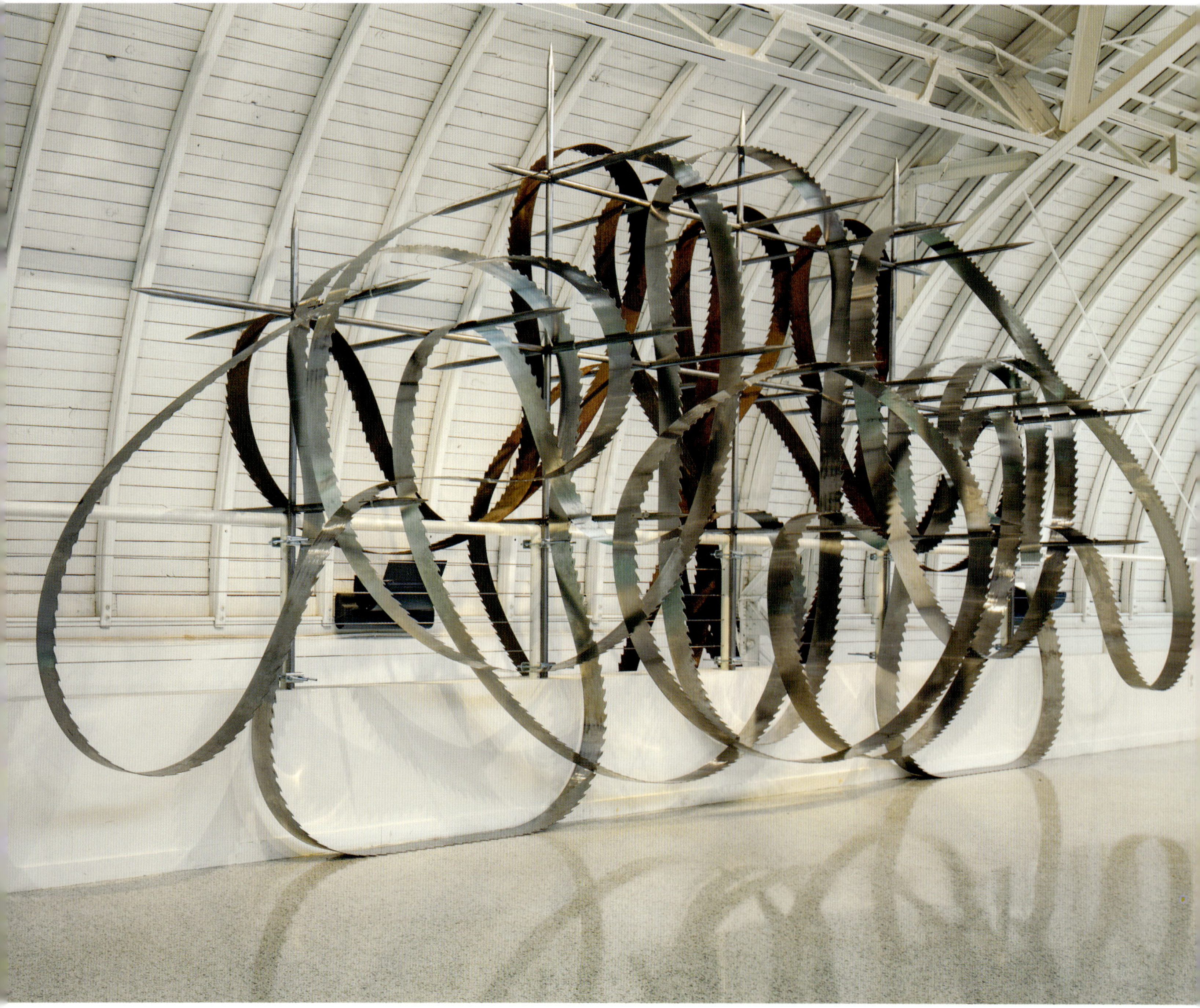

 Threshold, 2015/2019 (cat. 13)

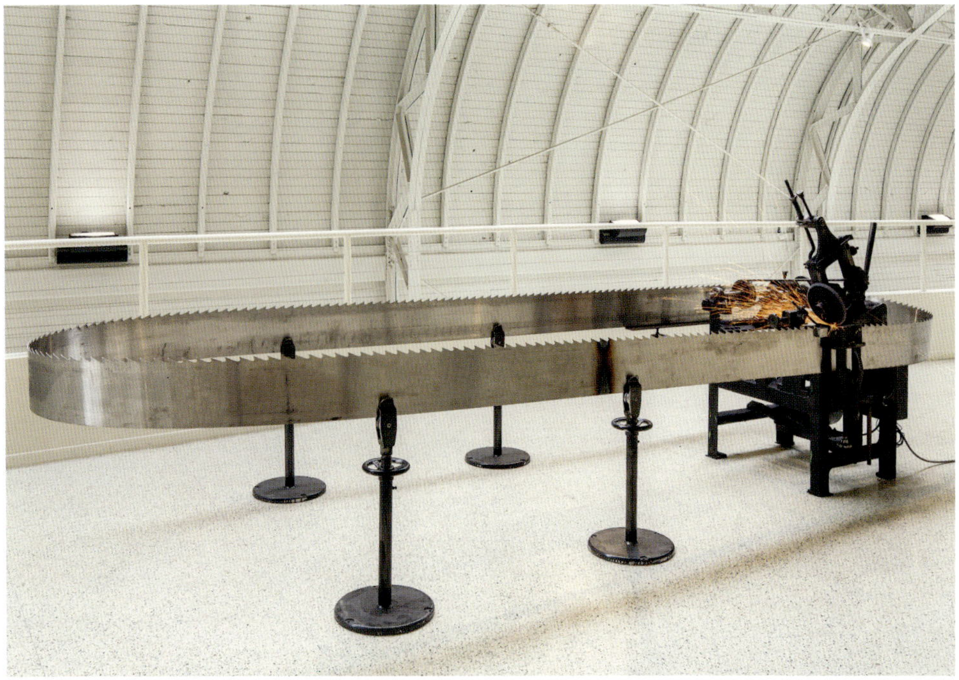

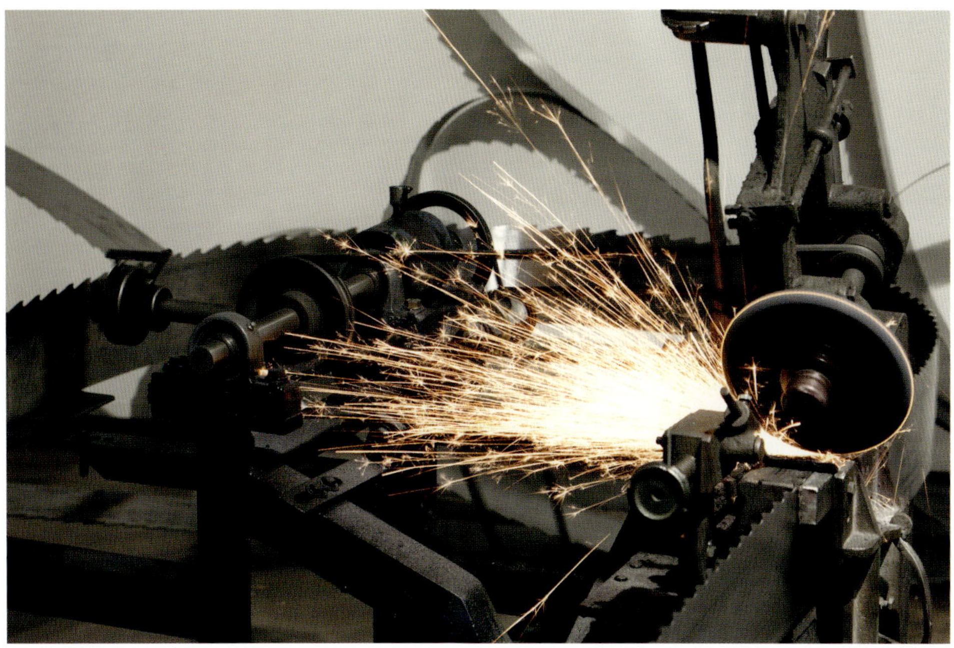

Tongue Twister, 2014 (cat. 11)

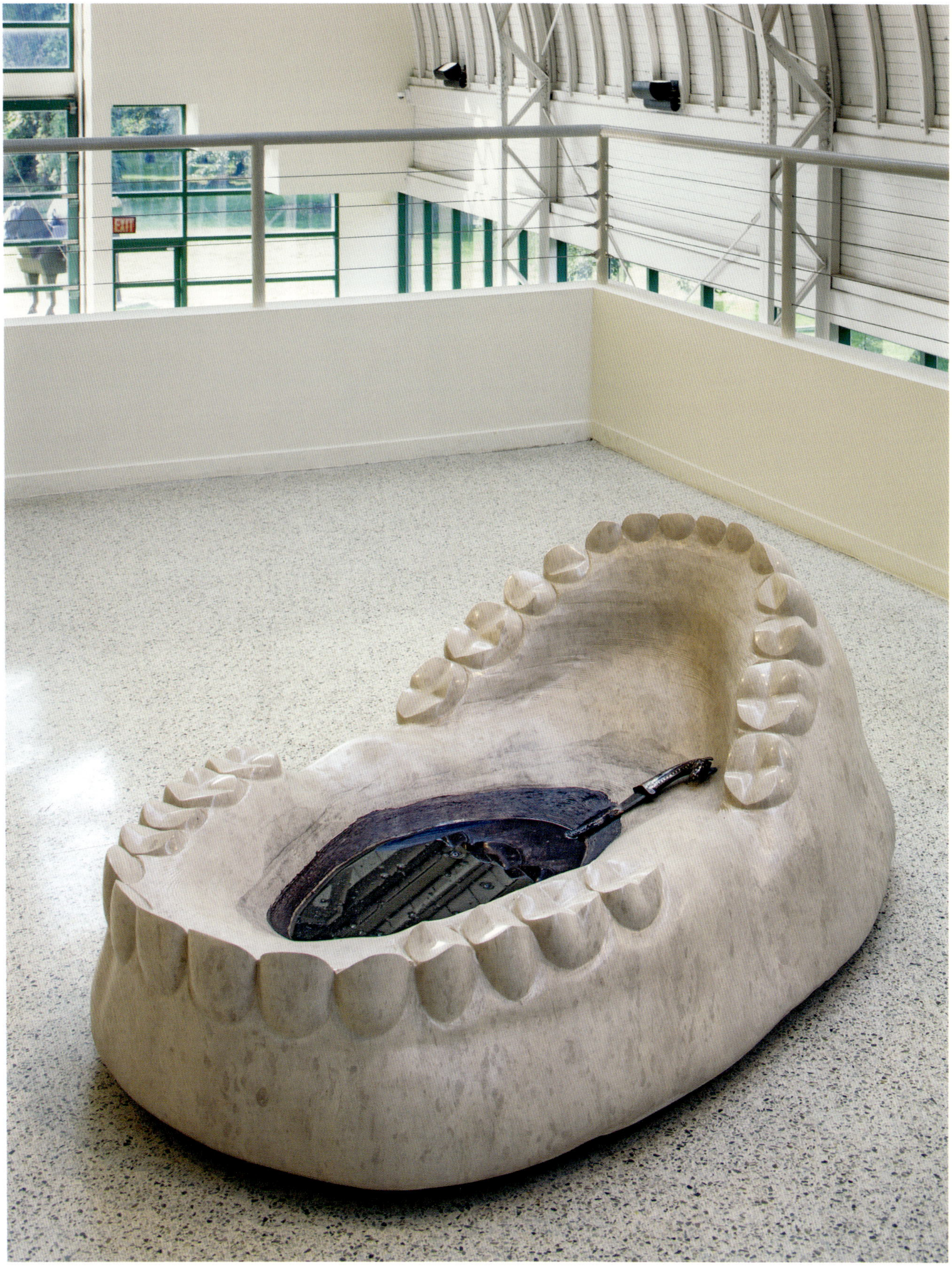
EXIT

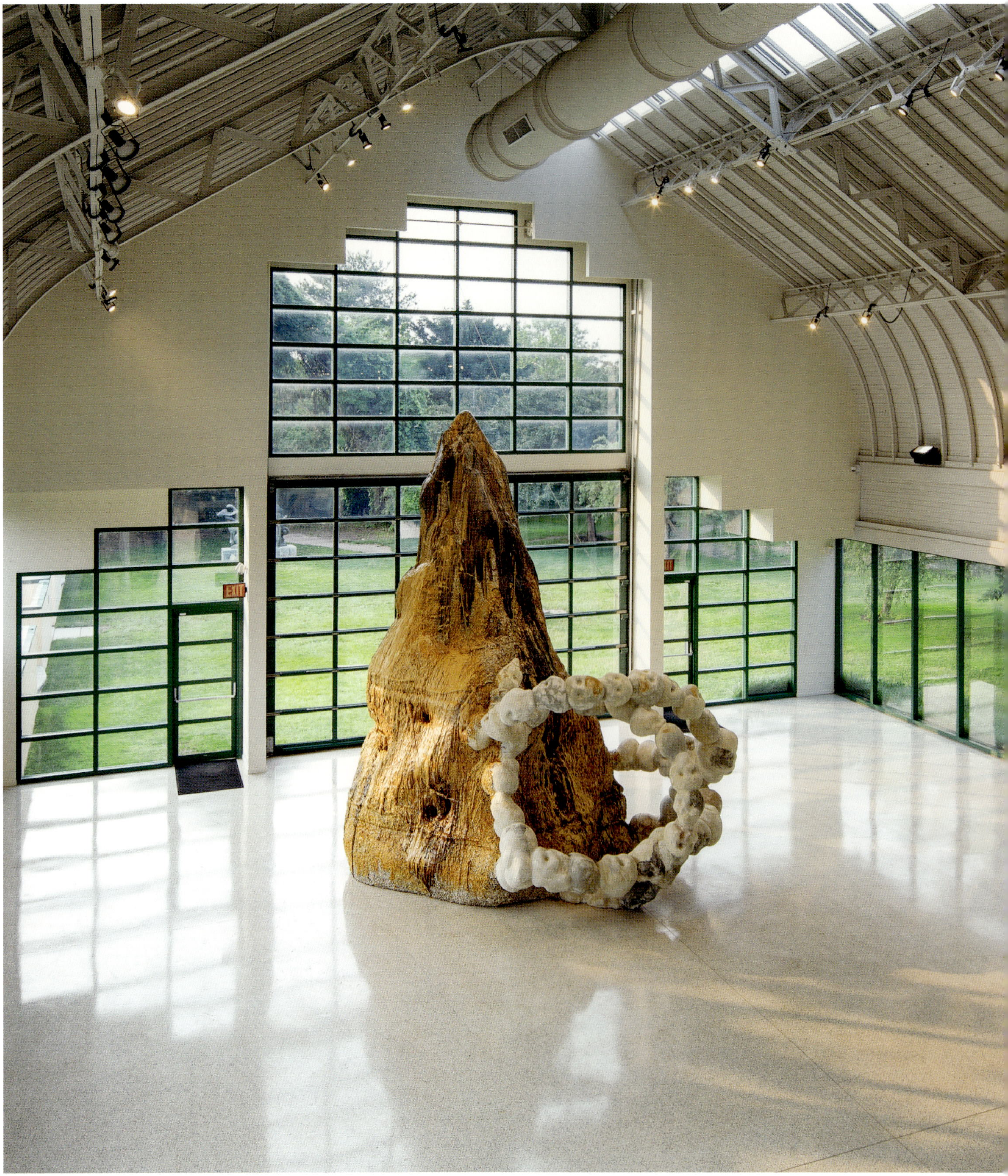

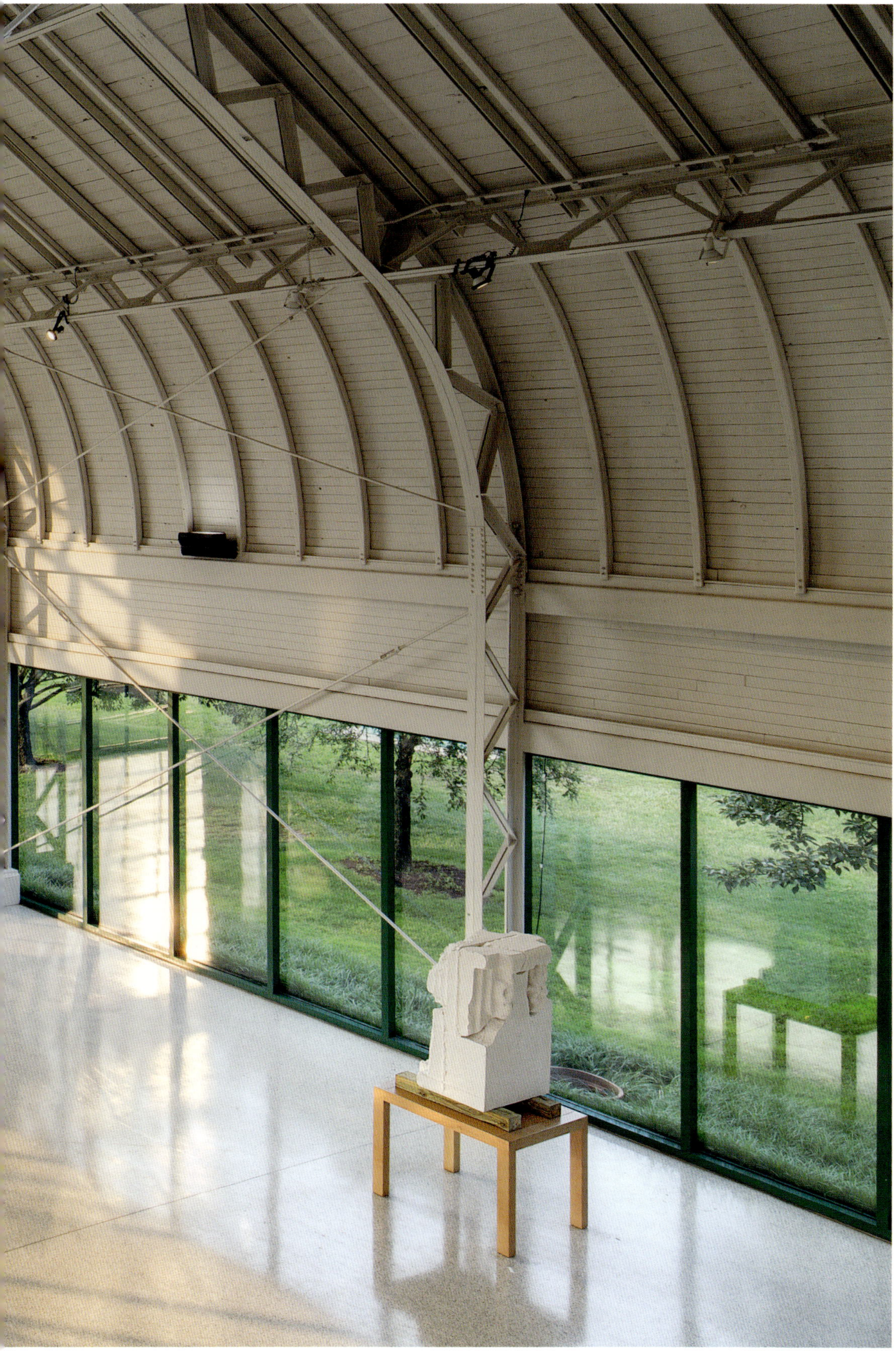

Fringe, 2019 (left, cat. 18)

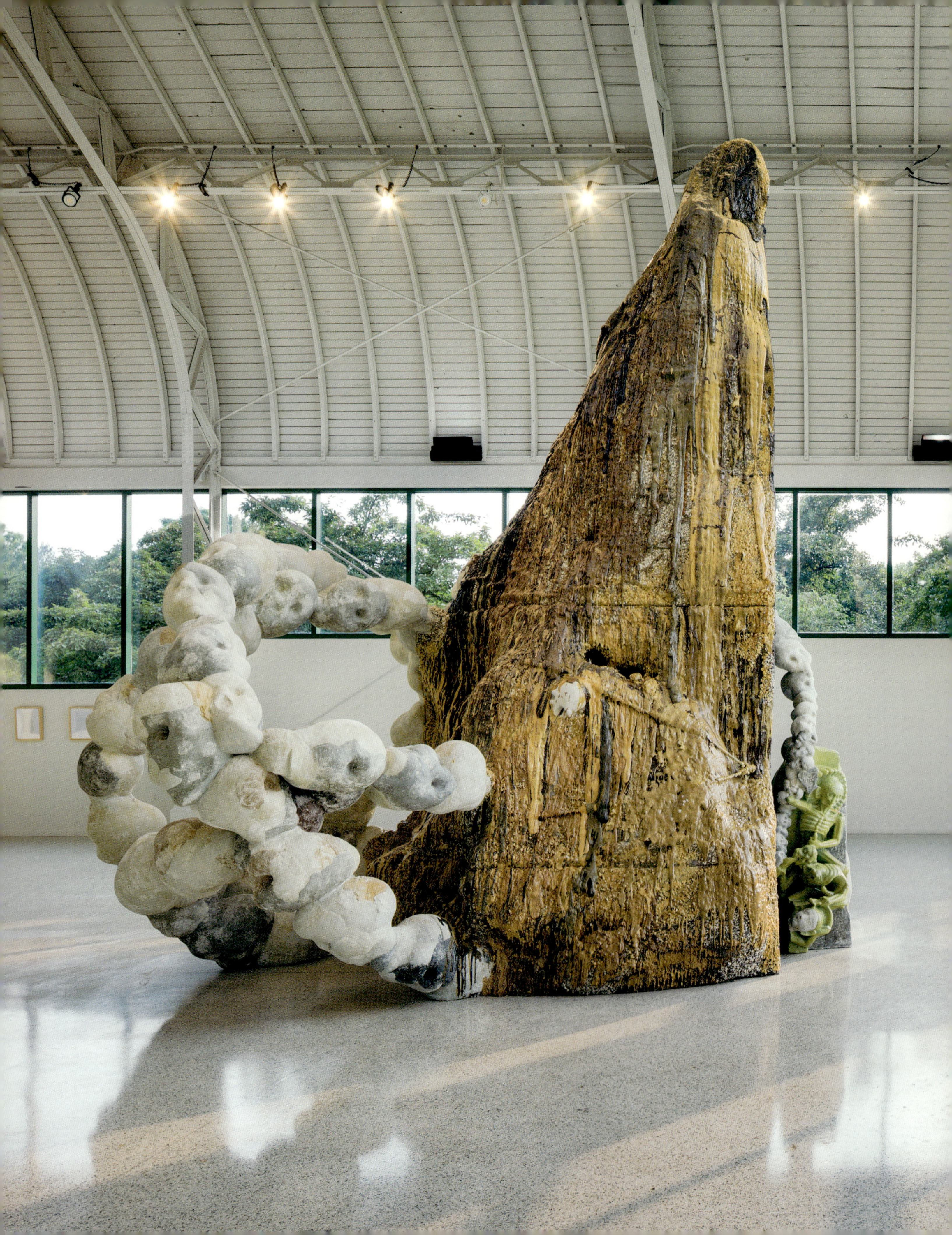

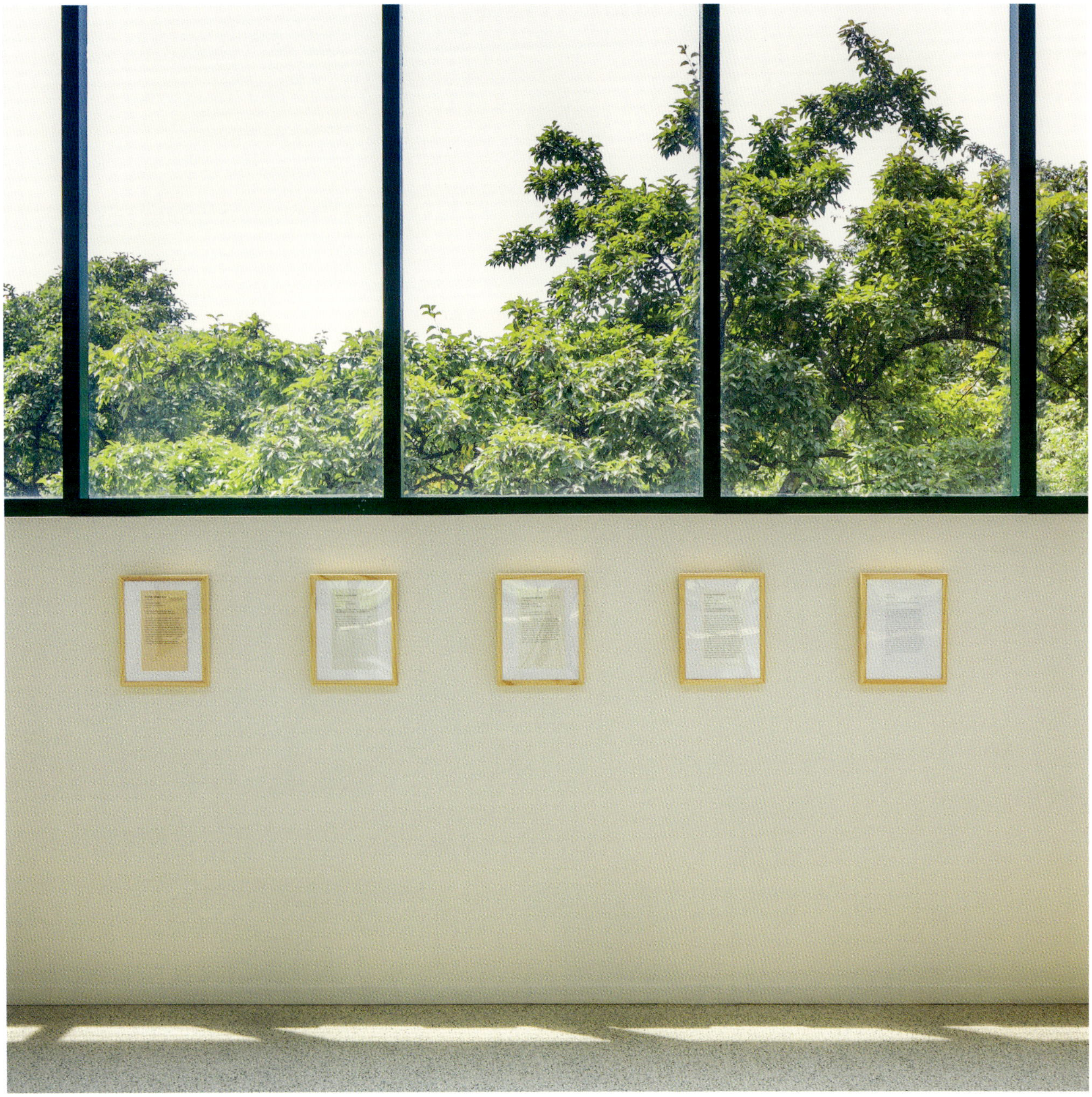

Fringe, 2019 (cat. 18)

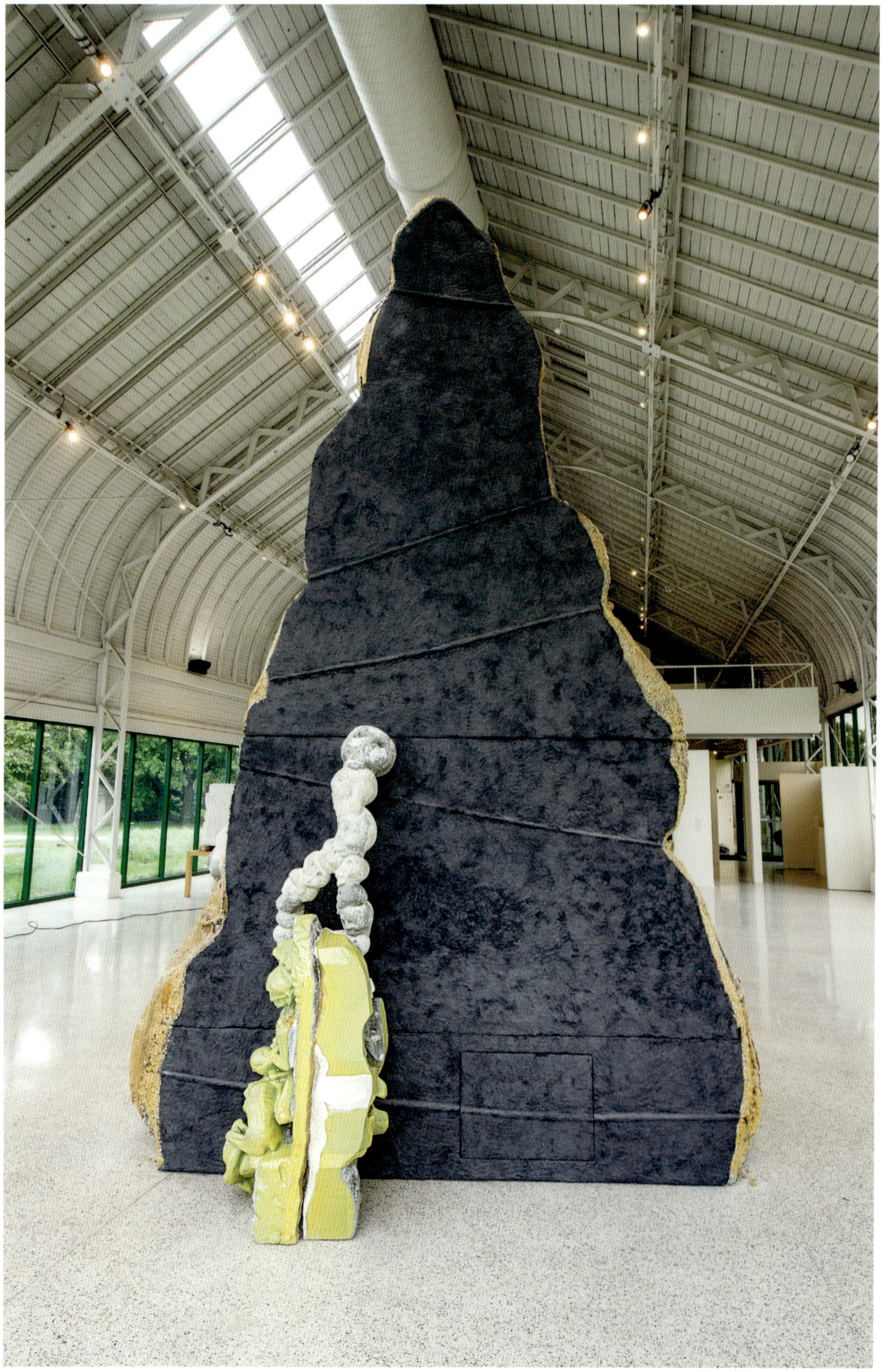

Fringe, 2019 (cat. 18)

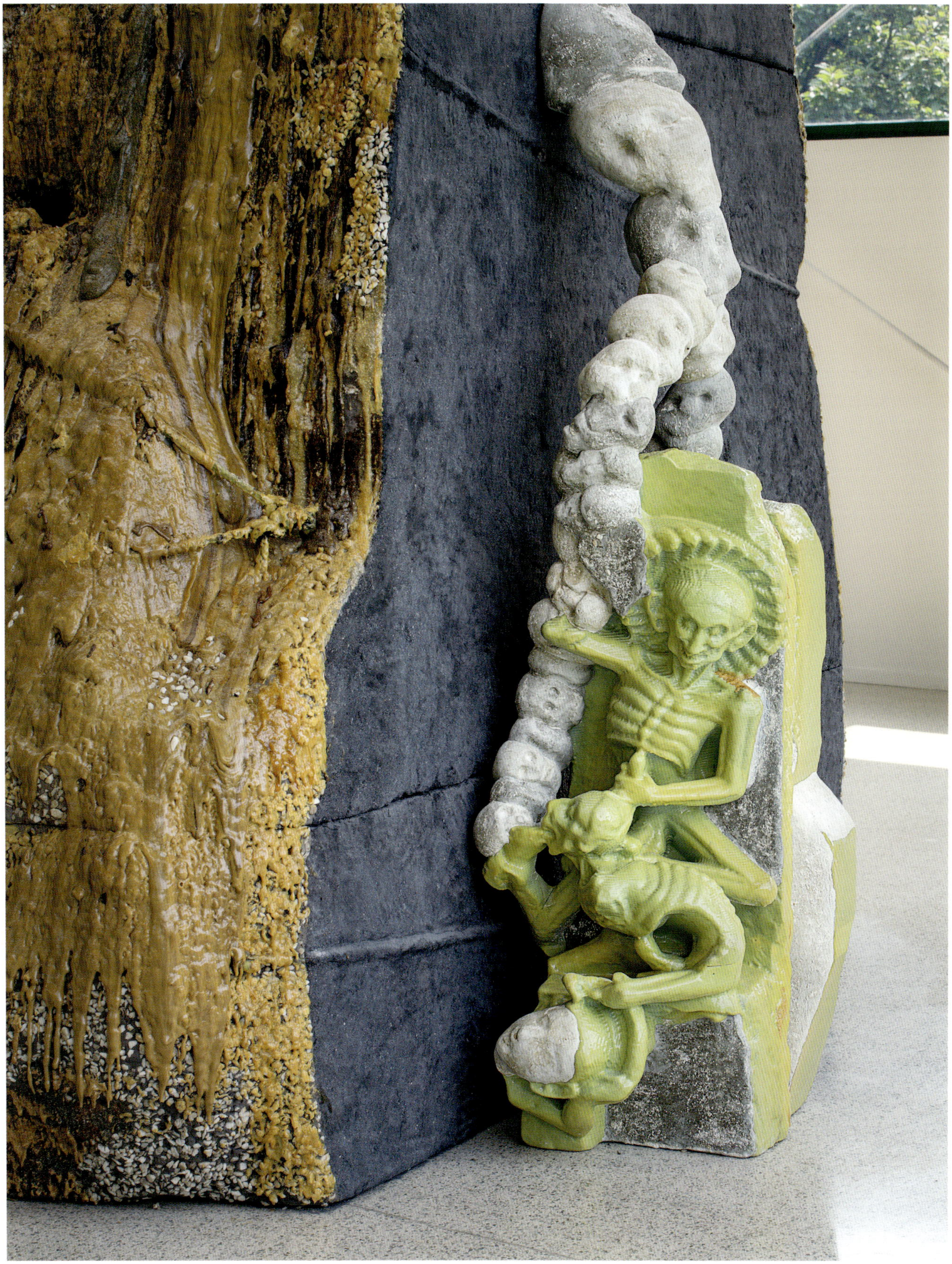

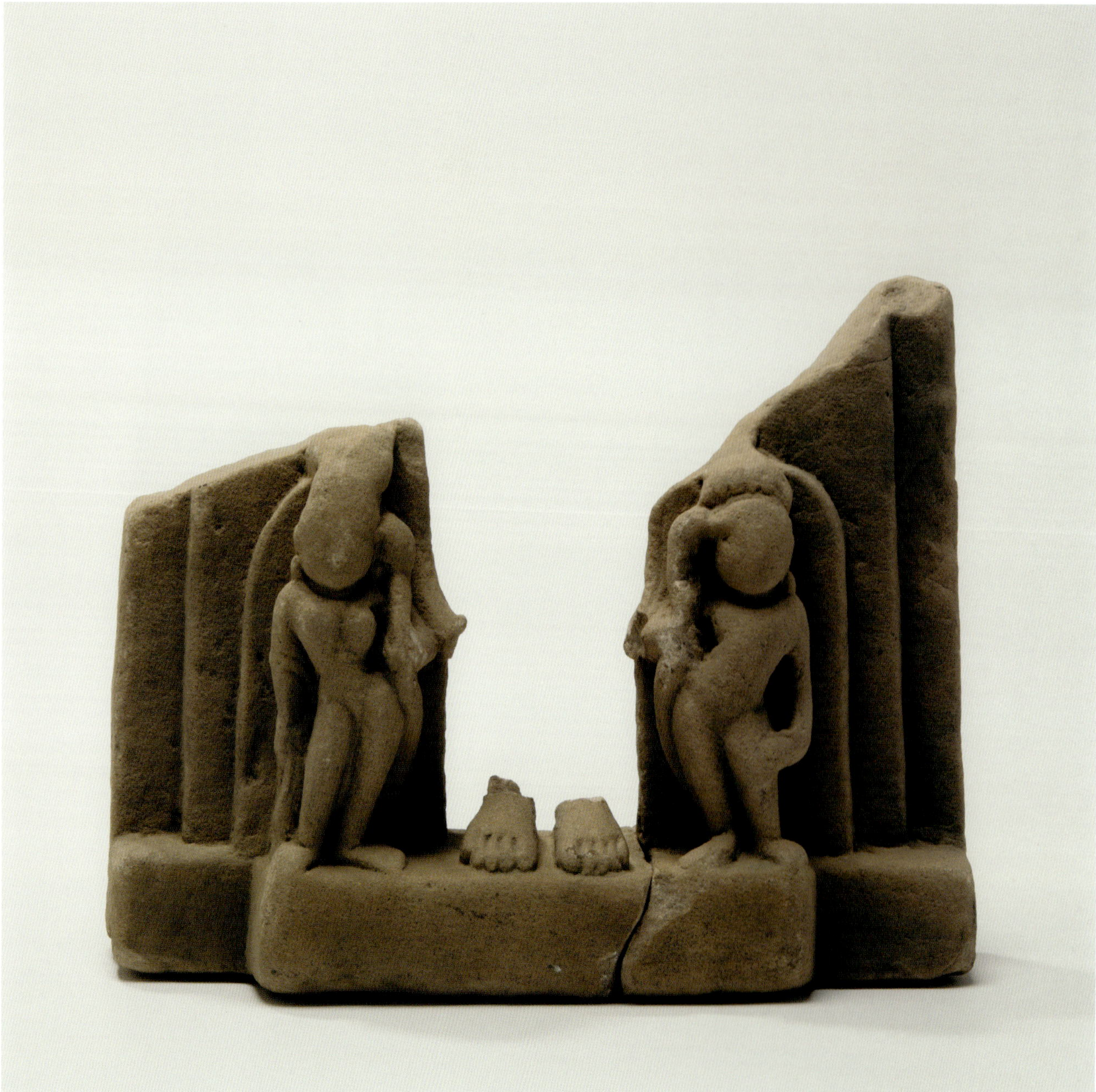

Artist unknown, India

Lower portion of a stele with deity in Samapada Sthanika flanked by female and male attendants, 9th–10th century (cat. 1)

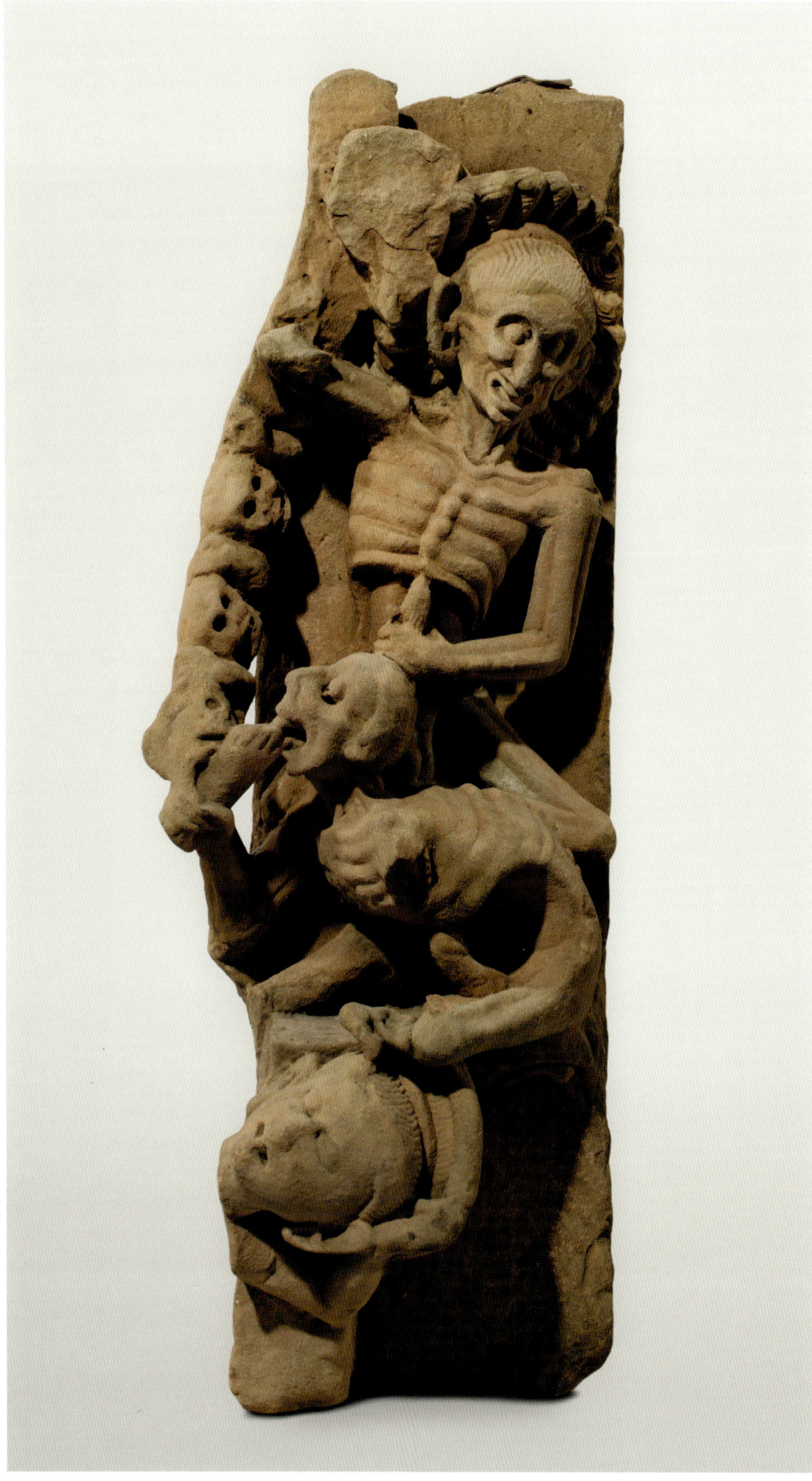

Artist unknown, India
Terrifying Attendant Spirits,
ca. 10th century (cat. 2)

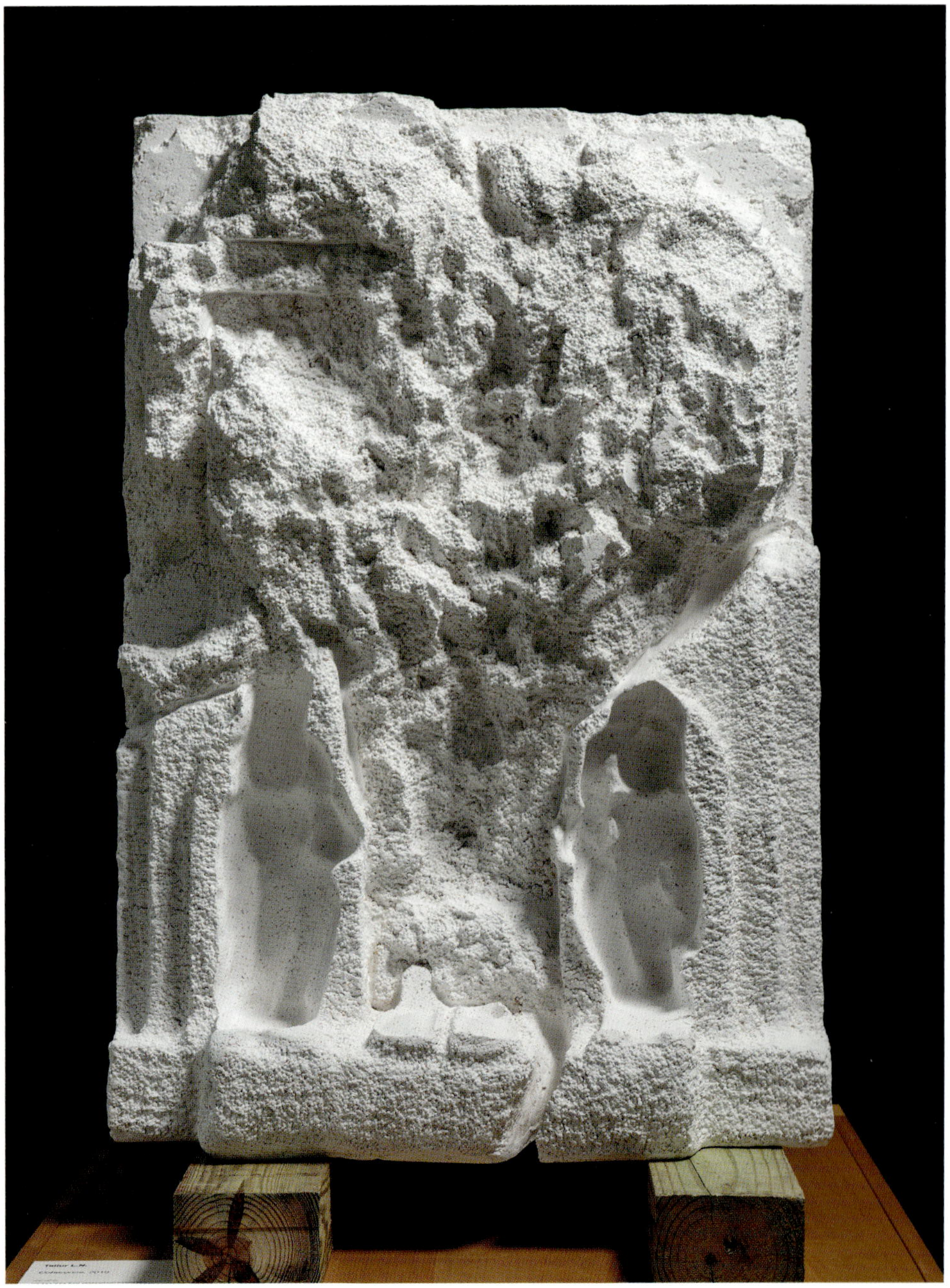

Coherence, 2019 (cat. 14)

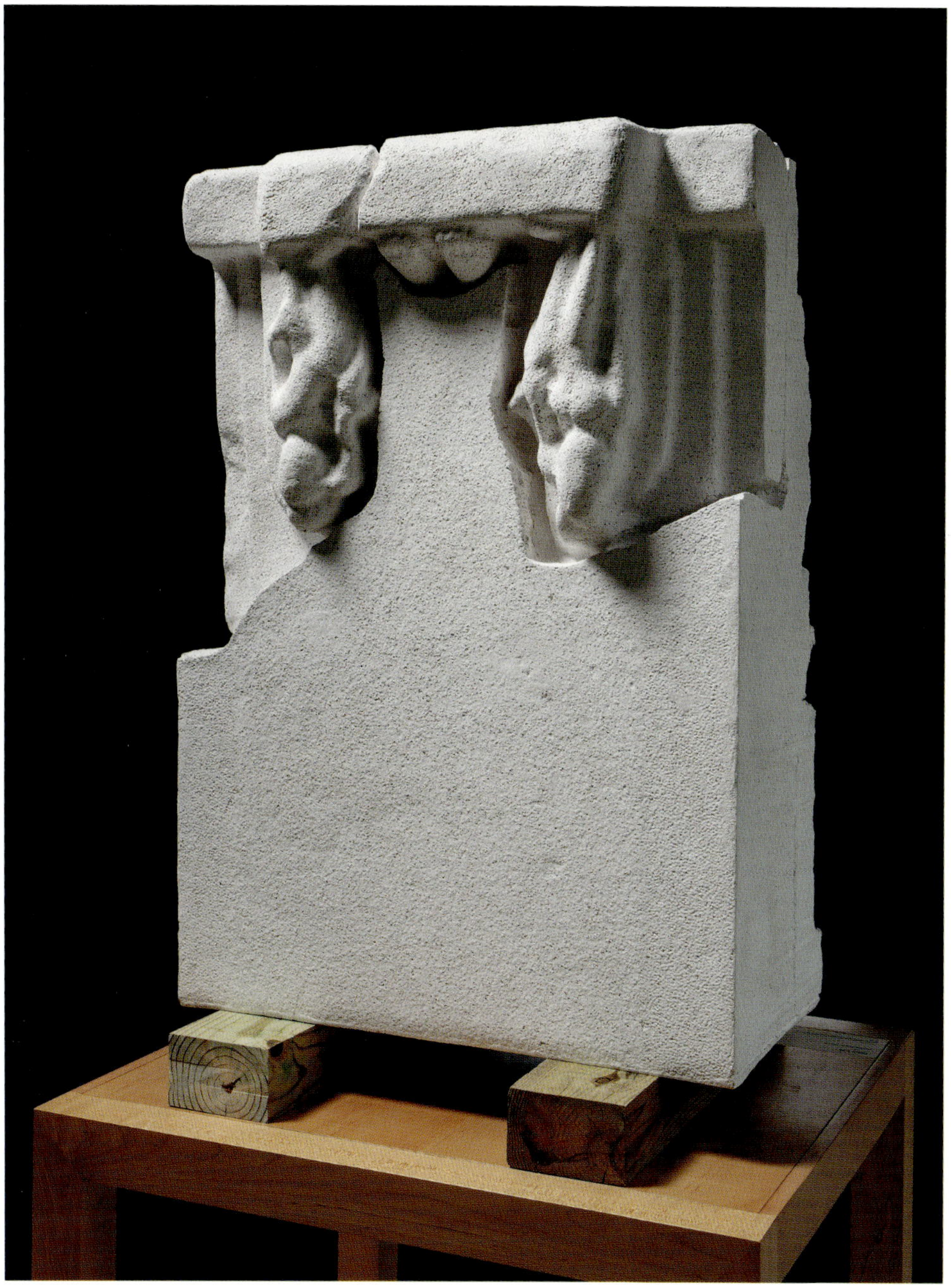

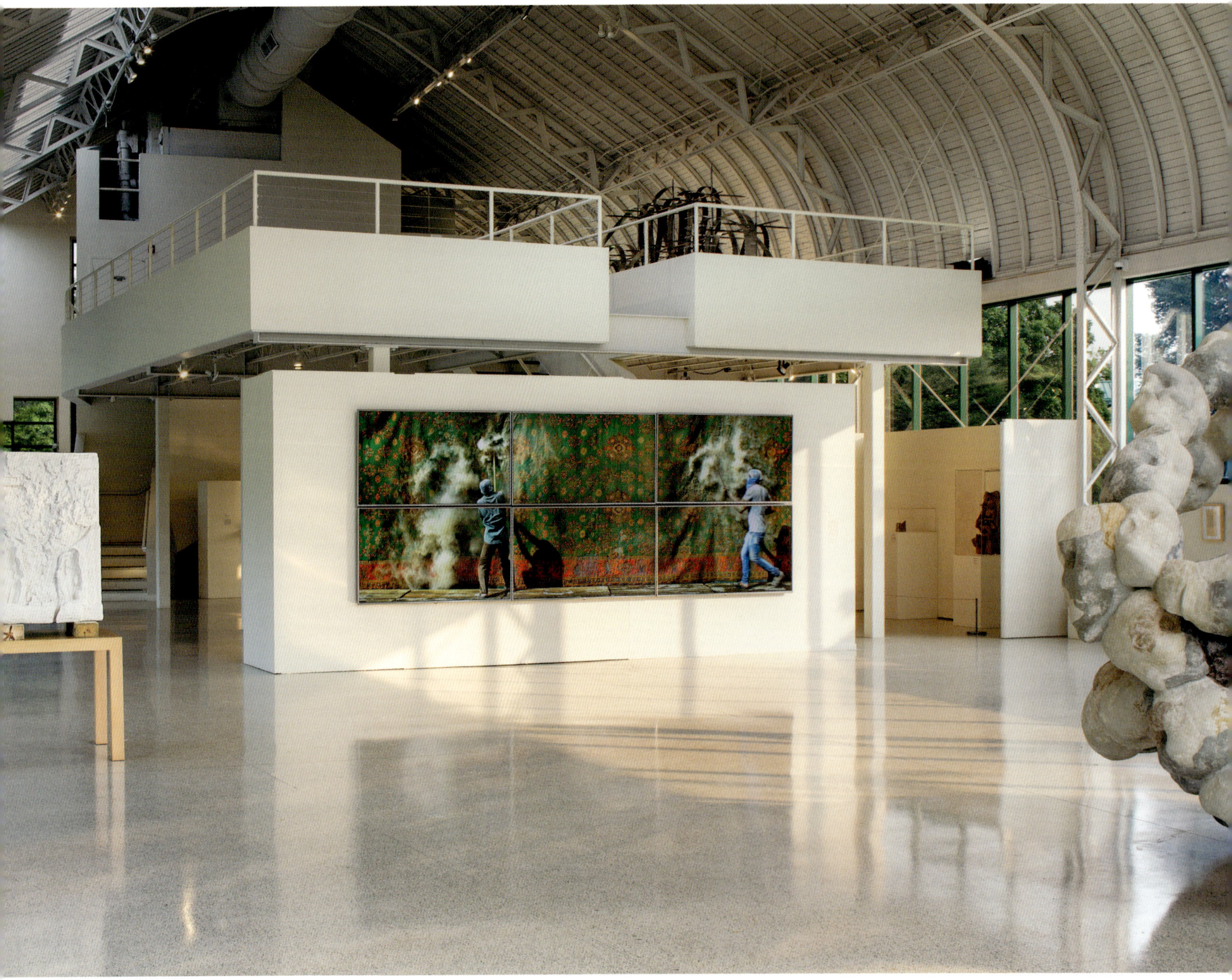

 Interference, 2019 (cat. 17)

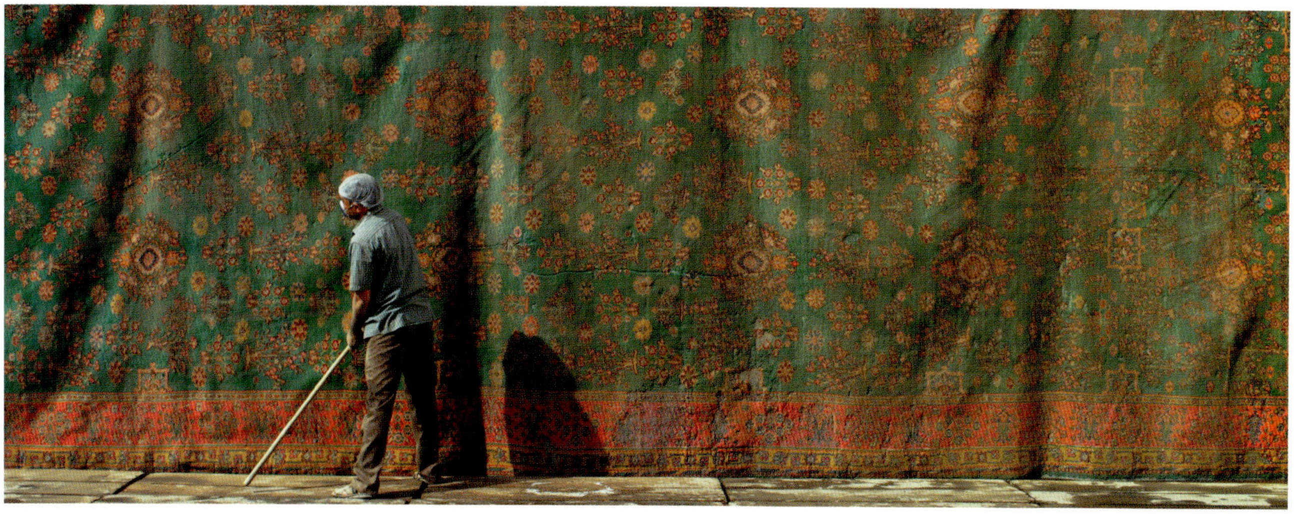

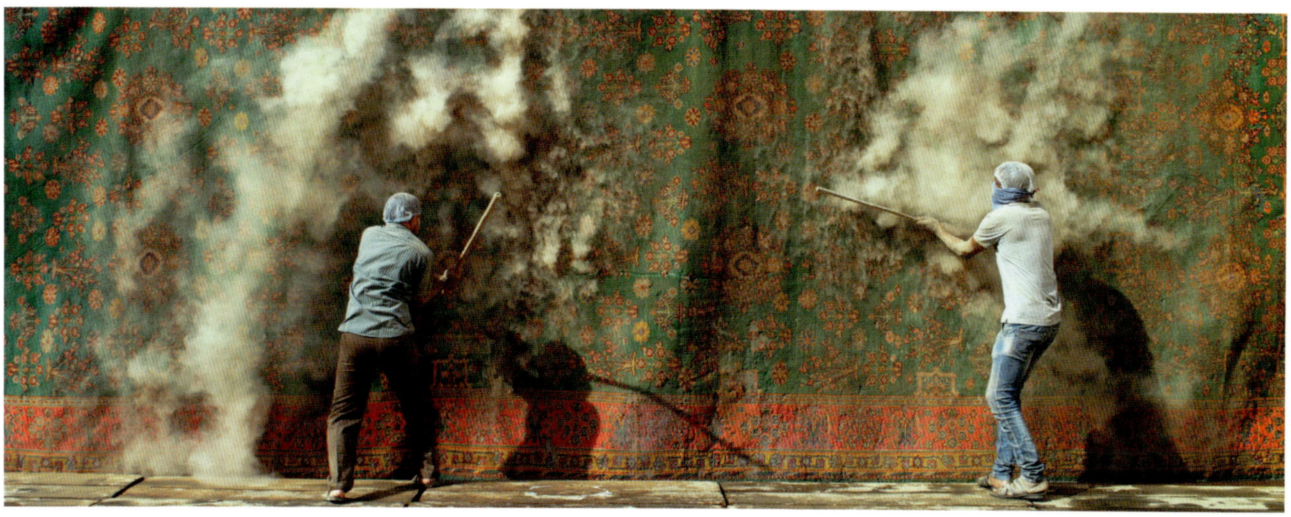

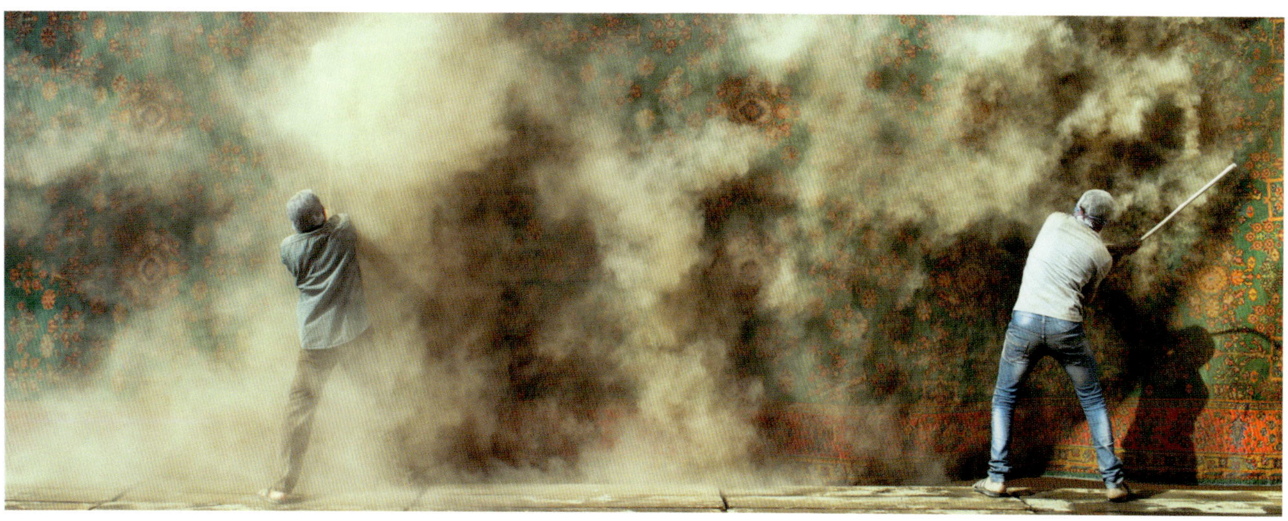

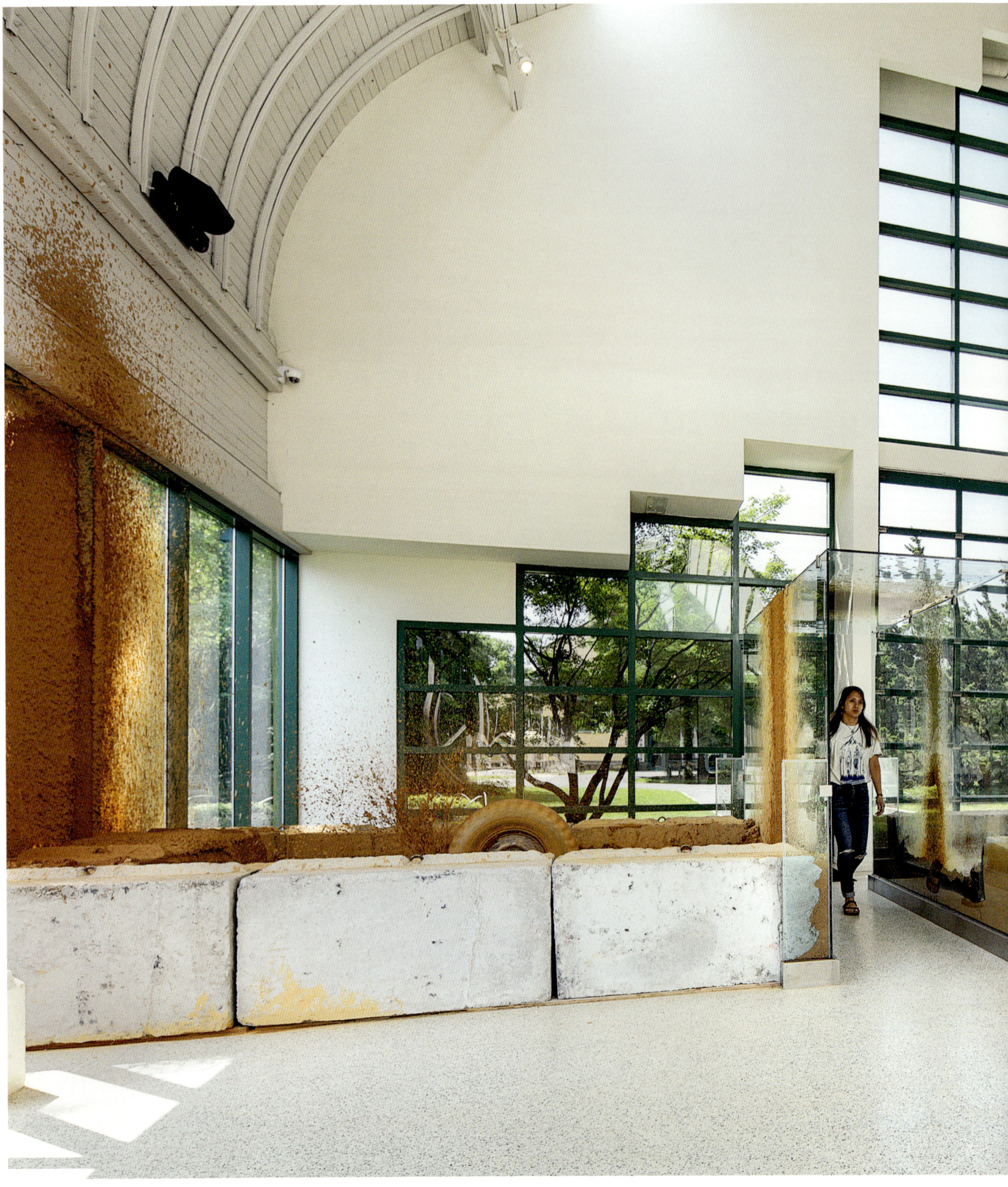

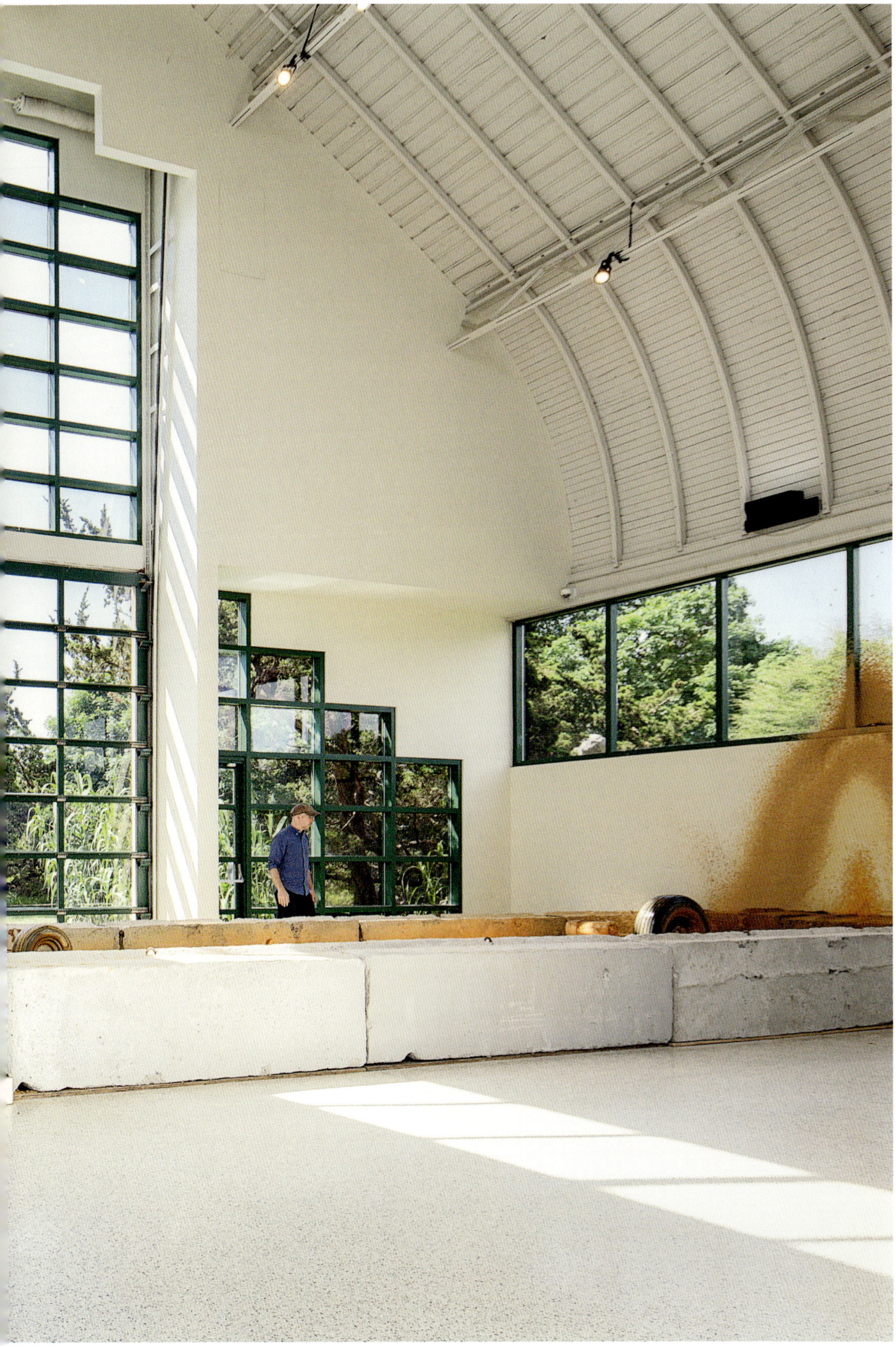

Path Breaker, 2019 (cat. 19)

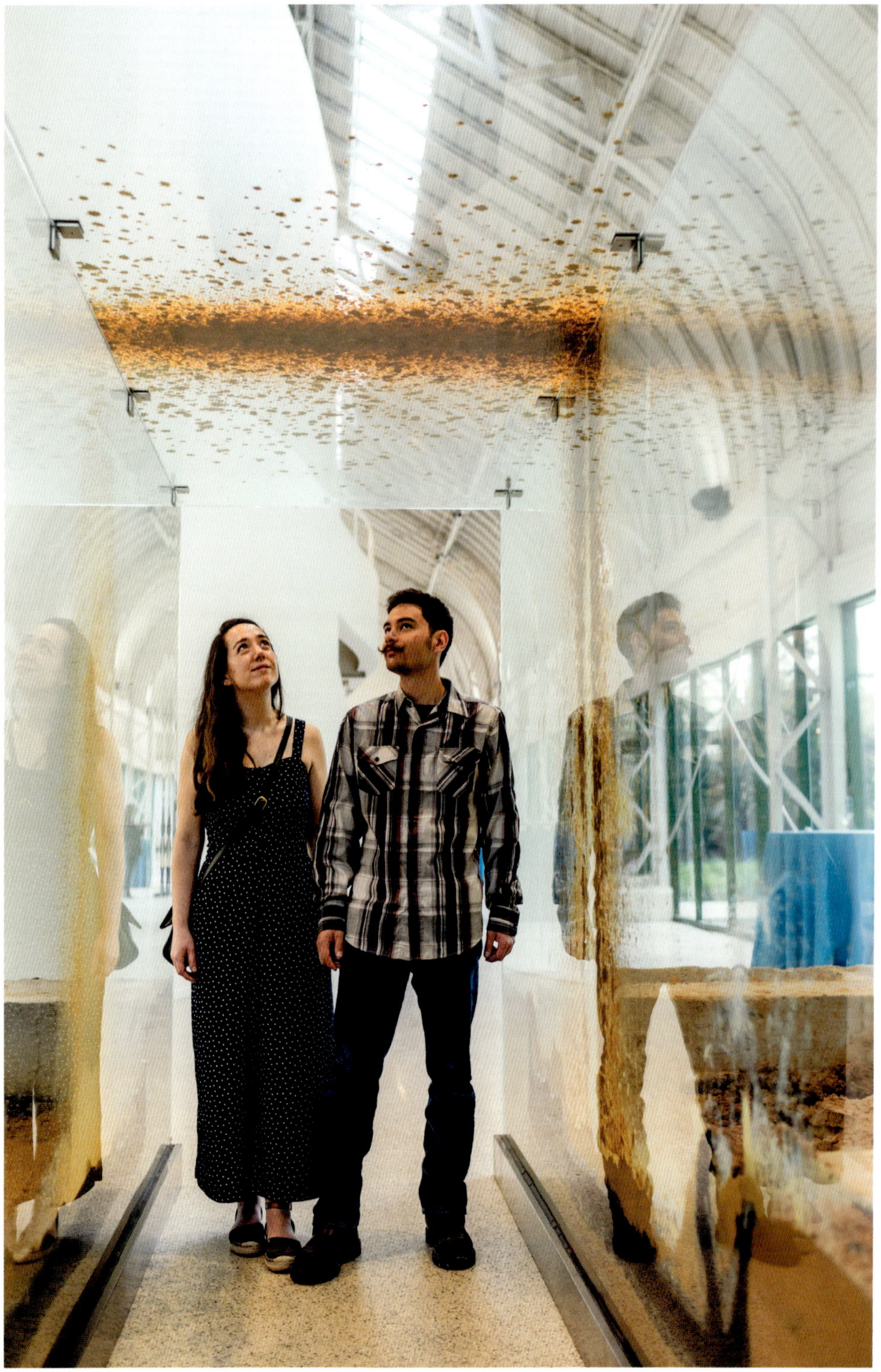

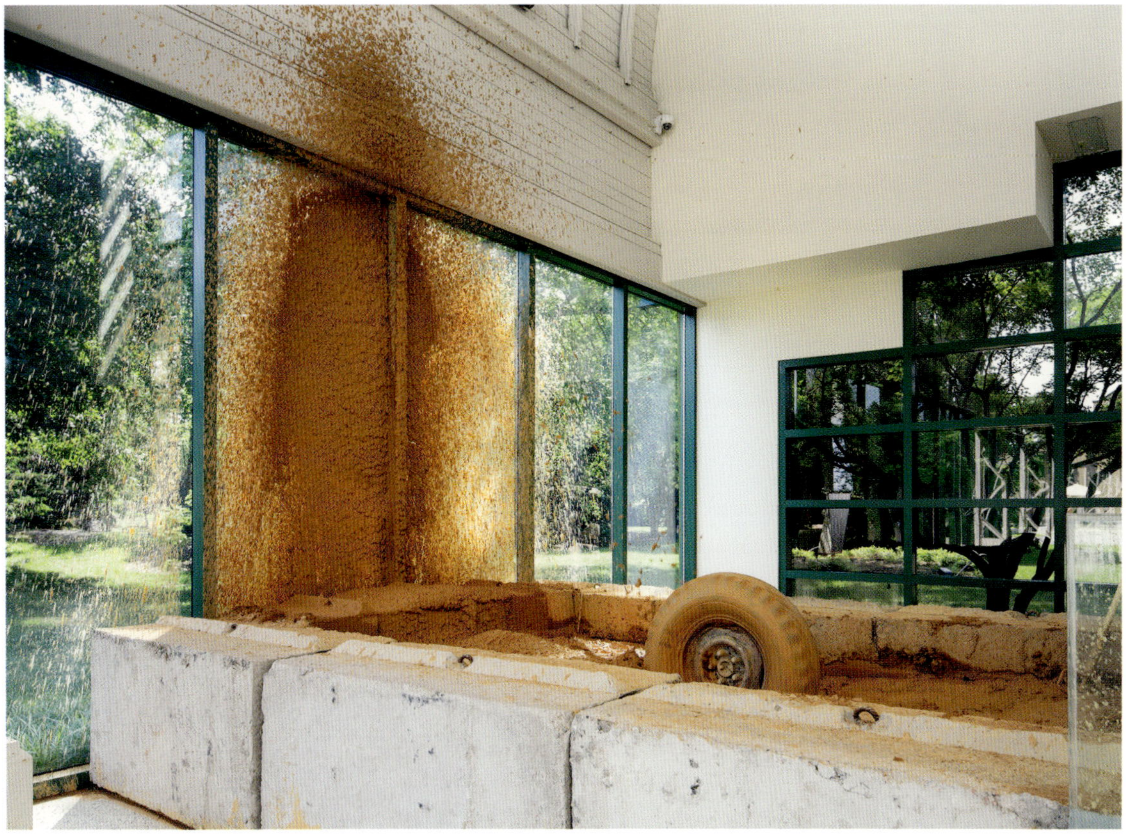

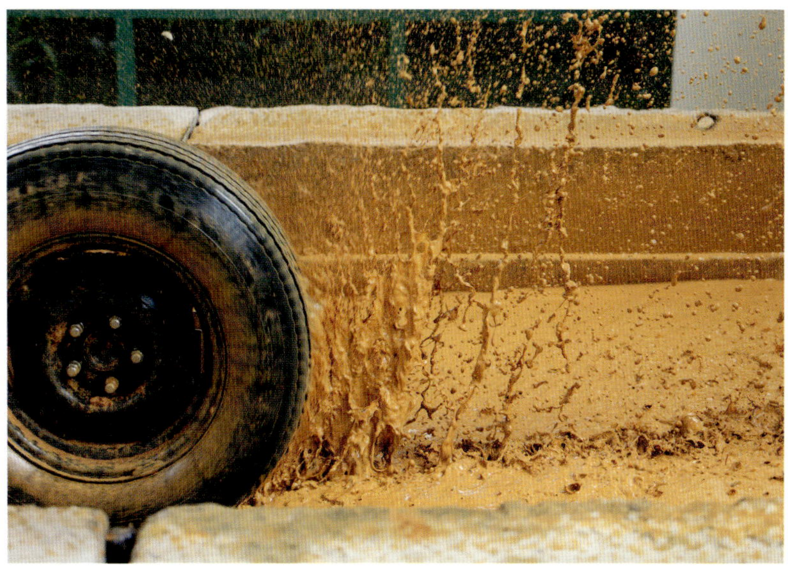

Path Breaker, 2019 (cat. 19)

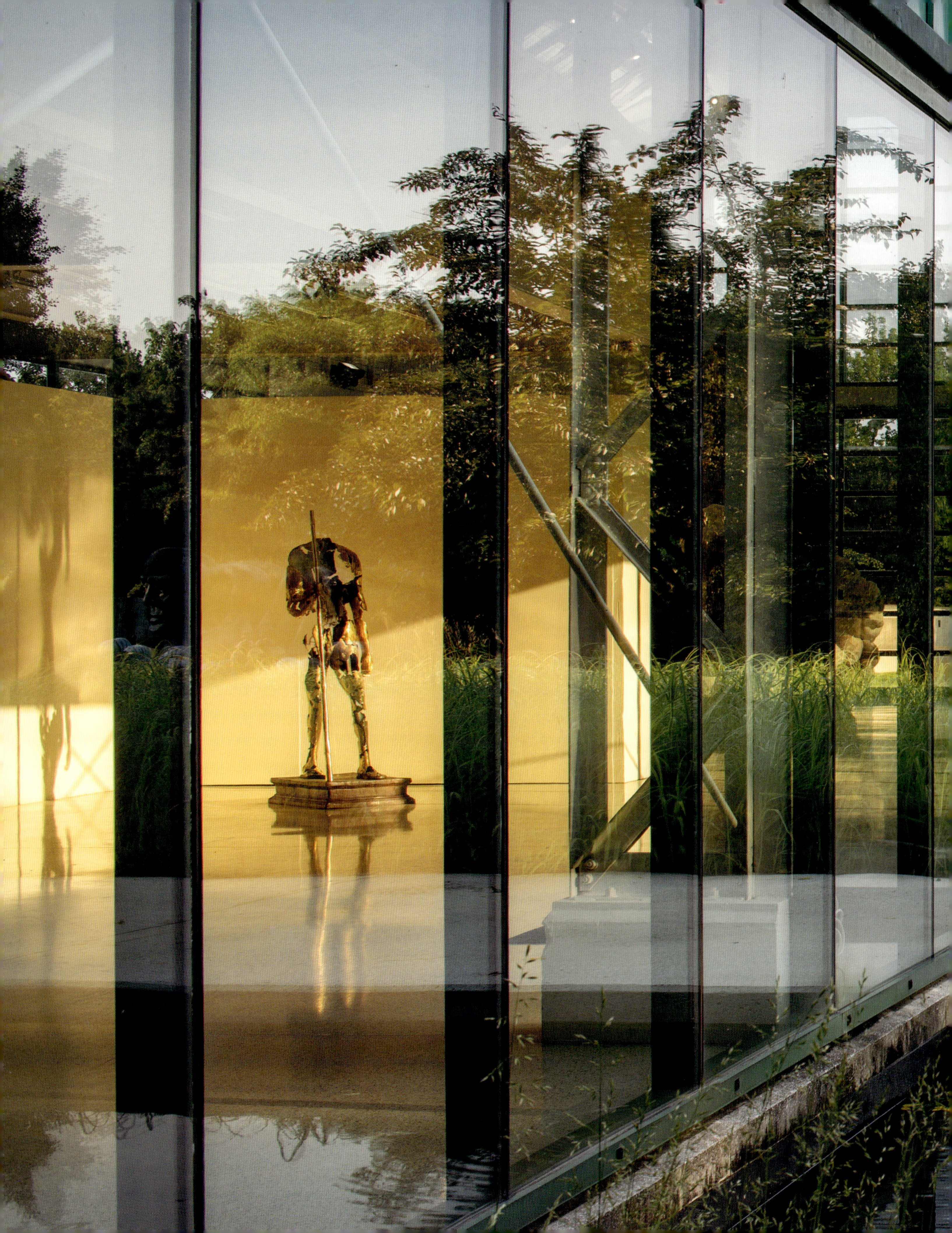

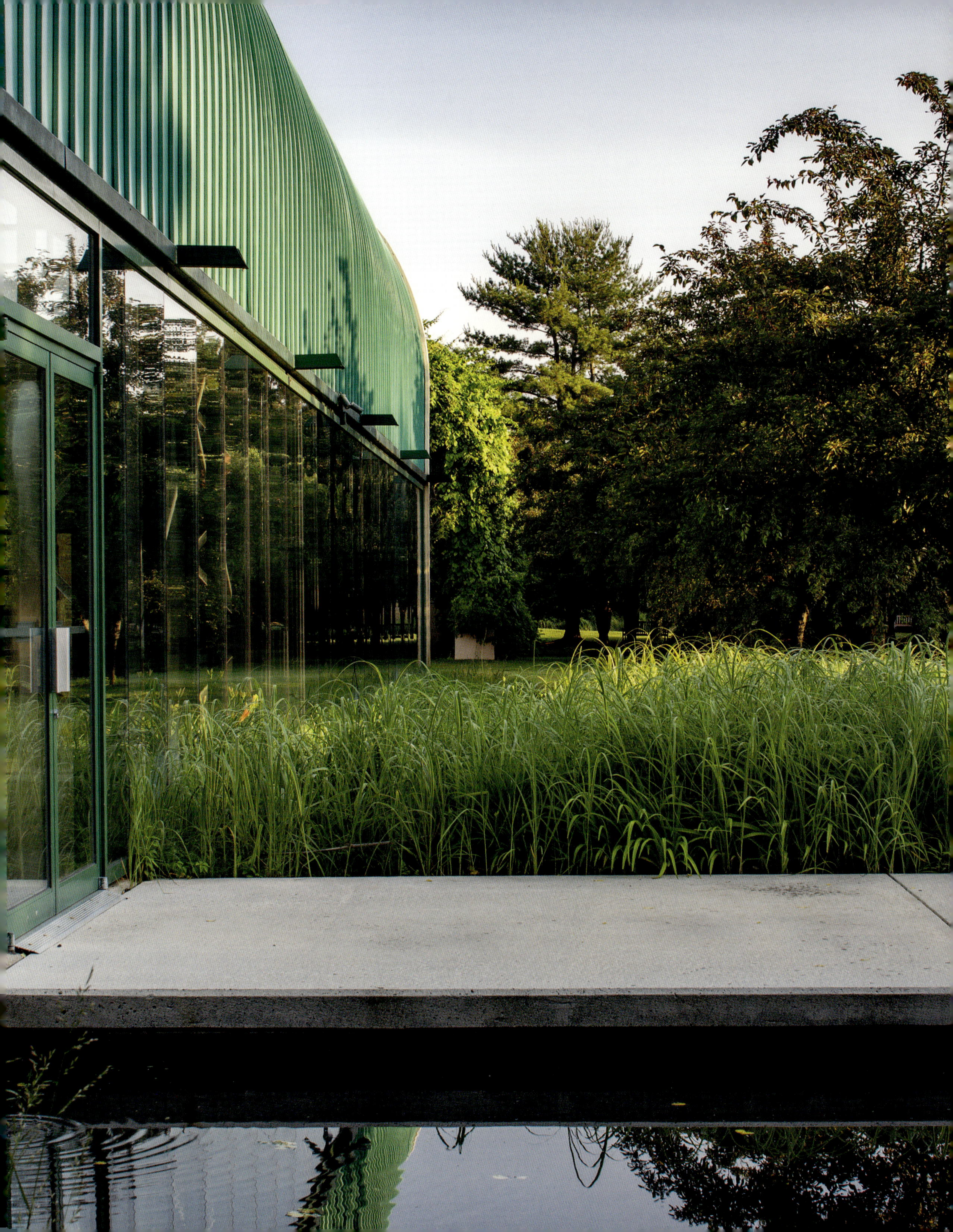

Exhibition Checklist

All works by Tallur L.N. unless otherwise noted

Artist unknown, India
1 **Lower portion of a stele with deity in Samapada Sthanika flanked by female and male attendants**, 9th–10th century
sandstone
two parts: 4½ × 5⅛ × 2½ inches and 5⅝ × 3⅛ × 2½ inches
Philadelphia Museum of Art, Gift of N. M. Heeramaneck, 1931
Pages 22, **102**

Artist unknown, India
2 **Terrifying Attendant Spirits**, ca. 10th century
sandstone
32¾ × 11 × 11½ inches
Philadelphia Museum of Art, Purchased with the Stella Kramrisch Fund, 2000
Pages 21, **103**

3 ***Panic Room***, 2006
jute bags, blowers
53 × 94 × 27 inches
Collection of Laura Lee Brown and Steve Wilson, 21c Museum Hotels
Pages 52, **66**, **67**

4 ***Alzheimer's***, 2006
termite and white ant–eroded wooden object, silver, clay
61 × 29 × 17 inches
Private collection, Chapel Hill, North Carolina
Pages 53, **75**

5 ***Apocalypse***, 2010
electromagnetic polishing system, pipe, wood, coins, certificate, vinyl lettering
dimensions variable
Courtesy of the artist and ARARIO
Pages 18, 59, **63**, **68–71**

6 ***0+0=0-0***, 2011
angle grinder, wooden statue, lighting
87 × 38 × 22 inches
Collection of Rajshree Pathy, Coimbatore
Page **73**

7 ***Chromatophobia***, 2012
granite, wood log, coins, hammers, vinyl lettering
91 × 78 × 89 inches
Courtesy of the artist and Jack Shainman Gallery
Pages 18, **62–65**

8 ***Eraser Pro***, 2012
cast bronze
78¾ × 37⅜ × 25⅝ inches
Courtesy of the artist and Jack Shainman Gallery
Pages 20, 53, **89**

9 ***Obituary Note***, 2013
cast bronze, burnt wood
72 × 59 × 46 inches
Grounds For Sculpture, Purchase
Pages 50, **81**

10 ***Iron Age***, 2013
cast iron
67 × 34 × 22 inches
Courtesy of the artist and Jack Shainman Gallery
Pages 53, **79**

11 ***Tongue Twister***, 2014
milled Turkish stone, iron dagger, water
22 × 62 × 37 inches
Courtesy of the artist and ARARIO
Page **95**

12 ***Milled History***, 2014
yellow teakwood sandstone
72 × 49 × 15 inches
Courtesy of the artist and ARARIO
Pages 19, **76–77**

13 ***Threshold***, 2015/2019
blade-sharpening machine, bandsaw blades, galvanized pipes
dimensions variable
Courtesy of the artist and ARARIO
Pages 4, 21, **90–92**

14 ***Coherence***, 2019
cast stone
42 × 30 × 22 inches
Collection of the artist, produced with support from Grounds For Sculpture, the Philadelphia Museum of Art, and Digital Atelier, Inc.
Pages 21, **104**, **105**

15 ***Tolerance***, 2019
yellow teakwood sandstone
68 × 32 × 14 inches
Collection of the artist
Pages 6, 52, **82**, **83**

16 ***Enlightenment Machine (Beta Version 3.0)***, 2019
wood, grinding machine, figurines
90 × 116 × 59 inches
Collection of the artist
Pages 19, 59, **84–87**

17 ***Interference***, 2019
4k video, television monitors
4:51 min.
Varia Kiran, videography; Vandita Jain, sound engineer; assistance from Junagadh Museum and Bhanu Pratap Singh
Collection of the artist
Pages 22, **106**, **107**

18 ***Fringe***, 2019
bone meal, bone char, and crushed bone with commercial adhesive on foam
18 × 25 × 20 feet
Collection of the artist, produced with support from Grounds For Sculpture, the Philadelphia Museum of Art, and Digital Atelier, Inc.
Pages 3, 10–11, 21, **96–101**

19 ***Path Breaker***, 2019
glass, concrete, metal plate, motor, tires, clay
dimensions variable
Collection of the artist
Pages 24, **108–111**

20 ***Scaffold***, 2019
mixed-media installation
dimensions variable
Courtesy of the artist
Pages 12, 15, **26–47**

Works included in *Scaffold* installation

21 ***Untitled (Elephant)***, 2008
wooden elephant, RCC pillar, steel construction rods
88 × 36 × 14 inches
Courtesy of the artist and ARARIO
Pages 12, **35**, 55

22 ***Bulimia 2***, 2008
jackfruit wood, white ant–eroded object coated in silver
39 × 24 × 44 inches
Private collection, New York
Pages **36–37**, 53

23 ***Lamp (Deepa Laxmi)***, 2010
cast bronze, concrete, red pigment
55⅛ × 39 × 24 inches
OZLO Collection, New Delhi
Pages **40**, **41**, 55

24 ***"?"***, 2011
bronze
35⅜ × 31½ × 35⅜ inches
Courtesy of the artist and Jack Shainman Gallery
Pages 17, **38**, **39**

25 ***Unicode***, 2011
cast bronze, concrete, coins
67 × 61½ × 47 inches
Collection of Dr. Robert B. Feldman, Cohoes, New York
Pages 17, **45**

26 ***Pedestal on Pedestal***, 2012
cast bronze, cement, coins, oil
39 × 35 × 39 inches
Courtesy of the artist and ARARIO
Pages 17, **39**

27 ***Hatha Yoga***, 2012
clay figurine in a vitrine, painted wood statue with nails, nail-covered replica, nail-manufacturing machine
machine: 47 × 33 × 39 inches;
angel: 78 × 37 × 18 inches;
nailed angel: 39 × 23 × 23 inches
Collection of Kiran Nadar Museum of Art, New Delhi
Pages 12, 15, **29–34**

28 ***Victory Pillar***, 2012
cast bronze, cement, coins, oil
98 × 20 × 20 inches
Collection of Ashish Jain, New Delhi
Pages 17, **40**, **42**, **43**, 55

Artist Biography and Exhibition History

1971 Born in Tallur, Karnataka, India

The artist divides his time between India and Korea

Education

1992–96 BFA in painting, Chamarajendra Academy of Visual Arts (CAVA), Mysore University, India

1997–98 MFA in museology, Maharaja Sayyajirao University of Baroda, Gujrat, India

2001–2 MA in contemporary fine art practice, Leeds Metropolitan University, United Kingdom

Solo Exhibitions

2018 *Coinage*, permanent public sculpture at UPM Circle Manipal, India

2017 *Smoke Out*, Chemould Prescott Road, Mumbai, India*

2015 *The Threshold*, Arario Gallery, Seoul, South Korea

2014 *UKAI (Cormorant Fish Hunting)*, Nature Morte, New Delhi, India

2013 *Balancing Act*, SCAD Museum of Art, Savannah, Georgia

New Yorked, Jack Shainman Gallery, New York, New York

2012 *Montessori: Lessons in Economics*, Gallery Nature Morte, Berlin, Germany

Pass word, Nature Morte, New Delhi, India

2011 *Quintessential*, Dr. Bhau Daji Lad Mumbai City Museum, Mumbai, India

Chromatophobia—The Fear of Money (Part 2), Nature Morte, New Delhi, India*

Chromatophobia—The Fear of Money (Part 1), Arario Gallery, Seoul, South Korea

2010 *Chromatophobia—The Fear of Money (Part 1)*, Arario Gallery, Beijing, China*

2009 *PLACEBO*, Chemould Prescott Road, Mumbai, India*

2008 *Antimatter*, Arario Gallery, New York, New York*

2007 *Bon Appetite*, Arario Gallery, Seoul, Korea*

1999 *Past Modern Interactive Art Objects*, Bose Pacia Modern, New York, New York

Past Modern Interactive Art Objects, Gallery Chemould, Mumbai, India*

Group Exhibitions

2017 *India and the World: History in Nine Stories*, CSMVS Museum, Mumbai, India, and National Museum, New Delhi, India

10 Contemporary Art Acquisitions, Dr. Bhau Daji Lad Mumbai City Museum, Mumbai, India

The Sculpture Park at Madhavendra Palace, Nahargarh Fort, Jaipur, India

Sub Plot; Language in the Vernacular, National Gallery of Modern Art, Mumbai, India (in collaboration with Sakshi Gallery)

Art in Counting House, 21C Durham, Museum Hotel, Durham, North Carolina

Persevering Traditions, Sakshi Gallery Mumbai, India, and Art District XIII, Delhi, India

2016 *Ramakrishna Behera | L.N. Tallur*, Nature Morte Gallery, New Delhi, India

The Dream Must Turn Speculative, Nature Morte Gallery, Kala Ghoda, Mumbai, India

Represented BDL Mumbai City Museum for India Art Fair, New Delhi

2015 *Constructs / Constructions*, Kiran Nadar Museum of Art, New Delhi, India

After Midnight: Indian Modernism to Contemporary India 1947/1997, Queens Museum, New York

Encounters, Art Basel Hong Kong

Daegu Contemporary Art Festival in Gangjeong, Daegu, South Korea

2014 *Mise En Scène*, The School, Jack Shainman Gallery, Kinderhook, New York

Beyond the Classical: Imagining the Ideal across Time, The National Academy Museum, New York, New York

By Destiny, Arario Museum, Jeju Island, South Korea

Universal Studio: Seoul, Seoul Art Museum, South Korea

The First International Biennial of Contemporary Art of Cartagena de Indias, Colombia

The Armory Show, representing Jack Shainman Gallery, New York, New York

India Art Fair, representing Nature Morte Gallery, New Delhi, India

2013 Busan Sea Arts Festival 2013, South Korea

Phantomata, Chemould Prescott Road, Mumbai, India

Art Unlimited, Art Basel, Switzerland

SKODA Prize show, National Gallery of Modern Art, New Delhi, India

Body Being Here, Daegu Art Museum, South Korea

2012 Kochi-Muziris Biennial, Kochi, India

The 7th Asia Pacific Triennial of Contemporary Art (APT 7), Queensland Art Gallery | Gallery of Modern Art, Brisbane, Australia

Critical Mass: Contemporary Art from India, Tel Aviv Museum of Art, Israel

2011 *MEDI(T)ATION*, 2011 Asian Art Biennial, National Taiwan Museum of Fine Art, Taiwan

Home Spun, Davi Art Foundation, New Delhi, India

Collectors Stage, Singapore Art Museum

Against All Odds, Lalit Kala Akademi, New Delhi, India

2010 *Place-Time-Play*, India-China Contemporary Art, West Heavens, Shanghai, China

The Empire Strikes Back—Indian Art Today, Saatchi Gallery, London, United Kingdom

La route de la soir, Tri Postal, Lille, France

Now through a Glass Darkly, Arario Gallery, New York, New York

2009 The Armory Show, representing Arario Gallery, New York, New York

Failed Plot, KIAF, Seoul, South Korea

2008 The 3rd Nanjing Triennial, China*

Pulse, Soho Studios, Miami, Florida

Passage to India, Initial Access—Frank Cohen Collection, Wolverhampton, United Kingdom

Mechanism of Motions, Anant Art Center, Delhi, India

2007 *Unholy Truths*, Initial Access—Frank Cohen Collection, Wolverhampton, United Kingdom

Arco 2007, Madrid, Spain

Hungry God, Art Gallery of Ontario, Toronto

The Armory Show, representing Arario Seoul, New York, New York

Subcontingent, Fondazione Sandretto Re Rebaudengo, Torino, Italy*

Hungry God: Indian Contemporary Art, Pusan Museum of Modern Art, Pusan, Korea*

2004–7 *Edge of the Desire: Recent Art in India*, curated by Chaitanya Sambrani (touring):

Art Gallery of Western Australia, Perth, September 2004–January 2005; Asia Society New York, February–June 2005; Tamayo Museum, Mexico City, August–October 2005; Museum of Contemporary Art, Monterrey, Mexico, January–March 2006; Berkeley Art Museum, California, June–September 2006; National Gallery of Modern Art, New Delhi, November–December 2006; National Gallery of Modern Art, Mumbai, January–February 2007*

2006 *Hyper Design*, 6th Shanghai Biennale, curated by Zhang Qing Shanghai Art Museum, China

9th Biennial de La Habana, Havana, Cuba*

Hungry God: Indian Contemporary Art, Arario Beijing, China*

Beautiful Cynicism, Arario Beijing, China*

2005 *Rites and Rewrites: Borders in Asia*, World Socialist Forum, Museum of Contemporary Art, Porte Alegre, Brazil*

Iconography in Transient Time, Gallery Sumakha, Delhi, India *

2004 Haste Modern, Nature Morte, New Delhi, India

Busan Binnale, Busan, South Korea*

Bifocal Vision: The Near and Far in Contemporary Indian Art, Lisbon, Portugal*

2003 *Crossing Generations: diVERGE*, Gallery Chemould, Mumbai, India

Eclectic, Total Museum, Seoul, South Korea, organized by Yellow Sea International, South Korea*

2002 *LMU*, Leeds Metropolitan University Gallery, United Kingdom

2000 *Millennium Logo*, National Gallery of Modern Art, Mumbai, India, organized by Art India Magazine, Mumbai

Art in the World 2000, organized by *BeauxArts* magazine, Paris, France*

1999 Asian Art Biennial, Dhaka, Bangladesh*

1997 *37th National Exhibition*, Lalit Kala Akademi, Chennai, India*

Awards

2012 The SKODA Prize, Delhi, India

2003 Sanskriti Award, Sanskriti Foundation, Delhi, India

2001 Commonwealth Scholarship, to study at Leeds Metropolitan University, United Kingdom

1999 Emerging Artist Award, Bose Pacia Modern, New York, New York

1997 Inlaks Fine Art Award, Inlaks Foundation, Delhi, India

1996 National Scholarship, Ministry of HRD, Government of India

1995 Karnataka Lalitkala Akademi Scholarship, to study at Maharaja Sayyajirao University of, Baroda, Gujrat, India

Research

"The Museum's Non-verbal Communication: 'Multi-sensory Approaches in Exhibition Design,'" MFA diss., Department of Museology, Maharaja Sayyajirao University of, Baroda, Gujrat, India

*Exhibition catalogue published.

Published on the occasion of the exhibition *Interference Fringe | TALLUR L.N.*
Organized by Gary Garrido Schneider, Executive Director, Grounds For Sculpture

On view at Grounds For Sculpture, Hamilton, New Jersey, May 5, 2019–January 5, 2020

NATURE MORTE

Published by
Grounds For Sculpture
80 Sculptors Way
Hamilton, NJ 08619
groundsforsculpture.org

Distributed by
ARTBOOK | D.A.P.
75 Broad Street, Suite 630
New York, NY 10004
artbook.com

The exhibition *Interference Fringe | TALLUR L.N.* and accompanying catalogue are supported, in part, by the National Endowment for the Arts, Art Works; Bank of America; the New Jersey Department of State, Division of Travel & Tourism; Chemould Prescott Road; Marriott Princeton; Nature Morte; Frank and Sharon Lorenzo; Umesh and Sunanda Gaur; and the following Exhibition Supporters: Gordon and Lulie Gund, Barbara Lawrence and Allen Laskin, and Eric B. Ryan.

General operating support is provided, in part, by the Atlantic Foundation; the Johnson Art and Education Foundation; the New Jersey State Council on the Arts, a partner agency of the National Endowment for the Arts; and the Geraldine R. Dodge Foundation.

Fringe (2019, cat. 18), commissioned for this exhibition, was created, in part, with support from the Digital Atelier, Inc. The artist and Grounds For Sculpture wish to acknowledge the Philadelphia Museum of Art for allowing access to their collection.

Produced by
Lucia | Marquand, Seattle
luciamarquand.com

Copy Editor: Kristin Swan
Proofreader: Ted Gilley
Designer: Thomas Eykemans
Photography: Nicholas Knight, Ken Ek
Typesetter: Brynn Warriner
Color Management: iocolor, Seattle
Printed and bound in Hong Kong by Paramount Printing Company, Ltd.

Library of Congress Control Number: 2019953168
ISBN: 978-1-64657-000-3

All artwork by Tallur L.N. unless otherwise noted
Front cover: Detail, cat. 8. Photo courtesy of Jack Shainman
Pages 3, 10–11: Installation views, cat. 18
Page 4: Installation view, cat. 13
Pages 62–63: *Interference Fringe | TALLUR L.N.* at Grounds For Sculpture, installation photo, 2019
Back cover: Detail, cat. 5. Photo courtesy of Chao Yong

Photography Credits
All works by Tallur L.N. © the artist
Unless otherwise noted, all photos by Nicholas Knight
Courtesy of the artist: pages 14, 16, 17 (thumbnail 1), 17 (thumbnail 3), 18 (thumbnail 2), 22, 23, 38, 41, 42, 43, 51, 53 (thumbnail 3), 55 (thumbnail 1), 58, 59, 70 (bottom), 75, 107
Photo by Cathy Carver: pages 35, 48, 54, 55 (thumbnail 1), 56 (top, bottom), 57
Photo by Ken Ek: pages 6, 17 (thumbnail 2), 21 (thumbnail 4), 26–27, 28, 29 (top), 30–31, 33, 34, 36–37, 39, 40, 52 (right), 64 (top), 70 (top), 82, 83, 100, 104, 105
Photo by David Michael Howarth Photography: pages 64 (bottom), 110
Courtesy of Jack Shainman Gallery: pages 17 (thumbnail 4), 20 (thumbnail), 45, 53 (thumbnail 1), 89
Photo by Himanshu Pahad: page 14
Courtesy of the Philadelphia Museum of Art: pages 21 (thumbnail 3), 102, 103
Photo by Sunil Raju: pages 16, 23
Photo by Dong Yeon Seo: pages 53 (thumbnail 3), 75
Photo by Chao Yong: pages 18 (right), 59 (left), 70 (bottom)